Dennis Jarosch

Native Web Applications

Dennis Jarosch

# Native Web Applications

## High-Performance Applications in the Cloud Through Native Code Execution

Südwestdeutscher Verlag für Hochschulschriften

**Impressum/Imprint (nur für Deutschland/only for Germany)**
Bibliografische Information der Deutschen Nationalbibliothek: Die Deutsche Nationalbibliothek verzeichnet diese Publikation in der Deutschen Nationalbibliografie; detaillierte bibliografische Daten sind im Internet über http://dnb.d-nb.de abrufbar.
Alle in diesem Buch genannten Marken und Produktnamen unterliegen warenzeichen-, marken- oder patentrechtlichem Schutz bzw. sind Warenzeichen oder eingetragene Warenzeichen der jeweiligen Inhaber. Die Wiedergabe von Marken, Produktnamen, Gebrauchsnamen, Handelsnamen, Warenbezeichnungen u.s.w. in diesem Werk berechtigt auch ohne besondere Kennzeichnung nicht zu der Annahme, dass solche Namen im Sinne der Warenzeichen- und Markenschutzgesetzgebung als frei zu betrachten wären und daher von jedermann benutzt werden dürften.

Coverbild: www.ingimage.com

Verlag: Südwestdeutscher Verlag für Hochschulschriften GmbH & Co. KG
Heinrich-Böcking-Str. 6-8, 66121 Saarbrücken, Deutschland
Telefon +49 681 37 20 271-1, Telefax +49 681 37 20 271-0
Email: info@svh-verlag.de

Zugl.: Berlin, Humboldt Universität zu Berlin, Diss., 2012

Herstellung in Deutschland (siehe letzte Seite)
**ISBN: 978-3-8381-3302-7**

**Imprint (only for USA, GB)**
Bibliographic information published by the Deutsche Nationalbibliothek: The Deutsche Nationalbibliothek lists this publication in the Deutsche Nationalbibliografie; detailed bibliographic data are available in the Internet at http://dnb.d-nb.de.
Any brand names and product names mentioned in this book are subject to trademark, brand or patent protection and are trademarks or registered trademarks of their respective holders. The use of brand names, product names, common names, trade names, product descriptions etc. even without a particular marking in this works is in no way to be construed to mean that such names may be regarded as unrestricted in respect of trademark and brand protection legislation and could thus be used by anyone.

Cover image: www.ingimage.com

Publisher: Südwestdeutscher Verlag für Hochschulschriften GmbH & Co. KG
Heinrich-Böcking-Str. 6-8, 66121 Saarbrücken, Germany
Phone +49 681 37 20 271-1, Fax +49 681 37 20 271-0
Email: info@svh-verlag.de

Printed in the U.S.A.
Printed in the U.K. by (see last page)
**ISBN: 978-3-8381-3302-7**

Copyright © 2012 by the author and Südwestdeutscher Verlag für Hochschulschriften GmbH & Co. KG and licensors
All rights reserved. Saarbrücken 2012

# Contents

| | |
|---|---|
| **List of Figures** | v |
| **List of Tables** | vii |
| **List of Abbreviations** | ix |
| **1. Introduction** | 1 |
| **2. Problem Statement and Approach** | 3 |
| **3. Background** | 5 |
|     3.1. Browser Plugins | 5 |
|         3.1.1. Netscape Plugin API | 6 |
|         3.1.2. ActiveX | 8 |
|     3.2. Web 2.0 | 9 |
|         3.2.1. Participation and User Generated Content | 9 |
|         3.2.2. Technological Advancements | 10 |
|         3.2.3. AJAX | 11 |
|         3.2.4. JavaScript | 12 |
|     3.3. Web Applications | 16 |
|         3.3.1. Native Applications vs. Web Applications | 17 |
|         3.3.2. Towards the HTML5 Standard | 19 |
| **4. The Web as a Platform** | 23 |
|     4.1. Beyond the Microsoft Windows Platform | 24 |
|     4.2. Platform Classification | 25 |
|         4.2.1. Level 1: Access API | 25 |
|         4.2.2. Level 2: Plugin API | 26 |
|         4.2.3. Level 3: Runtime Environment | 26 |
|         4.2.4. Criticism and Implications | 27 |
|     4.3. Components of the Web as a Platform | 27 |
|         4.3.1. Runtime | 28 |
|         4.3.2. Application Framework | 30 |
|         4.3.3. Tools | 31 |
|         4.3.4. Cloud Services | 32 |
|         4.3.5. Monetization | 33 |
|     4.4. Cloud Computing: Powering the Platform | 34 |
|         4.4.1. Cloud Computing Service Models | 36 |
|         4.4.2. Cloud Computing Deployment Models | 39 |
|         4.4.3. Cloud Applications and Services | 40 |
|     4.5. Challenges for the Web as Platform | 43 |

## Contents

**5. Native Web Applications**     **45**
- 5.1. Goals of Native Web Applications ... 45
- 5.2. Xax ... 46
  - 5.2.1. Architecture ... 47
  - 5.2.2. Implementation ... 50
  - 5.2.3. Capabilities ... 51
- 5.3. Native Client ... 53
  - 5.3.1. Architecture ... 53
  - 5.3.2. Implementation ... 55
  - 5.3.3. Portable Native Client ... 58
  - 5.3.4. Capabilities ... 58
- 5.4. Comparison of NaCl and Xax ... 60

**6. Performance Analysis**     **63**
- 6.1. Experimental Environment ... 64
- 6.2. Pi Benchmark ... 65
  - 6.2.1. Problem and Objective ... 65
  - 6.2.2. Theoretical Background ... 65
  - 6.2.3. Implementation Details ... 65
  - 6.2.4. Experimental Setup ... 67
  - 6.2.5. Execution ... 68
  - 6.2.6. Results ... 69
- 6.3. Pi-MT Benchmark ... 73
  - 6.3.1. Problem and Objective ... 73
  - 6.3.2. Theoretical Background ... 74
  - 6.3.3. Implementation Details ... 74
  - 6.3.4. Experimental Setup ... 76
  - 6.3.5. Execution ... 76
  - 6.3.6. Results ... 77
- 6.4. Gears Benchmark ... 81
  - 6.4.1. Problem and Objective ... 81
  - 6.4.2. Theoretical Background ... 82
  - 6.4.3. Implementation Details ... 85
  - 6.4.4. Experimental Setup ... 86
  - 6.4.5. Execution ... 87
  - 6.4.6. Results ... 88
- 6.5. Spectral Benchmark ... 92
  - 6.5.1. Problem and Objective ... 93
  - 6.5.2. Theoretical Background ... 94
  - 6.5.3. Implementation Details ... 100
  - 6.5.4. Experimental Setup ... 103
  - 6.5.5. Execution ... 104
  - 6.5.6. Results ... 105
- 6.6. Discussion ... 108
- 6.7. Further Investigations and Potential Solutions ... 111

**7. Evaluation, Effects, and Opportunities**     **113**
- 7.1. Comparison Criteria ... 113

|   |   |   |
|---|---|---|
| 7.2. | Evaluation | 114 |
|  | 7.2.1. 3D Graphics Performance | 114 |
|  | 7.2.2. Browser Neutrality | 114 |
|  | 7.2.3. Computational Performance | 115 |
|  | 7.2.4. Data Processing | 116 |
|  | 7.2.5. Maturity | 117 |
|  | 7.2.6. Openness | 117 |
|  | 7.2.7. OS-Independence | 119 |
|  | 7.2.8. Portability | 119 |
|  | 7.2.9. Porting and Code Reuse | 120 |
|  | 7.2.10. Security | 121 |
|  | 7.2.11. Conclusion | 123 |
| 7.3. | Drivers for NaCl's Adoption | 125 |
|  | 7.3.1. Technical Drivers | 125 |
|  | 7.3.2. Political Drivers | 126 |
|  | 7.3.3. Strategical Drivers | 127 |
|  | 7.3.4. Show-Stoppers | 128 |

## 8. Conclusion and Outlook   131

## A. Benchmarking Data   135
A.1. Pi Benchmark . . . . . 135
A.2. Pi-MT Benchmark . . . . . 136
A.3. Gears Benchmark . . . . . 137
A.4. Spectral Benchmark . . . . . 138

## Bibliography   139

# List of Figures

3.1. Global Market Penetration of Web Browser Plugins (May 2011) [StatOwl 2011] .... 6
3.2. Request and delivery of a static HTML page .................................. 10
3.3. Request, creation, and delivery of a Java-based dynamic web page ............ 11
3.4. Usage of client-side programming languages for websites [Q-Success 2011] ..... 13
3.5. SunSpider JavaScript benchmark results for 15 web browsers, as of June 25, 2010 [Kirsch 2010] ............................................................ 16
3.6. Structure of a three-tier web application .................................... 17
3.7. The HTML5 logo ............................................................ 19

4.1. OS market share as of June 2011 [Net Applications 2011] ..................... 24
4.2. Components of the Web as a platform ........................................ 28
4.3. Web application frameworks ................................................. 30
4.4. Average worldwide search traffic of the term "cloud computing", according to Google Trends ............................................................ 35
4.5. Cloud computing service models ............................................. 37
4.6. The Software as a Service cloud computing model ............................ 39
4.7. Cloud computing deployment models .......................................... 40
4.8. Why companies avoid infrastructure services [Forrester Consulting 2010] ...... 43

5.1. The Xax architecture ....................................................... 47
5.2. The interception of a Xax application system call using the ptrace kernel interface .. 51
5.3. The Native Client architecture .............................................. 54
5.4. Download, validation, and execution of an untrusted NaCl module ............. 56

6.1. Desktop web browser market share (Sept. 2011) [Net Applications 2011] ....... 64
6.2. A screenshot of the Native Client pi benchmark .............................. 66
6.3. Pi benchmark: running times of C, NaCl, and JavaScript ..................... 69
6.4. Pi benchmark: CPU utilization of C, NaCl, and JavaScript ................... 70
6.5. Pi benchmark: memory consumption of C, NaCl, and JavaScript ................ 71
6.6. Pi benchmark: web browser comparison ....................................... 71
6.7. Pi benchmark: web browser CPU utilization .................................. 72
6.8. Pi benchmark: web browser memory consumption ............................... 73
6.9. Pi-MT benchmark: running times of C, NaCl, and JavaScript .................. 77
6.10. Pi-MT benchmark: CPU utilization of C, NaCl, and JavaScript ............... 78
6.11. Pi-MT benchmark: memory consumption C, NaCl, and JavaScript ............... 79
6.12. Pi-MT benchmark: web browser comparison ................................... 79
6.13. Pi-MT benchmark: web browser CPU utilization .............................. 80
6.14. Pi-MT benchmark: web browser memory consumption .......................... 81
6.15. OpenGL line primitive types ............................................... 83
6.16. OpenGL triangle primitive types ........................................... 84
6.17. OpenGL quad primitive types ............................................... 84

## List of Figures

| | |
|---|---|
| 6.18. The OpenGL polygon primitive type | 84 |
| 6.19. A screenshot of the WebGLGears application | 86 |
| 6.20. Gears benchmark: FPS of C, NaCl, and JavaScript | 89 |
| 6.21. Gears benchmark: CPU utilization of C, NaCl, and JavaScript | 90 |
| 6.22. Gears benchmark: memory consumption of C, NaCl, and JavaScript | 91 |
| 6.23. Gears benchmark: web browser comparison | 91 |
| 6.24. Gears benchmark: web browser CPU utilization | 92 |
| 6.25. Gears benchmark: web browser memory consumption | 93 |
| 6.26. Spectrogram of the *LMAIntro.wav* audio sample | 94 |
| 6.27. Spectrogram of the *The Blooze.wav* audio sample | 95 |
| 6.28. Little-endian vs. big-endian byte ordering | 96 |
| 6.29. The canonical WAVE file format [Sapp 2003] | 97 |
| 6.30. Operation of a window function | 98 |
| 6.31. Schematic depiction of the STFT algorithm | 100 |
| 6.32. Examples of 8-bit numbers in the two's complement system | 101 |
| 6.33. Spectral benchmark: running times of C, NaCl, and JavaScript | 106 |
| 6.34. Spectral benchmark: CPU utilization of C, NaCl, and JavaScript | 107 |
| 6.35. Spectral benchmark: memory consumption of C, NaCl, and JavaScript | 108 |
| 6.36. Spectral benchmark: web browser comparison | 109 |
| 6.37. Spectral benchmark: web browser memory consumption | 110 |
| 6.38. Spectral benchmark: web browser CPU utilization | 110 |
| 7.1. The spider web of native application pros and cons | 122 |
| 7.2. The spider web of JavaScript strengths and weaknesses | 124 |
| 7.3. The spider web of NaCl strengths and weaknesses | 125 |

# List of Tables

3.1. Excerpt of browser plugins supported by the Mozilla Firefox web browser on different operating systems . . . . . . . . . . . . . . . . . . . . . . . . . . . . . . . . . . . 7
3.2. Statistics of the YouTube video-sharing community [YouTube 2011] . . . . . . . . . . 10
3.3. Key differences between native applications and web applications . . . . . . . . . . . . 18
3.4. Status of the HTML5 support in the leading web browsers, as of August, 2011 [Deveria 2011] . . . . . . . . . . . . . . . . . . . . . . . . . . . . . . . . . . . . . . . . . . . 20

4.1. Three levels of Internet platforms [Andreessen 2009] . . . . . . . . . . . . . . . . . . 26

5.1. A comparison of NaCl and Xax . . . . . . . . . . . . . . . . . . . . . . . . . . . . . . 60

6.1. Primitives supported by OpenGL and OpenGL ES 2.0 . . . . . . . . . . . . . . . . . 82
6.2. Audio files analyzed during the spectral benchmarking process . . . . . . . . . . . . 103
6.3. Web Workers usage in spectral benchmark implementations . . . . . . . . . . . . . . 104
6.4. Spectral benchmark: results of C, NaCl, and JavaScript . . . . . . . . . . . . . . . . 106
6.5. Spectral benchmark: web browser comparison . . . . . . . . . . . . . . . . . . . . . . 107

7.1. Evaluation of C, JavaScript, and NaCl . . . . . . . . . . . . . . . . . . . . . . . . . . 123

# List of Abbreviations

| | |
|---|---|
| ABI | Application Binary Interface |
| AJAX | Asynchronous JavaScript and XML |
| API | Application Programming Interface |
| ASP | Active Server Pages |
| AWS | Amazon Web Services |
| B2G | Boot to Gecko |
| BSD | Berkeley Software Distribution |
| CPU | Central Processing Unit |
| CSS | Cascading Style Sheets |
| DFT | Discrete Fourier Transform |
| DOM | Document Object Model |
| EC2 | Elastic Compute Cloud |
| FFT | Fast Fourier Transform |
| GLSL | OpenGL Shading Language |
| GPU | Graphics Processing Unit |
| GWT | Google Web Toolkit |
| HPC | High-Performance Computing |
| HTML | Hypertext Markup Language |
| I/O | Input/Output |
| IaaS | Infrastructure as a Service |
| IDE | Integrated Development Environment |
| IE | Internet Explorer |
| IPC | Inter-Process Communication |
| IT | Information Technology |
| JIT | Just-in-Time Compilation |
| JSON | JavaScript Object Notation |
| MPI | Message Passing Interface |
| NaCl | Native Client |
| NPAPI | Netscape Plugin Application Programming Interface |
| OS | Operating System |
| PaaS | Platform as a Service |
| PAL | Platform Abstraction Layer |
| PCM | Pulse-Code Manipulation |
| PDF | Portable Document Format |
| PPAPI | Pepper Plugin Application Programming Interface |
| RAM | Random Access Memory |
| REST | Representational State Transfer |
| RFID | Radio-Frequency Identification |
| RIA | Rich Internet Application |
| RIFF | Resource Interchange File Format |

## List of Abbreviations

| | |
|---|---|
| RSS | Resident Set Size |
| SaaS | Software as a Service |
| SDK | Software Development Kit |
| SFI | Software Fault Isolation |
| SOAP | Simple Object Access Protocol |
| SSD | Solid State Drive |
| STFT | Short-Time Fourier Transform |
| TCB | Trusted Code Base |
| TCO | Total Cost of Ownership |
| URL | Uniform Resource Locator |
| VM | Virtual Machine |
| VNC | Virtual Network Computing |
| W3C | World Wide Web Consortium |
| WAVE | Waveform Audio File Format |
| WHATWG | Web Hypertext Application Technology Working Group |
| XML | Extensible Markup Language |

# 1. Introduction

The World Wide Web (WWW) was released for public use in 1991, "with the philosophy that much academic information should be freely available to anyone" [Berners-Lee 1991]. In its original form, the Web was a network of information composed of websites. These websites consisted of HTML[1] pages that were connected with hyperlinks. The web browser was merely a viewer for static HTML content — used exclusively to surf the Web. As the Web evolved, so did its foundational technologies. The Web 2.0 revolution in the early 2000s finally transformed the Web from a network of information into a network of participation, with user generated content, blogging, and sharing at its core. During the Web 2.0 period, websites finally became much more dynamic and interactive. Today, the World Wide Web is amidst another transition from interactive websites to web applications — always accessible, regardless of the device that is being used to access them.

The distinction between websites and web applications is simple: Websites contain information, while web applications assist the user in performing tasks. The increasing popularity of web applications is dramatically changing the software industry in terms of software design, development, and distribution. Traditionally, native applications are developed for a certain operating system (OS) or computing platform, such as Microsoft Windows. One example of such native application is the web browser. Native applications are called native, because they are compiled to the machine language of a computer's processor(s). The fast-paced evolution of the Web has lead to the development of web applications that offer much of the functionality and complexity of traditional native applications. Web applications run in the web browser. Unlike native applications, they need not be installed before being usable and can be utilized anywhere, at any time. The only prerequisites for the usage of web applications are a web browser and an active Internet connection. Commonly, web applications are written in JavaScript, which, due to its nature as a dynamic programming language, is unable to match the computational performance of native applications.

An increasing number of people accomplish their daily computing tasks entirely with web applications — in the web browser. They use web applications to read and write e-mail, to engage in social networks, and to write documents in word processors. With the growing popularity of web applications, the World Wide Web itself has become a significant computing platform for application development: the Web as a platform. This platform is exceptional, because it decouples web applications from the underlying computing device and its operating system (OS). Web applications run on any device that features a web browser, including regular computers, mobile phones, modern TVs, and tablet computers. Two central components of the Web as a platform are the web browser and so-called *cloud*[2] services. Cloud computing is a recent movement that turns computing infrastructure, software, and data into services that are delivered over the Internet. These services are foundational to the back-ends of web applications. Being the runtime environment for web applications, the web browser has gained extensive capabilities for the development of highly interactive and responsive user interfaces.

While these technological innovations have led to the creation of web applications that have pushed the boundaries of what was considered possible in the browser, applications remain that cannot easily

---
[1]The Hypertext Markup Language is the predominant language to describe the structure and content of web pages.
[2]The term cloud is commonly used as a synonym for the Internet.

## 1. Introduction

be turned into web applications. For example, the absence of 3D graphics support has prevented web applications in the areas of 3D computer games, ray tracing, and 3D modeling. Deficits in the handling of large amounts of binary data and a general lack of computational performance have made it unfeasible to implement video editors and audio sequencers in the web browser.

It is the goal of this doctoral thesis to determine whether it is possible to combine the strengths of native applications and web applications — to enable browser-based applications that have so far not been possible. In addition, this work provides insight into the shortcomings of the Web as a platform and discusses possible solutions.

# 2. Problem Statement and Approach

Due to its inclusion in virtually all web browsers, HTML/JavaScript has established itself as the dominant application programming framework of the Web — it powers the front-ends of the vast majority of web applications. HTML5, the next revision of the HTML standard, adds new functionality to the web browser that enables offline web applications, hardware accelerated 3D graphics, and multimedia playback, among other features [Hickson 2010]. The goal of HTML5 is to provide building blocks for the Web as a platform that will eventually enable richer web applications. Although the final version of the HTML5 specification is still years away, many proposed features are already supported by modern web browsers.

HTML5 does not, however, address one of the foremost problems of the Web as a platform: it lacks the computational performance of compiled native applications. This limitation has prohibited the implementation of applications such as computer-aided design (CAD) tools, video editors, and large-scale scientific simulations as web applications. JavaScript, like other dynamic programming languages, remains handicapped by the computational overhead of interpretation[1] or just-in-time compilation[2]. Although the competition between web browsers has led to significant improvements in JavaScript performance, it is unlikely that JavaScript will ever be able to match the performance of compiled native applications [Kroeker 2009]. The question is whether JavaScript offers enough performance to facilitate the next generation of computationally demanding web applications, or whether an alternative is required?

In addition to its lack of performance, the Web as platform suffers from a second disadvantage: The majority of native applications and libraries were written in languages that are incompatible with web programming languages, e.g. C and C++ [Douceur et al. 2008]. This *legacy code*[3] embodies vast amounts of functionality that cannot currently be reused for the development of web applications. If legacy code could be made available for web application development, the development cycles of feature-rich web applications could be drastically shortened.

The execution of compiled native code in the web browser could facilitate the reuse of legacy code and bring higher computational performance to the Web as a platform. In this scenario, JavaScript web applications could be extended with native modules that implement performance critical parts. Ideally, these hybrid native/web applications would run in the web browser and yet provide low-level access to the computing hardware, combining the strengths of native applications with those of browser-based applications. This approach could complement the HTML5/JavaScript framework and enable a new class of web applications.

Browser plugins have allowed the execution of compiled native code in the web browser for almost two decades. Although they have achieved widespread adoption, browser plugins suffer from the lack of an effective security framework and their OS-dependency. New technologies are emerging that

---

[1] Interpretation refers to the execution of source code during or immediately prior to execution, instead of compilation in advance.
[2] Just-in-time compilation (JIT) is an optimization of Interpretation. It translates source code into machine language once and not repeatedly before every execution.
[3] Legacy code, in this context, refers to source code that is no longer supported for application development.

## 2. Problem Statement and Approach

employ the web browser as the runtime environment for untrusted native modules. For the first time, they make it possible to execute compiled native code on different operating systems without modifications. Sophisticated security frameworks contain and control the execution of untrusted native modules — protecting the system against viruses and other attacks. These innovative technologies are worth investigating because they allow the reuse of legacy code for web application development, without compromising on security and OS-independence. This doctoral thesis evaluates the effects and opportunities of compiled native code execution in the web browser, as a future technology for computationally demanding web applications in information technology.

This document is organized as follows: Chapter 3 provides an introduction to browser plugins and their security shortcomings. It explains the term Web 2.0 and discusses its technological foundations that are JavaScript and AJAX. The characteristics of web applications are outlined and compared to those of traditional native applications. In addition, the technological advancements of HTML5, the next revision of the HTML specification, are presented. Chapter 4 offers a classification of Internet platforms and defines the core components of the Web as a platform. It provides a description of cloud computing, including its service and deployment models. *Native Client* and *Xax*, two frameworks that allow the extension of web applications with compiled native code, are introduced in Chapter 5. Their goals, as well as their architectural and implementation-specific details are discussed. This chapter closes with a comparison of Native Client and Xax. In Chapter 6, the performance of traditional native applications, JavaScript web applications and Native Client web applications is analyzed. Four individual benchmarks are presented that evaluate different performance aspects. The benchmarking procedure and the results are discussed. Chapter 7 complements the results of the performance analysis with an evaluation of native applications, web applications, and Native Client web applications. For this sake, additional factors are defined and applied in order to determine the technical and non-technical strengths and weaknesses of each technology. Following the evaluation, the technical, political, and strategical drivers for Native Client's success are discussed. Chapter 8 provides a conclusion to the findings of this doctoral thesis and presents an outlook of their effects on the Web as a platform.

# 3. Background

In the early 1990s, when the World Wide Web was created, websites consisted primarily of static information. Their level of interactivity was low and they did not contain multimedia content. Web browsers were intended to visualize web pages — they lacked the functionality required for the creation of richer and more interactive websites. These shortcomings led to the development of browser plugin interfaces. These interfaces allowed third party developers[1] to create browser plugins that could handle multimedia content or embed interactive application code into websites.

The *Web 2.0* movement transformed the Web from an information network into a network of participation. User generated content, dynamic web sites, and sharing became the key elements of Web 2.0. Web browsers gained capabilities that facilitated the creation of interactive websites without the use of browser plugins. As interactive websites grew in complexity and began assisting users in performing tasks, they evolved into web applications. Web applications provide a level of functionality and a look and feel that is comparable to traditional native applications. However, they run entirely within the web browser. Modern web applications span a wide range of applications, e.g. image editors, e-mail, mapping tools, social networks, and word processors.

This chapter provides an introduction into web browser plugin interfaces, Web 2.0, and web applications. It discusses the benefits and drawbacks of prevalent plugin interfaces, outlines their security deficits, and explains why browser plugins were eventually superseded by web applications. Further, the term Web 2.0 is explained and the technological foundations of Web 2.0, AJAX and JavaScript, are reviewed. Web applications are defined and compared to traditional native applications. Finally, the feature-set of HTML5, the next major revision of the HTML standard that aims to facilitate richer web applications, is discussed.

## 3.1. Browser Plugins

A browser plugin is a small application that hooks into the web browser and extends its built-in capabilities. The desire to provide a standardized means of extending web browser functionality, in order to handle content other than HTML, lead to the development of a common plugin application programming interface (API): the Netscape Plugin Application Programming Interface (NPAPI). NPAPI made it possible for third party application developers to create browser plugins that allowed the web browser to handle and present richer content, e.g. audio and video. One of the earliest browser plugins was the Acrobat Reader plugin that made it possible to view PDF documents[2] inside the web browser, without launching the original Acrobat Reader application. The most successful browser plugin is arguably the Flash plugin, which revolutionized multimedia playback by bringing multimedia support to the browser — even today it delivers the vast majority of video content on the Web. Figure 3.1 illustrates the global market penetration of various browser plugins, as of May 2011.

---

[1] Third party developers refers to developers that are not involved with web browser development.
[2] The Portable Document Format (PDF) was created by Adobe as an open standard for document exchange.

## 3. Background

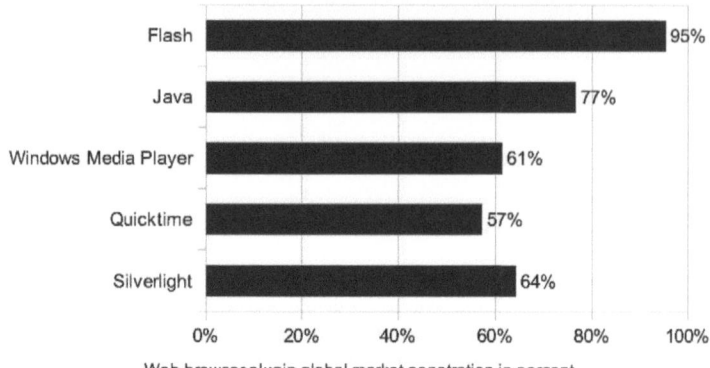

Figure 3.1.: Global Market Penetration of Web Browser Plugins (May 2011) [StatOwl 2011]

In the mid 1990s, the popular Java language and its APIs became available to web developers in form of a browser plugin. The plugin made it possible to embed Java applets into HTML websites and to execute these in the web browser. The richness of the Java API and the cross-platform approach of the Java programming language provided entirely new possibilities for the enhancement of websites. However, if visited with a plugin-less web browser, the space occupied by Java applets remained blank. At about the same time, Microsoft expanded its ActiveX technology to the Internet Explorer web browser, which allowed the extension of websites through native application code and core operating system libraries. Unlike the Java plugin, ActiveX was not designed for cross-platform use and it did not employ NPAPI.

### 3.1.1. Netscape Plugin API

NPAPI was first implemented in the Netscape Navigator as a cross-platform plugin architecture. Its goal was to provide a standard interface that allowed the extension of the web browser's capabilities in terms of content presentation through plugins — independent of the underlying operating system. NPAPI was subsequently adopted by other browser vendors and became the standard browser plugin interface. Plugins that target NPAPI automatically run in every web browser that supports this plugin interface. While NPAPI plugins are operating system dependent, i.e. they must be adapted to every supported operating system, the application programming interface was designed to be operating system agnostic. This is in contrast to the approach Microsoft pursued with ActiveX, which is deeply integrated with the Windows operating system. NPAPI went through several iterations before a final version was agreed on by the industry heavyweights Adobe, Apple, Macromedia, Mozilla, Opera, and Sun Microsystems in 2004 [Mozilla Foundation 2004].

NPAPI plugins are shared libraries, commonly written in C or C++, that are loaded into the web browser during runtime [Mozilla Developer Network 2011]. Originally they were executed within the main browser process — with full privileges. The lack of process isolation proved to be a major stability issue. When plugins crashed due to programming flaws, the entire web browser process was terminated as well. These stability problems eventually lead to the development of an out-of-process execution model, where plugins were placed in separate processes. NPAPI plugins are typically not

## 3.1. Browser Plugins

bundled with a web browser. Instead, they are downloaded and installed from the Internet. When a web browser comes across a website that requires a plugin that is missing, it will notify the user and contact a plugin finder service. It is then the user's responsibility to download and install the corresponding plugin. After a browser restart, the plugin becomes available and handles the dedicated content on the website.

Table 3.1.: Excerpt of browser plugins supported by the Mozilla Firefox web browser on different operating systems[3]

| Plugin | Windows | MacOS X | Linux (x86) |
|---|---|---|---|
| Adobe Flash Player | x | x | x |
| Adobe Reader | x | | x |
| Adobe Shockwave Player | x | x | |
| Firefox PDF Plugin | | x | |
| Flip4Mac WMV Plugin | | x | |
| Google Earth | x | x | |
| Java Plugin | x | x | x |
| QuickTime | x | x | |
| RealPlayer | x | x | x |
| Windows Media Player | x | | |
| MPlayer | | | x |

### Security Issues

The security concept of the NPAPI plugin architecture is based on the premise that plugins alone are responsible for security measures. The web browser does not restrict the permissions of plugins — in fact there are no restrictions at all. Plugin application code runs with the same privileges as the browser process and has full access to the underlying operating system. This is a severe security risk, especially as plugins have become "the single largest source of vulnerabilities in browsers today" [Grier et al. 2009]. These security vulnerabilities and the lack of a powerful plugin security model are the primary reasons for the shaping of a public opinion that regards native code execution in the web browser as unsafe. While the web browser itself does not provide any containment of plugin access and functionality, some plugins do provide security measures. For example, the Java plugin, which allows the execution of arbitrary Java application code in Java applets, employs a mechanism called *sandboxing*. The purpose of sandboxing is to contain application code and to restrict its access to the underlying computing environment. Typically, this involves limitations to file system and network access [Rubin and Geer 1998]. The strategy of placing the burden of security measures on the plugins instead has proven to be inadequate and was been repeatedly exploited in the past [Hopwood 1997]. The lack of a browser controlled security framework with containment for plugins is perhaps the most crucial shortcoming of the NPAPI plugin system.

Despite its security weaknesses, NPAPI is a success story. It has successfully opened the door for richer Internet content and multimedia playback. Most modern web browsers still support this interface for plugin development, although it is more than 15 years old. A notable exception is the Microsoft Internet Explorer, which has dropped NPAPI and replaced it with ActiveX in version 5.5

---
[3]http://plugindoc.mozdev.org/ and
http://www.google.com/earth/explore/products/plugin.html, last visited on October 18, 2011.

## 3. Background

SP2. The Google Chrome browser maintains support for NPAPI, but has since extended it with the Pepper Plugin API (PPAPI). PPAPI addresses the security issues of NPAPI in order to make plugins more portable and secure. For the first time, it permits the sandboxing of browser plugins [Sylvain 2008], [Schuh and Pizano 2010]. Google is currently the only major browser vendor working on PPAPI[4].

### 3.1.2. ActiveX

ActiveX is a framework that allows the creation of reusable software components. It was introduced by Microsoft in 1996 and builds on the Component Object Model (COM), the foundation of Microsoft's software component technology. Components that are built with ActiveX can be embedded into other applications as ActiveX controls. For example, this technology makes it possible to embed an Excel spreadsheet into a Word document and to edit it there. The Internet Explorer allows the embedding of ActiveX controls into web pages, bringing the functionality of the Windows operating system and its component model to the Web. Using ActiveX, web developers were supposed to "add animation, multimedia and other features to their Web sites" [Cohen and Franco 2006] — albeit only in the Internet Explorer and only on Windows. ActiveX was specifically designed for the Microsoft Windows operating system and its native Internet Explorer web browser. While, at first glance, the goals of ActiveX seem to align with those of NPAPI, i.e. to facilitate richer Internet content through browser plugins, there are several substantial differences. First of all, ActiveX goes far beyond the plugin approach. It makes it possible to reuse existing software components inside the web browser. Second, in order to achieve this goal, ActiveX was deeply integrated with the Windows operating system. The creators of ActiveX had no interest in introducing a cross-platform standard API, they wanted to bring Microsoft Windows components to the Web. While an ActiveX plugin (via NPAPI) was available for Netscape and Mozilla browsers, the primary target browser was the Internet Explorer. ActiveX components can be written in any programming language that supports COM development, for example C, C++, Borland Delphi, Visual Basic, and those supported by the .NET framework.

**Security Issues**

ActiveX provides unrestricted access to OS functionality. It does not employ sandboxing to isolate ActiveX controls from the rest of the system and there are no trust boundaries. In fact, "ActiveX controls either have full permissions or do not run at all [Hopwood 1997]. In order to provide at least a basic level of security, Microsoft implemented a code signing system for ActiveX called *Authenticode*. A code signing system maintains a white list of trusted entities and requires trusted components to be cryptographically signed. Upon downloading an ActiveX control, the Internet Explorer queries its white list and only automatically executes the control if it was signed by a trusted publisher. If not, the browser expects the user to decide whether to permit the execution of the ActiveX control. In practice, the code signing system has proven to be inadequate and was repeatedly compromised [Rubin and Geer 1998]. This situation is worsened by the fact that the Internet Explorer automatically downloads, installs, and executes ActiveX controls from trusted entities. Considering that, due to the lack of a security framework, a legitimate ActiveX control can potentially open the door for illegitimate traffic, the potential lack of user interaction places an additional security risk in ActiveX controls. Nevertheless, the reliance on user interaction is not an appropriate security measure. The burden of

---
[4]The current version of PPAPI is also referred to as Pepper 2.

deciding whether to trust a software component should not be placed on the user. Both NPAPI and ActiveX provide unrestricted access to the local machine. Therefore, neither technology should be considered superior over the other in terms of security.

Due to the market dominance of the Windows operating system and its Internet Explorer web browser, ActiveX controls reached a fair level of propagation on websites — despite their lack of cross-platform support and the security vulnerabilities. While ActiveX remains supported by the most recent versions of the Internet Explorer, its relevance has faded. ActiveX is no longer considered a significant technology for web development.

## 3.2. Web 2.0

The *Web 2.0* revolution swept across the World Wide Web in the early 2000s, when websites finally surpassed their original static appearance and allowed users to interact and to collaborate with each other. New technologies facilitated highly interactive dynamic websites, making it possible for consumers to contribute content to the WWW and to engage in social activities.

The term itself is closely associated with Tim O'Reilly and his company O'Reilly Media, who co-initiated the first *Web 2.0 Conference* in 2004. According to O'Reilly, the burst of the dot-com bubble in the fall of 2001 "marked a turning point for the web [...] with exciting new applications and sites popping up with surprising regularity" [O'Reilly 2005]. Although the version number indicates otherwise, Web 2.0 does not imply a revision of the technological foundations of the World Wide Web — instead it represents a step past its original use-cases. This view is challenged by Tim Berners-Lee, the inventor of the World Wide Web, who argues that "Web 1.0 was all about connecting people [...] Web 2.0 is, of course, a piece of jargon, nobody even knows what it means. If Web 2.0 for you is blogs and wikis, then that is people to people. But that was what the Web was supposed to be all along." [Laningham 2006]. Web 2.0 has become a buzzword in the Internet scene, with multiple definitions and implications. Subsequently, Tim O'Reilly clarified his understanding of Web 2.0, stating that "Web 2.0 is the business revolution in the computer industry caused by the move to the internet as platform, and an attempt to understand the rules for success on that new platform. Chief among those rules is this: Build applications that harness network effects to get better the more people use them." [O'Reilly 2006].

### 3.2.1. Participation and User Generated Content

Web 2.0 has transformed the World Wide Web from a network of information into a network of participation. Suddenly, anybody could contribute to and expose himself through the Internet, e.g. by blogging, or sharing photos and videos. New and emerging web services, such as YouTube, Gmail, and Google Maps, transcended the traditional idea of software products — never packaged, instead delivered as a service — continuous improvement instead of scheduled software releases — no sale or licensing, just usage. YouTube depends on its user base to create value. While it provides a platform to share, find, and view video content, the content itself is uploaded by users. Videos can be commented on and voted for, which in turn affects the results of search queries. YouTube is a good example for the harnessing of network effects. It allows users to add value while using the web service and the service itself improves as the selection grows. Table 3.2 provides statistics on the overwhelming success of the YouTube video-sharing platform. Another good example for the harnessing of network effects as a business model is Facebook. Users do not provide their personal data intentionally. They

## 3. Background

do this to interact with friends and to keep in touch. As a "side effect" users add value to Facebook as a company by providing access to their personal data and interests, thus facilitating data mining and personalized advertisement.

Table 3.2.: Statistics of the YouTube video-sharing community [YouTube 2011]

| | |
|---|---|
| 13 million hours of video content | were uploaded in 2010 |
| 3 billion videos | are viewed every day |
| 240,000 full-length films | are uploaded per week |
| 70% | of YouTube traffic comes from outside the US |
| 700 billion playbacks | were reached in 2010 |
| 100 million people | engage in social activities on YouTube every week |
| Nearly 17 million people | have connected their YouTube account to at least one social service |

### 3.2.2. Technological Advancements

Web 2.0 did not happen overnight. Several technological advancements laid the groundwork for dynamic and interactive websites. Interestingly enough, neither NPAPI nor ActiveX controls played a major role in this development.

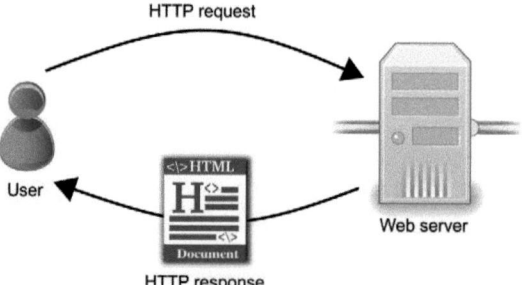

Figure 3.2.: Request and delivery of a static HTML page

The fundamental protocol of the Web is called *Hypertext Transfer Protocol (HTTP)*. HTTP is a request-response protocol that makes it possible for web browsers to request web content that is hosted on web servers. The web browser (or the client) issues a request to a web server and receives a response that is then presented to the user. HTTP is a stateless protocol, i.e. a server is not required to retain the status of a client, even if there are multiple requests. In order to attribute subsequent requests to a single user, websites commonly employ cookies[5] or server side sessions. In the early WWW, the content hosted on web servers consisted of static HTML pages. They were programmed by web developers and then served to web browsers. This process is illustrated in Figure 3.2. Advances in *server-side scripting* led to the concept of dynamic web pages. As the name indicates, dynamic web pages are dynamically created at a given time, instead of statically programmed. For example, consider a website that displays the current time. For obvious reasons, it does not make sense to

---
[5]Cookies allow a website to store information in web browsers that can be queried when the site is revisited.

create such a service as a static website — it would always be outdated. Instead, the HTML page containing the current time is created dynamically, when served to a web browser. This is achieved with server-side scripting. Server-side scripting allows the creation of a dynamic web page, based on the initial request — often by interfacing with databases or other data stores. Modern web servers support several server-side scripting technologies, such as PHP, Java, Perl, Python, and Microsoft's Active Server Pages (ASP). Figure 3.3 depicts the creation and serving of a dynamic web page, with the use of Java application logic and a database.

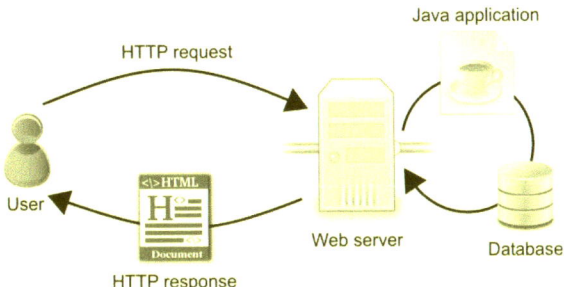

Figure 3.3.: Request, creation, and delivery of a Java-based dynamic web page

While dynamic web pages brought database technologies to the Web and made it possible to build HTTP responses that were tailored to users' requests, they did not make websites more interactive. Originally, individual pages of websites were requested by the web browser and returned as a whole by the web server. Each user request triggered the reload of an entire web page. This process was inefficient, e.g. a changed section caused a full page retransmit, and the user experience was impaired by flickering and delay. It was impossible to change *parts* of a web page — until *client-side scripting* became available. Client-side scripts are computer programs that are executed in the web browser. They make it possible to react on user input and to alter web pages without (necessarily) involving the web server. During the Web 2.0 wave, *Asynchronous JavaScript and XML (AJAX)* emerged as the most popular client-side scripting framework. It quickly replaced the NPAPI-based Java applets and Microsoft's ActiveX controls as the predominant technology for creating interactive websites. AJAX benefited from the fact that JavaScript had become a commodity and was supported by all modern web browsers, without requiring browser plugins.

### 3.2.3. AJAX

AJAX builds heavily on two underlying technologies that have been available much longer than AJAX itself: the *JavaScript* programming language and the *Extensible Markup Language (XML)*. JavaScript makes it possible to extend website functionality through client-side scripting. XML is a markup language to define the format of structured data in human-readable text files. It was inspired by the success of HTML and is very similar in syntax, albeit much less specific. For example, XML can be used to define custom file formats for data storage or high-level protocols for data exchange over a network. The combination of JavaScript and XML made it possible to dynamically change sections of a website — the term AJAX was born. The core principle of AJAX is that it allows the sending and receiving of data asynchronously from a web server and the subsequent modification of the structure of a web page. The data transfer occurs "in the background" and does not trigger a page reload. Instead

## 3. Background

of sending an entire HTML page, the web server sends slices of data that are encoded using XML. Upon receiving the web server's response, the web browser uses JavaScript to modify the *Document Object Model (DOM)* of the website. The DOM represents the structure of the web page itself. By modifying the DOM, a client-side script can modify the structure and contents of a web page without forcing a page reload. The advantages of AJAX are obvious:

1. *Reduced data volume*: less and more efficient data transfer
2. *Faster load times*: pages are updated quicker
3. *Improved presentation*: increased interactivity and less flicker due to page reload

Strictly speaking, neither XML nor JavaScript are requirements for AJAX programming. While these technologies have proven themselves in practice, there are alternatives for both data encoding and client-side scripting. For example, delivering plain text or HTML fragments are viable options, as these can easily be inserted into the DOM of a web page. Due to the verbosity of XML documents, the much more compact *JavaScript Object Notation (JSON)* has established itself as an popular format for data exchange. JSON[6] is a lightweight, text-based format that employs a key-value based structure [Crockford 2006]. It is human readable, yet easily parsable by machines, and, despite its name, not restricted to JavaScript. While JavaScript remains the most popular client-side scripting language for AJAX programming, due to its inclusion in all modern browsers, VBScript and ActionScript (Flash) are also capable of asynchronous data exchange and DOM manipulations. Two examples of the earliest and most groundbreaking AJAX web applications are Gmail (2004) and Google Maps (2005) — both built with JavaScript.

### 3.2.4. JavaScript

JavaScript is an object-oriented language that embraces the prototype-based object model[7]. Its primary design goal was to extend web sites with client-side executable code in order to allow client-side scripting. JavaScript was originally conceived by Brendan Eich of Netscape in 1995 and quickly gained acceptance among web developers. Eventually, Netscape submitted JavaScript for standardization, which resulted in the ECMAScript[8] language standard. Other implementations of ECMAScript include JScript, Microsoft's own JavaScript implementation for the Internet Explorer, and ActionScript, the scripting language that is used by Flash.

Despite its name, it is a common misconception that JavaScript is closely related to the programming language Java. This is not the case, although both share syntactic similarities that were borrowed from the C programming language. Semantically, JavaScript has much more in common with other dynamic programming languages, such as Smalltalk and Self. Ironically, JavaScript has long surpassed Java in terms of popularity for web development, although its APIs are far less powerful. The main advantage of JavaScript is its widespread availability — it is built into virtually all current web browsers[9] and not dependent on browser plugins. As illustrated in Figure 3.4, JavaScript has become the most widely used client-side scripting language for website programming. JavaScript is a cross-platform

---

[6]http://www.json.org, last visited on October 18, 2011.
[7]Prototype-based programming is an object-oriented programming model without classes that implements inheritance through cloning of existing objects, referred to as prototypes.
[8]ECMAScript defines a standardized scripting language.
[9]There are exceptions, e.g. the text-based lynx web browser, http://lynx.browser.org/; last visited on September 23, 2011.

## 3.2. Web 2.0

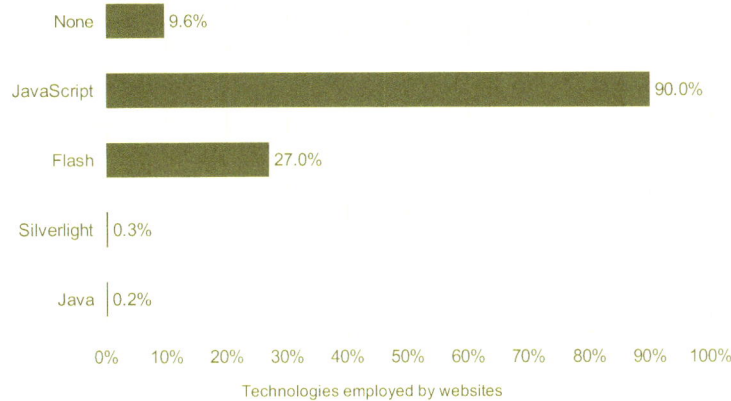

Figure 3.4.: Usage of client-side programming languages for websites [Q-Success 2011]

programming language and its applications run unmodified on any platform that provides a modern web browser.

**Characteristics**

JavaScript is a dynamic programming language that differs greatly from static programming languages, such as C and C++. A dynamic programming language is characterized by at least one of the following three attributes [Mikkonen and Taivalsaari 2007]:

1. *Dynamic typing*: types are associated with values, not with variables. Unlike static programming languages, most of their dynamic counterparts do not require variable and parameter types to be explicitly declared. The type of a variable is determined at runtime and may change over time.

2. *Interpretation*: source code is transfered into machine or byte code at runtime, i.e. during execution. This is in contrast to static programming languages, which employ a compiler to generate a binary representation of the source code before it can be executed.

3. *Runtime modification*: new classes, functions, variables, etc. can be added to classes and objects during execution. Static languages do not permit these modifications. On the contrary, structural and behavioral aspects of C, C++, and Java applications are unchangeable during runtime.

JavaScript fulfills all three characteristics. It is weakly typed, i.e. the types of variables must not be declared explicitly and are instead determined automatically during execution. This is in stark contrast to static languages that require variables to be explicitly defined and typed before they can be used to store values. Static programming languages usually employ a compiler to verify the source code and to compile, or translate it, into machine language. There is no explicit compiler for JavaScript — programming errors are detected and reported during execution. JavaScript source code is translated to machine language without the need for an intermediate byte code format. Finally, JavaScript

## 3. Background

permits the modification of source code while the program is running. This is impossible with static programming languages such as Java, C, and C++. Like Java, JavaScript features automatic memory management and garbage collection[10], plus it hides many low-level programming details from the developer. For these reasons, and due to its nature of a dynamic language, JavaScript development is often considered to be less demanding than C and C++ programming. On the other hand, JavaScript has the reputation of facilitating rapid application development and prototyping.

**Applications**

JavaScript has long been regarded as a "toy language", limited to bringing usability enhancements to websites [Mikkonen and Taivalsaari 2007]. Initially, these enhancements consisted of animated drop-down menues, simple pop-ups, etc. Its true potential as a full-featured programming language was discovered with the propagation of AJAX programming. Instead of providing mere enhancements to web pages, JavaScript was suddenly used to program complex websites that provided a level of functionality and interaction that was previously restricted to *real* applications. Following the success, popularity, and pervasiveness of AJAX-based web applications, JavaScript has long surpassed its original limitations of a scripting language within the web browser. For example, the applications of WebOS[11], the mobile operating system developed by Palm (now Hewlett Packard), are written in JavaScript. Among the reasons for this approach were the desire to tap into the growing community of JavaScript developers, rapid application development, tight integration with the Web, and advanced visual effects based on CSS transforms. While WebOS fell short of its expectations commercially, it is regarded as a highly polished and innovative mobile operating system that has recently extended its reach to tablets. Another example of a real world JavaScript product outside the web browser is GNOME Shell[12], the user interface shell of the very popular GNOME 3 desktop. GNOME Shell brings several innovative ideas to the desktop by adding an overlay for application and task management.

Although this application is far beyond its original scope, JavaScript is also gaining significant traction in server-side web development — most notably due to the *Node.js*[13] framework. Node.js is an event-driven JavaScript environment that simplifies the creation of scalable network programs, such as web servers. Instead of employing complex and error prone thread-based networking, Node embraces the asynchronous, or non-blocking, network programming model. Blocking I/O[14] halts the execution of an application until the I/O has been completed. Non-blocking I/O is more complex to program, but does not block the application in order to wait for the completion of I/O operations. Virtually all Node functions perform non-blocking I/O, which benefits the responsiveness and performance of Node applications. In addition to performance considerations, Node provides web developers with the advantage of using the same programming language for server and client development. Node.js is based on the V8[15] JavaScript engine of the Google Chrome browser, which is renowned for its speed. However, Node applications are not executed in the web browser. Instead, they run on a stand-alone version of the V8 engine that is distributed with Node.js.

---

[10] A garbage collector is a key component of automatic memory management that detects and frees memory occupied by objects that are no longer used by a computer program.
[11] https://developer.palm.com/, last visited on October 18, 2011.
[12] https://live.gnome.org/GnomeShell, last visited on September 23, 2011.
[13] http://nodejs.org/, last visited on October 18, 2011.
[14] Input/output, refers to the communication between a computer and another external entity, such as a hard drive, a second computer, or a human being.
[15] http://code.google.com/p/v8/, last visited on October 18, 2011.

## 3.2. Web 2.0

These examples underline the findings of Mikkonen and Taivalsaari who concluded that "we have found the JavaScript language to be a lot of fun" and their "experiences suggest that the JavaScript language can be used for developing real applications and even system software" [Mikkonen and Taivalsaari 2007].

### Performance

Although JavaScript has become the predominant client-side scripting language, it suffers from the performance disadvantages of dynamic languages. Since JavaScript source code is not compiled prior to execution, it must be translated into machine language during, or just-in-time for, execution. This additional overhead is costly in terms of performance, especially when compared to compiled applications that can be executed immediately. Whereas just-in-time compilation works well for statically typed virtual machine based languages, such as Java, it is a challenging task for JavaScript applications. Since many of these are short-lived scripts, it is not a trivial task to just-in-time compile them in an amount of time that guarantees a responsive browser during page loading. This is a problem and presents significant performance challenges, "because JavaScript blocks downloads and rendering in the browser" [Souders 2008].

These performance problems became increasingly apparent as the complexity of interactive websites grew. Mikkonen and Taivalsaari argued in 2007 that "a lot of room is left in optimizing JavaScript performance" and that "there is no fundamental reason for JavaScript VMs to run two orders of magnitude slower than Java virtual machines" [Mikkonen and Taivalsaari 2007]. When Google, one of the foremost proponents of interactive websites and web applications, entered the browser market in 2008 with the Chrome browser, the company set security and JavaScript performance as its primary goals. Soon afterwards, JavaScript benchmarks confirmed Chrome's outstanding JavaScript performance. As JavaScript performance became a marketing instrument, it fueled the competition between the major browsers that are Mozilla Firefox, Apple Safari, Opera, Google Chrome, and Microsoft Internet Explorer. With almost every new release, a different browser takes the lead in popular JavaScript benchmarks, such as SunSpider[16], V8[17], and Dromaeo[18]. Figure 3.5 depicts the impressive performance gains that have resulted from this development. Despite these achievements, Chang al. concluded in 2009 that "JavaScript performance has become one of the bottlenecks preventing the development of even more interactive client side applications" [Chang et al. 2009].

Although benchmarks confirm that the *browser wars* have generally led to higher JavaScript performance, doubts remain as to whether real applications can directly benefit from these improvements [Ratanaworabhan et al. 2010]. The quest for JavaScript performance is ongoing and new strategies such as tracing have found their way into modern JavaScript engines [Chang et al. 2009]. Despite these efforts, "it is unlikely that JavaScript performance will catch up to the speed of native code execution" [Kroeker 2009]. This realization may not be crucial for many web applications, but it can prevent the creation of web applications that need to get as much performance out of the computing hardware as possible.

---

[16]http://www.webkit.org/perf/sunspider/sunspider.html, last visited on October 18, 2011.
[17]http://v8.googlecode.com/svn/data/benchmarks/v6/run.html, last visited on October 18, 2011.
[18]http://dromaeo.com, last visited on October 18, 2011.

## 3. Background

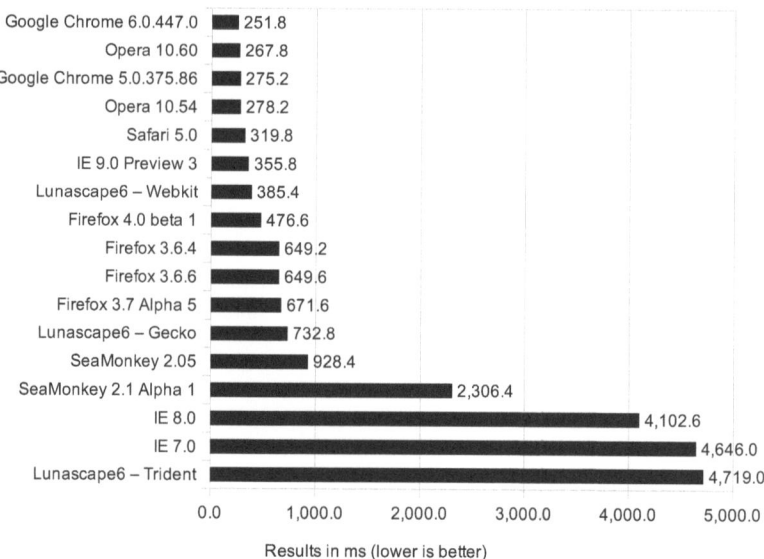

Figure 3.5.: SunSpider JavaScript benchmark results for 15 web browsers, as of June 25, 2010 [Kirsch 2010]

## 3.3. Web Applications

Web applications are applications that run in the web browser. While Websites contain information, web applications assist the user in performing tasks. Modern web applications provide a similar look and feel and a level of functionality comparable to that of traditional native applications. Web applications need not be installed before being usable and they can be accessed from mobile devices — any time, anywhere. Their only preconditions are the availability of Internet access and a modern web browser.

Every web application consists of at least two parts: a client-side part that runs in the web browser and a server-side part. In its simplest from, the server-side part consists of a web server that distributes the web application when accessed with a web browser. This structure is referred to as a two-tier architecture. Depending on the complexity of a web application, its structure may be organized in several *tiers*. Every tier is a layer in the web application structure that performs specialized tasks. Figure 3.6 depicts the structure of a three-tier web application architecture that adds a storage component. The level of tiers is also affected by the amount of functionality that is incorporated in the web application. A *rich Internet application (RIA)*, in which most of the functionality is concentrated in the front-end, might not require a particularly feature-rich back-end. For this approach a two-tier structure could be sufficient. In return, a simple front-end could be backed by complex application logic in the cloud that must be organized into several tiers, in order to provide a reliable and scalable service.

Several programming languages are available for web application development. However, the combi-

## 3.3. Web Applications

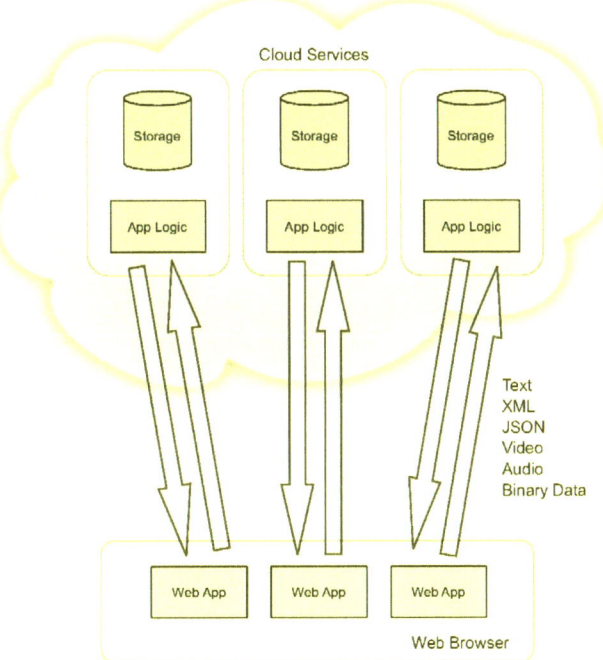

Figure 3.6.: Structure of a three-tier web application

nation of JavaScript and HTML5[19] has emerged as the prevalent web application framework. It is the only web application framework that is built into virtually every modern web browser.

### 3.3.1. Native Applications vs. Web Applications

Native applications are called native, because they are compiled to machine language for a computer's central processing unit (CPU) architecture. This approach provides low-level access to the hardware and leaves it up to the developer to deal with complex issues such as memory management. Writing complex native applications is challenging, but provides two major advantages: speed and efficiency. Many popular applications are native applications, e.g. web browsers, Microsoft Office, Adobe Photoshop, Apple Logic, and virtually all sophisticated computer games, just to name a few. The predominant form of monetization for native applications is licensing, i.e. the consumer buys a copy of the application which he may install and use on his computer. Because native applications are usually distributed as packages, regardless of whether they are purchased in stores or downloaded over the Internet, they are developed in scheduled releases. Bug fixes and new features are made

---

[19] HTML5 is the next major revision of the HTML specification.

## 3. Background

available through the next release and not immediately after being implemented. The complexity of native applications and the packaging overhead require thorough testing, before a new version can be released to the public. Once an update is released, all users must upgrade their applications in order to benefit from the improvements of the new version.

Native applications are developed for a certain operating system or computing platform, such as Microsoft Windows, i.e. they are operating system dependent. Ensuring that a native application runs on several competing computing platforms, e.g. Windows, Apple Macintosh, and Linux distributions, is a substantial undertaking that increases the application's overall complexity.

The modern web browser has evolved into a feature-rich runtime for applications that transcends its original purpose of a viewer for static content. It provides seamless Internet access, high level programming languages such as JavaScript, and the flexibility of the Document Object Model (DOM) for graphics presentation and user interaction. These features are the foundations of modern web applications. Web applications run in the web browser and differ greatly from native applications. They are not developed for a specific operating system. On the contrary, web applications are operating system independent. Any operating system that provides a modern web browser will be able to run the same web application without modifications. Web applications are delivered as a service. Neither must they be packaged and distributed to the consumer, nor must they be installed before being usable. It suffices to direct the web browser to the web application's URL and the program becomes accessible. This is a huge advantage over the prerequisites of native applications, because web applications can be used anywhere, anytime, from any computer or mobile device — as long as there is an Internet connection.

Table 3.3.: Key differences between native applications and web applications

| | Native Applications | Web Applications |
|---|---|---|
| Distribution | Packages must be installed | Delivered as a service |
| Updates | Must be performed individually | Seamless |
| Target platform | Operating system | Web browser |
| Operating system independent | No | Yes |
| Monetization | Licensing model | Pay-per-use, subscription |
| Release management | Scheduled | Immediate |
| Can be used anywhere, anytime | No, must be installed first | Yes |
| Require Internet connectivity | No | Yes, mostly |

The software licensing model that has proven to be successful for native applications is not suitable for web applications, as there is no copy to be bought or installed. Instead, advertising and subscription-based or pay-per-use models have emerged as the primary forms of web application monetization. Advertising has been accepted by consumers because it keeps many popular web applications available for free, e.g. Google and Yahoo Mail, Facebook, Google and Bing Search, and Flickr. Since web applications are not distributed as packages and must not be installed, it is much simpler for developers to provide updates on a regular basis. Whenever a new version of a web application is made available, all users immediately gain access to the improvements. In most cases, they will not even be aware of the changes, except that things that were broken yesterday suddenly work today. Web application developers gain a level of control over the software versions in use that cannot be matched by native applications. For example, the Internet Explorer 6 remains one of the most widely used web browsers to date, even though it is considered outdated and was superseded by three major versions (Internet Explorer 7, 8, and 9). The ease of distribution and update management are among the most compelling advantages of web applications. The key differences between native applications and web applications are compared in Table 3.3.

### 3.3.2. Towards the HTML5 Standard

HTML is the markup language that is used to describe websites in the World Wide Web. "HTML was primarily designed as a language for semantically describing scientific documents, although its general design and adaptations over the years have enabled it to be used to describe a number of other types of documents" [Hickson 2010].

Figure 3.7.: The HTML5 logo

The next major revision of the HTML standard is called *HTML5* and it adds several new syntax features to the language. HTML5 lays the foundation for richer web applications and aims to provide functionality that is equivalent to that of Adobe Flash, Microsoft Silverlight, and Java FX — without requiring the installation of these proprietary application frameworks. In fact, it is one of the goals of the HTML5 initiative to move the Web away from closed, proprietary technologies and to provide an open development framework for web applications. HTML5 and JavaScript are closely related. The HTML5 APIs complement JavaScript's very limited own core APIs, thus facilitating the development of modern web applications. The HTML5 standard is currently work in progress and has not yet been finalized. Nevertheless, modern web browsers have begun supporting features of the current draft proposals. The HTML5 specification is being developed by the Web Hypertext Application Technology Working Group (WHATWG) and the World Wide Web Consortium (W3C) in a joint effort.

**Functionality**

Although the specification is very specific about the functionality it defines, HTML5 has become the umbrella term for next generation browser APIs — even those that are not strictly part of the HTML5 specification. Among the most prominent new APIs of the HTML5 specification are [O'Reilly 2009], [van Kesteren 2011]:

- AUDIO: the ability to play back audio content
- CONTENTEDITABLE: enables documents with editable areas
- DRAG AND DROP: allows the dragging and dropping of objects

## 3. Background

- OFFLINE SUPPORT: support for web applications that can be used offline
- VIDEO: the ability to play back video content

Other features that are commonly associated with HTML5 but not part of the HTML5 specification, as published by the W3C, include:

- CANVAS: allows the drawing of 2D shapes and images
- GEOLOCATION: provides location information of a device to web applications
- WEBGL: allows the creation of 3D web applications using the OpenGL ES 2.0 API
- WEB SOCKETS: enable bidirectional communications with server-side processes
- WEB WORKERS: facilitate the execution of background tasks, without blocking the user interface

Table 3.4.: Status of the HTML5 support in the leading web browsers, as of August, 2011 [Deveria 2011]

|  | Chrome 13 | Firefox 5 | IE 9 | Opera 11 | Safari 5 |
|---|---|---|---|---|---|
| AUDIO |  |  |  |  |  |
| CANVAS |  |  |  |  |  |
| CONTENTEDITABLE |  |  |  |  |  |
| DRAG AND DROP |  |  |  | Not supported |  |
| GEOLOCATION |  |  |  |  |  |
| OFFLINE SUPPORT |  |  | Not supported |  |  |
| VIDEO |  |  |  |  |  |
| WEB SOCKETS |  |  | Not supported | Partially supported |  |
| WEB WORKERS |  |  | Not supported |  |  |
| WEBGL | Partially supported |  | Not supported |  |  |

These features make it possible to build richer web applications in the web browser. Perhaps their necessity is best underlined by the rate of adoption of key HTML5 elements by browser vendors and web developers — although the HTML5 specification is still not finalized. For example, despite a lack of agreement and ongoing discussion regarding the supported video formats, several video portals, such as Vimeo[20] and YouTube[21], are already offering HTML5 powered videos instead of Adobe Flash based videos. Google has recently added drag and drop support to its Gmail product, which makes it possible to drag files from the desktop into the web browser in order to attach them to an e-mail — a

---

[20] http://vimeo.com/tag:html5, last visited on October 18, 2011.
[21] http://www.youtube.com/html5, last visited on October 18, 2011.

## 3.3. Web Applications

feature that has been available in native applications for a long time. The Google Docs team is said to be working on incorporating the new offline capabilities into Google Docs, making the Documents, Spreadsheet, and Presentation applications usable without of an active Internet connection. HTML5 "is not just a markup language but a computing platform that will make Web apps even more powerful than they are now" [Berners-Lee 2010].

### Limitations

HTML5 adds many exciting new APIs to modern web browsers that facilitate the development of richer web applications. While it does close the gap to alternative web development frameworks such as Flash, several limitations and open issues remain. The HTML5 support for video was welcomed by many as an alternative to the use of Flash. However, it has been set back by disagreements over the video formats that should be supported. While Mozilla favored free and open source codecs, Apple and Microsoft pushed for the adoption of the H.264, a video codec that contains patented technology. Because of these and other technical limitations, e.g. HTML5 does not yet provide support for webcams and microphones, YouTube drew the conclusion in December 2010 that HTML5 is not yet ready to replace Flash as the standard for video on the Web[22].

HTML5 does not offer any support for multi-touch gestures, which are very popular on mobile devices, and it is hampered by naming inconsistencies in the implementations of different browser vendors. Until the final specification arrives, which is expected to be in the second quarter of 2014[23], web developers will need to take these into account. Despite these shortcomings, there is no doubt that HTML5 is the future of web development.

---

[22]http://www.technewsworld.com/story/70333.html?wlc=1312454709, last visited on Oct. 18, 2011.

[23]http://www.wired.co.uk/news/archive/2011-02/15/html5-2014-what-next, last visited on October 18, 2011.

# 4. The Web as a Platform

Web 2.0 services and the growing relevance of web applications have turned the Internet into an extension of individual computers [McFedries 2008]. Users have become accustomed to employing web applications for their daily computing tasks and to storing their data in the cloud — videos on YouTube, e-mail in Gmail, and contacts in Facebook. The availability of high-speed Internet connectivity in many parts of the (Western) world has provided the basis for ubiquitous computing, where information and computing become everyday objects that are generally available. With everything and everybody being interconnected, the network has become the operating system for "a megacomputer that encompasses the Internet, all its services, all peripheral chips and affiliated devices from scanners to satellites, and the billions of human minds entangled in this global network" [Kelly 2005]. Or, as Nicholas Carr puts it: "The World Wide Web has turned into the World Wide Computer" [Carr 2008].

Simply put, the Web has evolved into a significant computing platform. A computing platform facilitates the development and execution of applications. "The World Wide Computer, like any other electronic computer, is programmable." [Carr 2008]. It allows the creation of services and applications that are provided over the Internet. For the first time, a computing platform was successfully decoupled from the underlying operating system — web applications are operating system neutral and do not target OS-specific APIs (see Section 3.3). The Web as a platform belongs to no one and can be programmed by anyone, therefore "Mozilla believes that the web can displace proprietary, single-vendor stacks for application development" [Mozilla Foundation 2011].

While web applications running in the web browser constitute the front-end of the Web as a platform, the back-end is powered by cloud computing, a new Internet buzzword. In the cloud computing model, data and applications reside within the cloud, i.e. the Internet. Cloud computing turns computing infrastructure, platforms, and applications into services that are often provided on a pay-per-use basis. Examples of these services include search, identity, the social graph, location, communications, media access, as well as calendar and e-mail services. Today, users often own several Internet-enabled devices, for example a PC, a smartphone, and a tablet. Storing personal data on any of these devices has become a limitation, as it prohibits access and use from the remaining devices. A user's music library should, ideally, be accessible from any of these devices — even on the go. The synchronization of personal data through the Internet is becoming the obvious solution to this problem. The downside of this approach is that personal data is transfered to the Internet, or the cloud, transcending the reach and control of its individual owners. Challenges remain for cloud computing in terms of governance, data protection, and data lock-in.

This chapter provides insight into the historical dominance of the Microsoft Windows platform and the growing significance of the Web as a platform. It offers a classification of computing platforms into three categories, access API, plugin API, and runtime environment platforms, and explains their benefits and drawbacks. Further, the Web as a platform is defined and its central components are introduced and explained. An introduction to cloud computing is given and innovative cloud services are presented. Finally, the challenges of the Web as a platform are discussed.

4. The Web as a Platform

## 4.1. Beyond the Microsoft Windows Platform

During the Web 2.0 period, the predominant platform for application development was the Microsoft Windows platform. In those times, before the rise of smartphones and tablets, the personal computer (PC) was the only widely used personal computing device. In other words, the computing experience was very homogeneous. Although alternative platforms continued to exist, e.g. Apple Mac OS, Linux, and different flavors of the UNIX operating system, the vast majority of PCs was powered by the Windows OS. There were good reasons for this market dominance: Microsoft invested heavily into developer tools, provided necessary APIs for application development, and guaranteed that old software would work with new iterations of the Windows platform. Plus, the Windows OS promised the greatest user base and thus the largest potential group of potential customers on the market. The feature-rich Windows API facilitated all kinds of applications, ranging from games to office productivity suites, but it also locked developers and users into the Windows platform. However, this downside was generally accepted by both parties. Perhaps the advantages of the Windows platform and the simplicity of targeting a *single* application platform outweighed the drawbacks. Neither the Java platform, with its promise of cross-platform application development, nor the open source movement around the Linux OS were able to challenge the dominance of the Windows platform, although both platforms have reached a notable market share in the server sector. Linux is still waiting for its breakthrough on the desktop and Java has lost its significance in the consumer space — with the notable exception that it serves as the underlying technology for the successful Android mobile phone operating system.

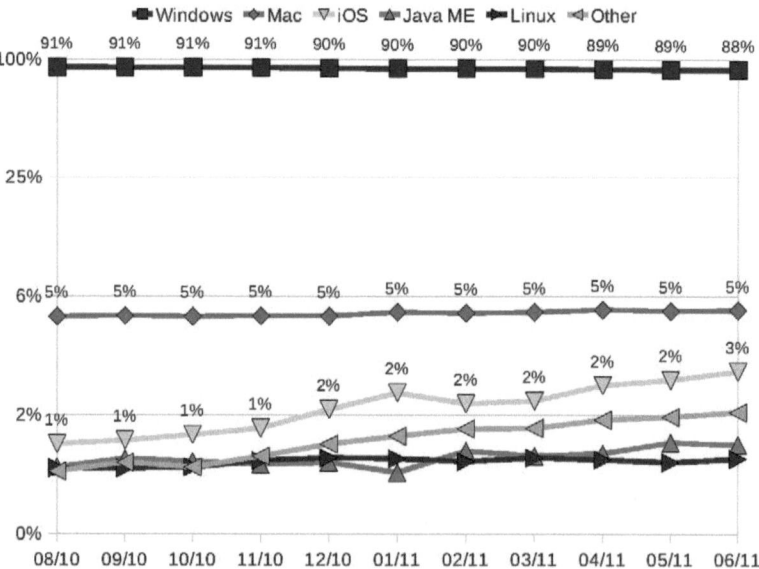

Figure 4.1.: OS market share as of June 2011 [Net Applications 2011]

Meanwhile, however, a substantial part of the Windows/PC equation has changed. With the appearance of the Apple iPhone and other smartphones, computing devices have suddenly become heterogeneous. The Apple iPad sounded the bell for the breakthrough of tablet computers, an entirely new form factor that abandoned keyboard and mouse altogether. These new devices run a variety of operating systems, most of which are not manufactured by Microsoft. The market share of mobile devices is exploding and cannibalizing that of low-cost personal computers. For instance, in the first quarter of 2011, Apple sold more than twice as many iPads and more than five times as many iPhones as computers[1]. The impact of these new devices on the Windows platform is (still) marginal but clearly visible. As depicted in Figure 4.1 the market share of the Windows operating system has dropped below 90% — for the first time in decades. Although Windows remains the most used operating system by far, it has lost market share to mobile operating systems, most notably iOS and Android. The market for mobile devices is fragmented — there is much more competition than in the traditional PC sector. Although Apple's iOS and Google's Android mobile platforms are battling for the lead in terms of market share, several other competitors are striving to sell their mobile products. The only thing all platforms, mobile or the PC, have in common is their support for modern, standard-compliant web browsers. Web applications, built on top of the Web as a platform, have the potential to become a means of developing applications that run on all devices and all operating systems.

## 4.2. Platform Classification

In the year 2009, Marc Andreessen, best known as co-founder of Netscape and co-author of mosaic, the first widely-used web browser, offered a classification of Internet platforms. Andreessen argued that the Internet platforms of the future would be delivered as online services, instead of as products. They would not require developers to download and install SDKs (Software Development Kits) — applications would be developed in the web browser. In an attempt to describe and distinguish the models of popular web services, Andreessen defined three levels of Internet platforms: Level 1, Level 2, and Level 3 [Andreessen 2009]. They are compared in Table 4.1.

### 4.2.1. Level 1: Access API

An access API platform is typically provided in the form of a web services API, usually accessed using the REST, SOAP, or comparable protocols. In this service model, the platform offers access to its web services via the Internet. Developers of web applications can integrate these services into their web applications — hence the name access API. The key characteristic of the access API platform is that applications live, and are executed outside of the platform, e.g. on servers provided and maintained by the application developer. This approach is currently the most common Internet platform and employed by eBay, Paypal, Flickr, Delicious, and many others.

The downside of the access API platform is that it places the entire responsibility of building, deploying, and running applications on the developer. In terms of both technical expertise and financial resources, this is a considerable demand, as it involves the maintenance of the runtime system, programming language, database solution, servers, storage, networking, bandwidth, and security. While it is the simplest platform to create, the Level 1 platform is the most difficult to program. Therefore, the propagation of web services APIs has fallen short compared to previous widespread native application platforms, such as Microsoft Windows or the Apple Macintosh.

---

[1] http://www.apple.com/pr/library/2011/07/19Apple-Reports-Third-Quarter-Results.html, last visited on October 18, 2011.

*4. The Web as a Platform*

## 4.2.2. Level 2: Plugin API

A plugin API platform allows the extension of its core functionality by making it possible to plug applications into the platform. This concept has seen widespread adoption within native applications. For example, both the Adobe Photoshop image manipulation program and many web browsers allow third-party developers to add missing functionality in the form of plugins (see Section 3.1). One of the first and most important Level 2 Internet platforms is the Facebook platform[2]. Instead of providing Level 1 web services APIs, the Facebook platform makes it possible to develop applications that become part of the Facebook user experience — applications can be plugged into Facebook. This approach is seen as a role model for upcoming Internet services, as it allows developers to add functionality, while retaining the branding of a platform.

Just like in a Level 1 platform, the applications of a Level 2 platform reside outside the platform and also run somewhere else. Again, the burden of creating and running applications is placed on developers, who need to provide and maintain the necessary infrastructure. The technical expertise and financial resources required to deploy and operate applications on Level 2 platforms remain very high, which limits the adoption of these platforms. The major advantage of Level 2 platforms, on the other hand, is that they provide a distribution channel that allows developers to market and monetize their applications. For example, the Facebook platform boasts more than 500 million users [Zuckerberg 2010], which makes it a very attractive platform for application developers. Level 2 platforms are substantially more complex than Level 1 platforms and must deal with the technical, quality assurance, and security issues of plugging external applications into their user experiences.

Table 4.1.: Three levels of Internet platforms [Andreessen 2009]

|  | Level 1 | Level 2 | Level 3 |
|---|---|---|---|
| Provides web services APIs | x | x | x |
| Applications become part of the user experience |  | x | x |
| Applications run on the platform |  |  | x |
| Developers must provide infrastructure | x | x |  |
| Complexity of creating the platform | low | medium | high |

## 4.2.3. Level 3: Runtime Environment

The major difference between the Level 3 Internet platform and the other platforms is that applications actually run on the platform, inside the core system. In other words, the platform provides the *runtime environment* for the execution of third-party applications. Developers no longer need to maintain their own infrastructure — they simply upload their code into the platform, where it is executed. The implication that third-party code runs inside a platform generates substantial issues for a platform provider in terms of security, quality, and reliability. Therefore, the creation of a Level 3 platform is much more complex than that of a Level 1 oder Level 2 platform.

The advantages of the runtime environment platform are that the technical and financial prerequisites of developing and deploying a applications drop to a minimum. This makes it possible for developers who would be technically or financially incapable of embracing Level 1 or 2 platforms to implement and

---
[2]http://developers.facebook.com/, last visited on September 27, 2011.

deploy their applications. The Level 3 platform offers a multitude of possibilities, such as sharing code in an open source fashion, or even selling code through a marketplace. The traditional Windows/PC platform is a typical Level 3 platform — its applications are created for, are deployed on, and run on the platform, i.e. the computer. The advantages of this type of platform are compelling and have lead to the development of several Level 3 Internet platforms, e.g. Google AppEngine, Microsoft Azure, the Saleforce platform — and most notably the Apple iOS mobile platform.

### 4.2.4. Criticism and Implications

Critics argued that Andreessen's definition of Internet platforms defines platforms on the platform, i.e. on top of the platform that is the Web. In addition, his enthusiasm for the level 3 platform was seen as a bias towards the Ning platform[3], which Andreessen co-founded [Wilson 2007]. While Andreessen's classification of Internet platforms is certainly debatable, it provides the basis of understanding why platforms are built and embraced.

In addition to facilitating the development of applications, a strong platform can provide extra benefits to its developers, such as access to user bases and data, distribution channels, marketing efforts, and ways of monetization — things that developers cannot easily build themselves. These factors can determine the popularity and success of a platform, as they have done with Facebook and the Android and iOS mobile platforms. For instance, Zynga, a company that develops and operates browser games[4] on social networks, as well as its on own web sites, has flourished in the undertow of Facebook. Zynga's top 50 games are being played by almost 200 million users every month [AppData] and the revenue for the year 2010 is expected to be as high as $500 million [Helft 2010]. The company has successfully been able to tackle the technical challenges of building a popular gaming platform and scaling it to to millions of users, but it is questionable whether Zynga would have had the amount of success, had they not been able to tap into the vast amount of users and the distribution channel that the Facebook platform provides.

Josh Catone asks, "If the entire web is a platform, why would a developer choose to cede control over his app by locking himself into a single, third-party platform?" and then provides the answer himself: "The answer is that these platforms give developers access to something they can't easily build themselves — such as users, data, or development tools" [Catone 2007]. It is one of the greatest challenges of the Web as a platform to evolve into a compelling development platform that encompasses these extra benefits.

## 4.3. Components of the Web as a Platform

Unlike the Microsoft Windows or the Apple iOS platform, the Web as a platform is not controlled by a single (commercial) entity. Instead, it is a "system without an owner, tied together by a set of protocols, open standards and agreements for cooperation" [O'Reilly 2005]. The evolution of the Web itself has determined the evolution of the Web as a platform. Its central meta components are illustrated in Figure 4.2: runtime, application framework, tools, cloud services, and monetization.

---

[3] Ning is an Internet platform (level 3) that provides the necessary building blocks for people to create their own social networks. http://www.ning.com/; last visited on October 18, 2011.
[4] Browser games run inside the web browser and usually need not be purchased. Instead gamers repeatedly pay for extra features or in game advantages, thus generating revenue.

## 4. The Web as a Platform

Several different implementations exist for each meta component, e.g. a web browser, the runtime of the Web as a platform, is available as a product from Microsoft, Apple, Mozilla, Google, Opera, and several smaller vendors. This level of multi-vendor support applies the other components as well and is achieved by the embracement of open protocols and promises of interoperability. Although, or maybe because the Web has no owner, the implementations of the foundational meta components are mostly interchangeable. This makes the Web as a platform more open and more flexible than any single-vendor owned platform for software development. This section introduces and defines the central meta components of the Web as a platform.

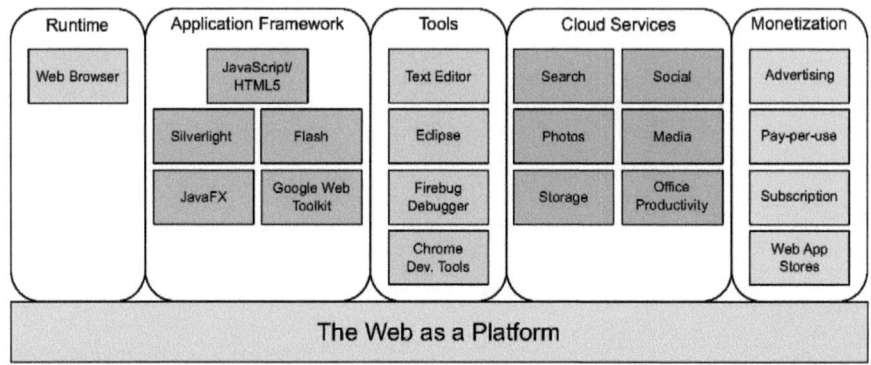

Figure 4.2.: Components of the Web as a platform

### 4.3.1. Runtime

It is frequently claimed that the web browser itself has become a new platform for application development, or even a new operating system that permits the execution of programs. The browser is indeed an integral part of the new platform that is the Web, as it allows the client-side execution of web applications. However, the functionality of browser-based web applications would be decisively limited without the functionality provided by cloud services in the back-end. Therefore, it seems more appropriate to refer to the web browser as a *runtime* for web applications, instead of a platform itself.

The modern web browser has long surpassed its original purpose as a content viewer for static information. Today, it provides the core functionality for the implementation and execution of web applications:

1. Seamless Internet access
2. High-level programming languages
3. HTML, DOM, and CSS for interactive highly user interfaces
4. Profiling and debugging tools

The HTTP and HTTPS (secure and encrypted HTTP) protocols are the core protocols of the Web. They are supported by all web browsers and provide seamless access to Internet resources. HTTP

## 4.3. Components of the Web as a Platform

and HTTPS allow the request and transfer of data between web browsers and web servers. They also allow the integration of cloud services with web applications.

As explained in Section 3.2.4, JavaScript has become the dominant programming language for the development of web applications. However, other programming languages are available as parts of alternative application frameworks. These will be discussed in detail in Section 4.3.2.

Like modern websites, web applications employ HTML and Cascading Style Sheets (CSS) for the layout and design of their user interfaces. CSS is a styling language that describes the design of an HTML document. The use of CSS makes it possible to separate the structure of a web application from its styling. While the general layout and document structure is defined in HTML, CSS is used to define the look of user interface elements and to determine their positioning. The CSS support in modern web browsers is constantly improving to meet the needs of web developers. New CSS versions permit animations[5] and other user interface effects that previously had to be implemented using JavaScript. AJAX and DOM manipulations remain core technologies of interactive web applications. Their foundational technologies, JavaScript, XML, JSON, are well supported by modern web browsers.

Since the JavaScript programming language does not include a compiler for the validation and compilation of its programs, these tasks must be handled by the JavaScript engines of modern web browsers. These engines are responsible for the parsing, validation, interpretation/compilation, error handling, and execution of JavaScript programs. Since the web browser already provides the tools to validate and execute JavaScript applications, this functionality can be reused to inspect or debug JavaScript programs during execution. Many browsers feature built-in debugging[6] and profiling[7] tools that assist the developer in finding applications bugs and performance bottlenecks.

As the runtime for web applications, the web browser is responsible for their secure execution and containment. A lot of work has gone into the security frameworks of modern browsers. The Google Chrome browser was the first browser to isolate its JavaScript engine, HTML renderer, and other key browser components from the underlying operating system using sandboxes [Barth et al. 2008]. This security measure restricts the damage that malicious or flawed web application code can do to the underlying system. Chrome also employs process isolation to separate web applications that run in different browser tabs from another [Reis and Gribble 2009]. As explained in Section 3.1.1, browser plugins, which were initially executed in-process, have been moved out-of-process in order to improve stability and security. Instead of running with the same privileges as the main browser process, web browser plugins are now restricted in permissions. While not all web browsers implement all of these security mechanisms, the security measures for web application execution have certainly improved — including the speed in which security vulnerabilities are being fixed. Some browser vendors even proactively issue bounties for the detection of security weaknesses.

The main disadvantage of the web browser as the runtime for web applications lies in its heterogeneity. The browser market is fragmented and highly competitive, which is positive for innovation. On the other hand, web developers must ensure that their websites and web applications are compatible with a variety of web browsers — all with different versions, functionality, and bugs. From a web developer's perspective this can be a lot of work and a frustrating experience in general. The fragmentation of the web browser market is the price for the openness of the Web as a platform.

---

[5] CSS transforms have been introduced as part of the CSS 3 specification.
[6] A debugger makes it possible to step through the execution of a computer program and to inspect the contents of its variables.
[7] A profiler is used to optimize computer programs, by analyzing its use of system resources.

## 4. The Web as a Platform

### 4.3.2. Application Framework

An application framework is comprised of a set of programming languages and their core APIs, which can be used by software developers to create applications. The Web as a platform can be programmed with HTML5/JavaScript and various external application frameworks — namely Flash, Silverlight, and JavaFX.

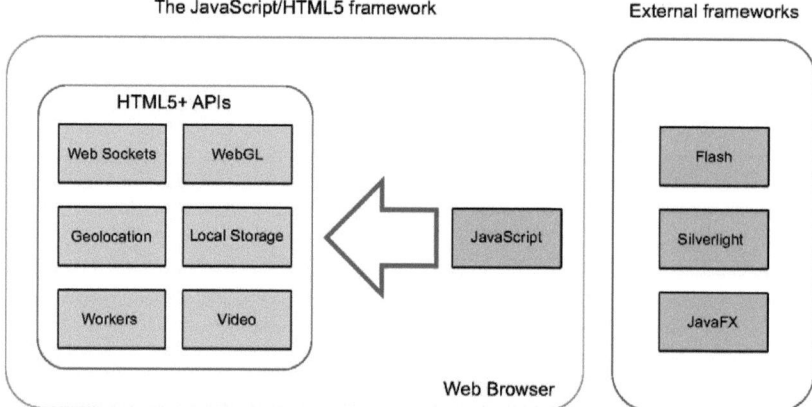

Figure 4.3.: Web application frameworks

Flash was originally introduced as a multimedia framework, but is now positioned as a general purpose web application development framework. Flash applications are programmed in ActionScript, which, being an implementation of the ECMAScript specification, shares many syntactical similarities with JavaScript. Silverlight was created by Microsoft as an alternative to Flash. It is based on the .NET framework, which is the modernized core framework for application development on the Windows platform. Silverlight embraces the C# programming language, a modern garbage-collected language that borrows a lot from Java in terms of its design and syntax. Silverlight has failed to gain a critical amount of traction for web application development, but remains a core technology of Microsoft's mobile devices strategy. JavaFX aims to bring the Java API to web applications and introduces a new scripting language called JavaFX Script. Its impact on real world web application has so far been minor.

Although Flash, Silverlight, and JavaFX have long provided most of the functionality that is now being introduced with HTML5, they suffer from three major disadvantages. First, they are not built into modern web browsers and must be installed as browser plugins[8]. Second, they are controlled by single commercial entities, which limits the influence of third parties. Third, the support for Flash, Silverlight, and JavaFX on mobile devices is poor — with the exception of the Microsoft Windows Phone 7 platform that is largely based on Silverlight. Apple explicitly refused to allow Flash support for its leading iOS operating system that powers the iPhones and iPads. Even competitors that have invested heavily in Flash support, in order to gain a USP over iOS, have so far been unable to deliver a satisfying user experience. Flash applications on mobile devices are often hampered by poor usability and performance deficits. HTML5 and JavaScript, on the other hand, are widely supported

---

[8] An exception, to some extent, is the Flash plugin that has since been built into the Google Chrome browser.

by all modern mobile operating systems. According to a study by ABI Research, "more than 2.1 billion mobile devices will have HTML5 browsers by 2016, up from just 109 million in 2010" [Taylor 2011]. Together with the rich feature set that HTML5/JavaScript are gaining, this duo has become a compelling application framework for web developers.

A very interesting framework for the development of web applications is the *Google Web Toolkit (GWT)*[9]. The goal of GWT is to facilitate the development of complex, yet highly optimized, JavaScript-based web applications, without the need to focus on browser specific behavior. Somewhat surprisingly, GWT applications are not written in JavaScript, but in the Java programming language. The GWT software development kit (SDK) provides core Java APIs for the development of AJAX web applications in Java. A Java GWT application is then translated into highly optimized JavaScript code that can be executed on all major browsers, including those of the leading mobile devices. GWT even makes it possible to test and debug its Java applications in the web browser, without requiring an initial translation to JavaScript. The Google Web Toolkit is an open source framework that offers many advantages for rapid web development, especially for developers that are accustomed to Java. It is used for various Google projects.

### 4.3.3. Tools

High-quality developer tools are important for a platform. One of the reasons for success of the Windows platform were its outstanding tools and the support Microsoft provided to its application developers. Unlike the Windows platform, the Web is an open platform for web application development. Therefore, there are no "official" tools for the development of web applications. Countless tools have appeared — developed by commercial vendors, open source initiatives, and individuals. Web developers are free to choose between several text editors and full featured integrated development environments (IDEs) for web application development. Eclipse, one of the most popular open source IDEs, provides integrated debuggers and build automation tools for several programming languages. It is also easily extensible and allows projects like GWT to plug into its core functionality.

The web browser plays an essential part during the development and testing of web applications. Since JavaScript applications need not be compiled, changes to the source code become effective immediately after an application reload in the browser. Unlike native desktop or mobile platforms, the Web as a platform does not require the use of emulators[10] for the development of web applications — a web browser is sufficient. Many modern browsers have development tools such as debuggers and profilers built in. Alternatively, as in the example of the excellent *Firebug* debugger for Mozilla Firefox, these are available as browser extensions. Browser extensions differ from browser plugins in the sense that they allow the extension of a web browser's functionality, instead of its ability to present web content [Barth et al. 2009]. Extensions are commonly written using HTML, CSS, and JavaScript, instead of native code.

In compiler development, a major breakthrough is achieved when the compiler is self-hosting, i.e. it is able to compile its own source code. On a similar note, web-based development tools, making it possible to develop web applications in the web browser, are starting to appear. One of the most prominent projects was the Mozilla Bespin/Skywriter project, which has recently been merged into the Ace project[11]. Ace is a code editor, written in JavaScript, that supports features such as syntax highlighting, auto intention, search using regular expressions, and matching parentheses — all in the

---
[9] http://code.google.com/webtoolkit/, last visited on October 18, 2011.
[10] An emulator allows software development in a simulated a computing environment.
[11] http://ace.ajax.org/, last visited on October 18, 2011.

## 4. The Web as a Platform

web browser. The openness of the Web as a platform has fueled the development of innovative tools for web development, with no end in sight.

Although many tools are already available for the development of applications for the Web as a platform, there is also room for improvement. Current tools often lack the polish and level of integration of IDEs for native applications — or even the tools for Silverlight and Flash. Especially non-programmers, e.g. web designers, are held back by the lack of professional authoring tools[12] for HTML5/JavaScript. With the market shifting towards HTML5 instead of Flash and Silverlight, initial products are starting to appear, e.g. Adobe Edge[13].

### 4.3.4. Cloud Services

Cloud computing, or utility computing, is currently one of the biggest buzzwords in the Internet business. Essentially, cloud computing is about turning everything — infrastructure, platforms, software — into services that are delivered over the Internet. In addition, cloud computing promises seemingly infinite computing and storage resources, while relieving service providers from the burden of maintaining their own computing infrastructure. In this sense, it drastically simplifies the creation of Level 1 and Level 2 Internet platforms and services.

Cloud services are a vital part of the Web as a platform stack. They provide the back-end infrastructure for web applications and extended functionality as a service. Among the most important cloud services of the Web as a platform are:

- Search
- Calendars and e-mail
- Identity and social networks
- Location
- Storage
- Communications
- Media access

By integrating these cloud services into web applications, a service level can be achieved that surpasses the abilities of network-less applications by far. For example, consider a photo management web application. In order to use the web application, a user must log into the service using an identity service, such as Facebook Connect or his Google Account. His photographs are stored on the Internet and retrieved through a cloud service. The application allows the editing of photos — changes are transferred back to the originals through the cloud service that stores the data. In case a photograph contains location information that determines where the snapshot was taken, the application queries a location service in order to visualize the location on a map. Further, the application employs social cloud services to directly share favorite photos with friends. A built-in communication service allows the collaboration with other photographers during the editing of photographs.

The interconnection of services, data, or functionality from several sources in form of a new web application or service is called a *mashup*. Mashups aim to combine existing services in order to make them more useful in a new context. Cloud services provide the back-end functionality for web

---

[12]Authoring tools allow non-programmers to create animated web content.
[13]http://labs.adobe.com/technologies/edge/, last visited on September 30, 2011.

applications and the interconnection with external services that can be openly accessed. Since all photographs in this example are stored on public servers on the Internet, they are also accessible by mobile devices. Using the browser, it is possible to show friends and family a slide show of the latest vacation on a tablet computer, without requiring prior synchronization. Cloud applications have the potential to synchronize and distribute content between multiple devices and platforms.

### 4.3.5. Monetization

Monetization has historically been one of the key challenges for commercial websites and it remains a key challenge for web applications. Fortunately, with the general acceptance of e-commerce, consumers have become accustomed to spending money in the World Wide Web. The subscription-based model, where consumers pay a monthly fee in order to be able to access a service, is suitable for certain types of websites and enterprise grade web applications. Consumers, on the other hand, often enjoy the free services that advertising provides.

Advertising is a fundamental pillar of monetization in the WWW and the foundation of the gigantic revenues of companies such as Google and Facebook. The equation is simple: the more page impressions, the more ads served and sold. Advertising also works very well for mobile and web applications, especially for those that are offered free of charge. Consumers have long accepted the trade-off of being served ads in their, otherwise free, favorite web applications.

The pay-per-use business model, which was popularized by cloud computing and its everything as a service approach, is also a practicable model for web applications. As the name indicates, customers pay for their usage of web applications, with the time being the major factor. Additional factors, e.g. the amount of data transfered, can be relevant as well. This approach is in contrast to traditional software, which is commonly monetized by selling licenses (compare with Section 3.3.1). Together with the advantages of web applications — no need to install, instantly usable with a web browsers, accessible from mobile devices — the pay-per-use model could, once consumers have realized they do not need to own software, reach entirely new groups of buyers.

The application store business model has successfully established itself in the context of mobile devices and has been a key driver of their success. Initially introduced by Apple, the application store makes it possible for developers to sell their applications through a centralized repository, solving two key issues for developers: discoverability and monetization. An application store is basically a catalog of applications that are available for a certain platform. Consumers can browse this catalog and easily purchase and install applications. The simplicity of finding and installing applications is a key advantage for consumers that were used to having to go to a physical store or to search the Internet for applications.

The Apple App Store for mobile iOS devices hosts more than 500,000 iPhone applications[14], which currently makes it the leading mobile platform in terms of variety — and the number is steadily rising. Apple embraces popular and creative applications in marketing efforts and makes it easy for a large audience to find the applications they are looking for. Since the App Store is a closed and restricted environment, iOS Apps must be approved before being accepted into the store, Apple exercises full control over the primary monetization channel of their platform. The company charges developers with a 30% fee and provides the handling of payments in return — plus millions of potential buyers. For developers this can be a profitable model, as their only responsibility lies in the conception and creation of the application. Despite being locked into the iOS platform, the advantages of a large

---

[14]http://www.apple.com/iphone/built-in-apps/app-store.html, last visited on October 18, 2011.

## 4. The Web as a Platform

user base, discoverability, distribution, and monetization seem to have convinced developers to make Apple's AppStore the most populated mobile application store on the market. Consumers too are locked into the platform, because they are unable to take their applications with them when switching to a new mobile device. Following the massive success of the mobile App Store, Apple has since extended the concept to its regular computers.

Google, on the other hand, has attempted to bring the application store concept to the Web. Its Chrome Web Store is a catalog for free and commercial web applications. It focuses on two major challenges that Google sees as crucial for the adoption of web applications: How do users discover new and exiting web applications and how can developers finally make money by developing these applications? The Chrome Web Store is restricted to Google's own Chrome browser and marks an attempt to strengthen its Chrome platform, which has recently been complemented with Chrome OS[15]. According to Andreessen's classification, the Chrome platform is a level 2 platform. It permits plugins and extensions to the Chrome browser, but the applications, which can be regular and existing websites, run outside the platform. Web applications can be "installed" into an application dashboard in the Chrome browser — which merely saves a bookmark containing the web application URL. Critics argue that the Chrome Web Store provides a solution for a non-existing problem, especially since there is "no actual software to deliver and no updates to manage and roll out" [Paul 2010]. Considering that payment is no longer a crucial problem on the Web, this leaves discoverability as the main benefit of a web application store. In order for this model to be successful on the Web, consumers must be convinced that there is added value in web applications that are listed in the store, compared to those that are not.

## 4.4. Cloud Computing: Powering the Platform

The rise of cloud or *utility* computing is often compared to the evolution of electrification. During the industrial revolution, manufacturers initially operated their own power producers in order to generate electricity for their machinery. When centralized power plants appeared and started providing electricity as a utility, manufacturers eventually abandoned their own electrical facilities and plugged into the electric grid — the provision of electricity as a utility lowered operating costs and allowed them to focus on their core businesses. Likewise, cloud computing turned computing infrastructure and applications into a utility.

Amazon[16] is widely recognized as an online retailer that started selling books and now sells everything from Apple products to Zippo pocket lighters [Rivlin 2005]. What is not commonly known, however, is that Amazon is also one of leading providers of cloud services, the so-called *Amazon Web Services*[17]. How could an online retailer become one of the leaders in cloud services and technologies? Amazon built gigantic data centers, filled with computing infrastructure, in order to be able to handle peak times, e.g. during Christmas season. However, during low and regular times, the computing infrastructure was underutilized. Estimates of server utilization in data centers commonly range between 5% and 20% — these statistics most probably apply to Amazon as well [Armbrust et al. 2010]. This level of overprovisioning is necessary to handle peak times, but at the same time translates into higher costs. In order to optimize the utilization of its computing infrastructure, Amazon decided to offer its overcapacities to customers, as infrastructure services on a *pay-per-use* basis. Amazon entered the

---
[15]Chrome OS is an operating system that is designed to run only web applications.
[16]http://www.amazon.com, last visited on September 13, 2011.
[17]http://aws.amazon.com, last visited on September 13, 2011.

## 4.4. Cloud Computing: Powering the Platform

Infrastructure as a Service (IaaS) market in 2006, by launching its Elastic Compute Cloud (EC2)[18] platform, and quickly became the market leader.

Although IaaS is often used as a synonym for cloud computing, cloud services have long transcended the concept of providing on-demand infrastructure alone. However, for such as widely used term, the definition of cloud computing is surprisingly difficult. Whereas the *cloud* itself is frequently used as a metaphor for the Internet, a single and precise definition of *cloud computing* has never been agreed on. It has been described as "a recent trend in IT that moves computing and data away from desktop and portable PCs into large data centers" [Dikaiakos et al. 2009] or as "both the applications delivered as services over the Internet and the hardware and systems software in the data centers that provide those services" [Armbrust et al. 2009]. IBM defines cloud computing as "an emerging style of computing in which applications, data and IT resources are provided to users as services delivered over the network" [IBM Corporation 2010]. The National Institute of Standards has developed a comprehensive definition that defines cloud computing as "a model for enabling convenient, on-demand network access to a shared pool of configurable computing resources (e.g., networks, servers, storage, applications, and services) that can be rapidly provisioned and released with minimal management effort or service provider interaction" [Mell and Grance 2011]. These and most other definitions find common ground in the agreement that cloud computing describes the delivery of computing resources as services over a network.

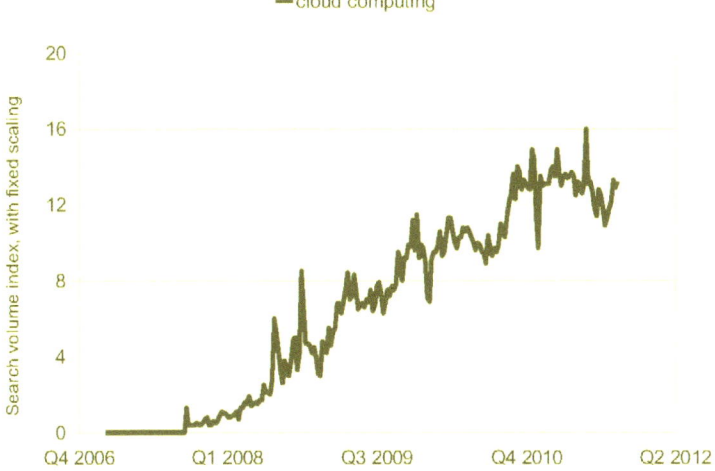

Figure 4.4.: Average worldwide search traffic of the term "cloud computing", according to Google Trends

Cloud computing has evolved from on-demand and grid computing and marks a paradigm shift away from the client-server model that was introduced in the 1980s. According to Google Trends[19], searches for *cloud computing* have started becoming relevant in October 2007 and have since grown steadily. The growth of worldwide search traffic for the term *cloud computing* is illustrated in Figure 4.4.

---
[18] The Amazon Elastic Compute Cloud platform provides virtual computing infrastructure on a pay-per-use basis.
[19] Google Trends is a service that provides information about the popularity of search keywords; http://www.google.com/intl/en/trends/about.html, last visited on September 28, 2011.

## 4. The Web as a Platform

According to an estimate computed by RightScale, a company that specializes in cloud computing management, approximately 15.5 million server instances were launched on Amazon's EC2 platform at the time of October 2009 [Rightscale]. The number of instances requested daily was calculated to be around 50,000. Cloud computing is more than a hype and quickly gaining traction. But what exactly is cloud computing and how does it differ from other service oriented architectures?

The National Institute of Standards and Technology list five essential characteristics of cloud computing [Mell and Grance 2011]:

1. *On-demand self service*: computing capabilities are provided to customers unilaterally and without the need of human interaction from the side of the cloud provider.

2. *Broad network access*: "capabilities are available over the network and accessed through standard mechanisms that promote use by heterogeneous thin or thick client platforms (e.g., mobile phones, laptops, and PDAs)" [Mell and Grance 2011]

3. *Resource pooling*: Cloud computing infrastructure is shared among customers and services are provided using the multi-tenant model. The customer generally has no knowledge or control over the physical location of the computing infrastructure.

4. *Rapid elasticity*: seemingly infinite computing resources are available, with the ability to quickly scale up and down with demand.

5. *Measured service*: resource usage is paid per use and monitored, controlled, and reported in a way that is transparent to customers.

Armbrust et al. argue that there are three *new* aspects of cloud computing, "from a hardware provisioning and pricing point of view" [Armbrust et al. 2010]. First, the availability of seemingly infinite computing resources on demand, accessible quickly enough to counter load surges, thus eliminating the need for overcapacities and far ahead planning. Second, the reduction of financial upfront investments, allowing new businesses to start small and to scale up their hardware resources with their needs. Third, the ability to pay only for the duration of the usage of computing resources and the ability to acquire and release them on a short-term basis.

### 4.4.1. Cloud Computing Service Models

Cloud computing companies deliver a wide range of services over the Internet. These services can be categorized into three basic service models of cloud computing: Infrastructure as a Service (IaaS), Platform as a Service (PaaS), and Software as a Service (SaaS). Figure 4.5 illustrates the cloud computing service models and their foundational technologies.

**Infrastructure as a Service (IaaS)**

The term *Infrastructure as a Service* describes the provision of computer infrastructure, such as processing, storage, and networking, as a service over the Internet. These infrastructure services resemble virtual computers — like real computers, they can be used to deploy operating systems and to execute arbitrary applications. The provision and maintenance of the underlying cloud infrastructure is the responsibility of the IaaS service provider.

For example, instead of buying and maintaining its own server hardware, a company may chose to pay for the usage of infrastructure services, supplied by Amazon or any other IaaS provider. There are

## 4.4. Cloud Computing: Powering the Platform

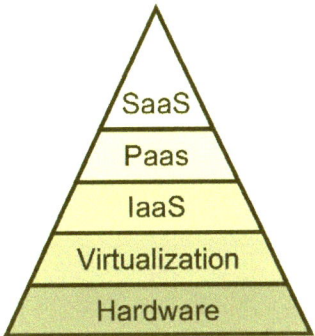

Figure 4.5.: Cloud computing service models

several advantages to this approach. First of all, the company does not need to buy server hardware, which reduces upfront investments. Second, the IaaS provider is responsible for the operation and maintenance of the computer infrastructure, while the company can focus on its core business model and does not need to develop expertise in this area. Third, the company can start with a single server instance and quickly scale up to multiple instances within mere hours, if its services prove to be accessed more frequently than expected. The total costs are influenced by several factors, with the duration of the usage and the bandwidth for data transfers being the most prominent. Microsoft and Amazon offer pay-per-use software licenses for Windows Servers and Windows SQL Server on Amazon EC2, which make these products $0.05 more expensive per hour than comparable open source alternatives.

The foundational technology of the IaaS concept is *virtualization*[20]. Virtualization provides an abstraction of computer hardware and makes it possible to run several *virtual computers* on the hardware of a single physical computer. These virtual computers run inside so called virtual machines (VMs) that share the physical computer's resources but otherwise create protected and independent computing environments. Whenever a customer requests a new virtual computer, a so-called instance is created inside a VM. By running several VM instances in parallel, the utilization of the physical computer is increased. Virtualization makes it possible to create and provide new instances to customers within minutes — a flexibility that is referred to as elasticity. Virtualization is by no means a technology that is restricted to cloud computing. Other use cases include the development and testing of software, e.g. for mobile devices that are simulated in a VM on a regular computer. By employing virtualization, several different operating systems and their dedicated applications can be installed and executed on a single computer. Virtualization was the key driver for IaaS and made it possible for Amazon to monetize its overcapacities, by selling computing infrastructure to customers in form of virtual machine instances.

### Platform as a Service (PaaS)

The *Platform as a Service* model providers a higher level of abstraction than the IaaS model. As the name suggests, PaaS provides a *platform* for application development, instead of raw computing

---
[20] Virtualization is frequently used as a synonym for hardware virtualization.

## 4. The Web as a Platform

infrastructure. The platform provides capabilities, such as programming languages, tools, and application programming interfaces (APIs) that can be employed by customers in order to build and deploy applications. In the PaaS model, customers surrender the control over the infrastructure of the platform. The PaaS provider controls the underlying cloud infrastructure, its operating systems, as well as networking and storage facilities. Customers remain in control of their applications.

PaaS offerings are usually not compatible or interchangeable[21]. This means that applications developed for a certain cloud platform are tied to the APIs of this platform and cannot easily be migrated to a different PaaS provider. In this sense, PaaS is more restrictive than IaaS, since applications are developed directly for a specific cloud platform and not for an (interchangeable) OS instance. Therefore, customers should evaluate the potential dangers of being locked into a platform, before selecting a cloud service provider for their businesses.

On the other hand, the PaaS service model offers many advantages to application developers over IaaS. Instead of having to develop everything by themselves, they can make use of existing functionality, e.g. authentication and billing services, that are provided by the PaaS provider as part of the platform. This reduces the complexity and the time to market of applications that are developed for a cloud platform. In addition, modern PaaS offerings provide automatic load balancing and scaling, as well as high availability mechanisms. While IaaS offerings can provide additional virtual computers within a short period of time, they are unable to offer automatic scaling according to demand. Two examples of significant cloud platforms are Google AppEngine and Microsoft Azure. While the AppEngine platform can be programmed using the Python and Java programming languages, Azure supports application development using Microsoft .NET.

### Software as a Service (SaaS)

The *Software as a Service* model provides the highest level of abstraction of the three cloud computing service models. SaaS describes the provision of applications to customers as a service. These applications are commonly web applications. SaaS offerings are often monetized through the pay-per-use and subscription models. Figure 4.6 illustrates the principle of SaaS: Cloud infrastructure services are employed to power web applications, which are in turn provided to customers as a service. In the SaaS service model, customers have the least amount of control over the infrastructure and application services. However, SaaS providers often allow the customization of specific parts of an application to suit customer needs. Two examples of significant SaaS offerings are the Salesforce Customer Relationships Management (CRM) system[22] and Google Apps[23].

One of the key principles of SaaS is multi-tenancy. A multi-tenant application "can satisfy the needs of multiple tenants (companies or departments within a company, etc.) using the hardware resources and staff needed to manage just a single software instance" [Salesforce.com 2008]. In other words, a single application instance is shared by multiple customers, which dramatically reduces the overhead of setting up new customers and providing them with application services. In contrast to virtualization, the separation of multi-tenancy is designed and implemented at the application level, instead through independent environments on an infrastructure level.

---

[21] A notable exception is the Deltacloud project, which provides a single API to several cloud providers; http://incubator.apache.org/deltacloud, last visited on September 27, 2011.
[22] http://www.salesforce.com/, last visited on September 13, 2011.
[23] http://www.google.com/apps, last visited on September 13, 2011.

Figure 4.6.: The Software as a Service cloud computing model

### 4.4.2. Cloud Computing Deployment Models

#### Public Cloud

In a *public cloud*, IaaS, PaaS, and SaaS services are provided over the Internet by data centers that are publicly accessible. The public cloud principle is the most significant deployment model of cloud computing. The Amazon EC2 platform, Microsoft Azure, and Google AppEngine are public clouds. A key attribute of a public cloud is resource sharing. Since the technology infrastructure is usually virtualized, it is likely that physical servers, running VM instances, are shared between customers. In other words, the data and applications of competing businesses might physically reside on the same physical computer — separated only by the boundaries created through the VMs. While resource sharing makes it possible to increase the utilization of the cloud infrastructure, privacy and data integrity concerns have led to the conception of *private clouds*.

#### Private Cloud

In a private cloud, computing resources are not shared between customers. A private cloud is built with the goal of retaining exclusive control over data and computing infrastructure. While this initially meant that companies employing private clouds remained responsible for the operation of the cloud infrastructure, several large cloud operators have started offering private clouds as a service. In this case, a private cloud differs from a public cloud in the exclusive use of its computing infrastructure. Private clouds make sense for companies that already sustain the necessary computing infrastructure and are unwilling to outsource the governance of their data, or for those that simply dread the potential dangers of resource sharing.

#### Hybrid Cloud

A hybrid cloud is a combination of the public and the private cloud models. It attempts to combine the benefits of both deployment models. An organization might outsource parts of its activities and functions to public cloud providers, but keep mission critical data and functionality within its own control. Figure 4.7 illustrates the relationship of the public, private, and hybrid cloud computing deployment models.

## 4. The Web as a Platform

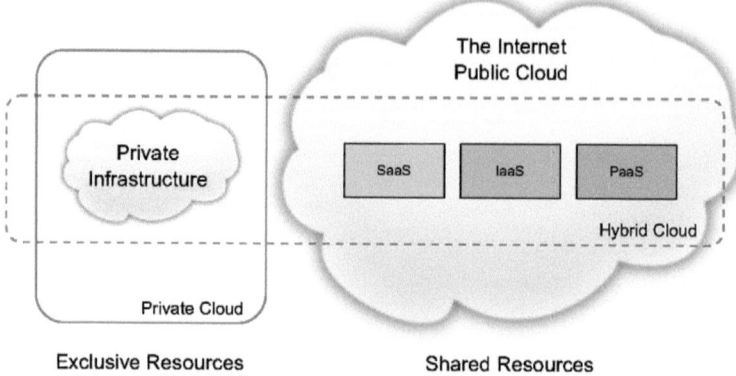

Figure 4.7.: Cloud computing deployment models

**Community Cloud**

According to the National Institute of Standards and Technology, a community cloud is distinguished by the fact that its infrastructure is "shared by several organizations and supports a specific community that has shared concerns (e.g., mission, security requirements, policy, and compliance considerations)" [Mell and Grance 2011]. The infrastructure may exist either on or off premise and may be managed by the organizations themselves or a third party. One example of a community cloud is Google's *Gov Cloud*[24] for the City of Los Angeles [Claburn 2009].

### 4.4.3. Cloud Applications and Services

Cloud computing has enabled a number of innovative services and applications that would not have been possible without the combination of virtualization, elastic computing, broad network access, online storage facilities, and the pay-per-use business model. This section presents and discusses a selection of these applications and cloud services.

**Supercomputing**

The IaaS service model was one of the crucial drivers for the adoption of cloud computing. IaaS is very a useful tool when the demand for a service varies over time, as it removes the need for overprovisioning. In addition, its elastic scaling abilities make it possible to deploy new services without having to determine the exact demand that is to be expected. However, the flexibility of IaaS also makes it very suitable for batch analytics and batch processing, e.g. in supercomputing. On March 1, 2011, a 10,000-core supercomputer was assembled from 1,250 Amazon EC2 instances

---
[24]The plan was to shift 30,000 city workers from Novell GroupWise to Google Apps within the year 2010, with cost savings amounting to approximately $6 million over five consecutive years.

with 8 computing cores each — "it took 45 minutes to provision the whole cluster[25]" [Brodkin 2011]. The supercomputer spent eight hours examining proteins for the biotechnology company Genetech, at a total cost of $8,500. These costs were cheap compared to the financial investments that would have been required to build a comparable conventional cluster. With cloud computing however, 1,000 instances running one hour cost the same as one instance running 1,000 hours. There is an enormous potential in IaaS for scientific computations that can be parallelized, as it provides the performance of a supercomputer on demand.

### Chrome OS and the Litl Webbook

Google generated a lot of interest and discussion when it announced its ambitious *Chrome OS* project in July, 2009. Chrome OS is an operating system that was designed to run *only* web applications inside the web browser. This marks a radical departure from the conventional approach of giving the user the freedom to install native applications at will. On the other hand, the removal of native applications gave Google engineers the opportunity to rethink fundamental computing paradigms. Chrome OS was designed from the ground up with security as a primary focus. The system is self-healing, keeps itself up to date automatically, and greatly simplifies computing as a whole. The hardware specifications of Chrome OS demand the use of a solid state hard drive (SSD), instead of a much cheaper magnetic hard disk. SSDs are faster, more reliable, and use less energy than their magnetic counter parts. However, the SSD inside a Chrome OS computer is not even used to store user data — documents, photos, e-mail, bookmarks, and all other personal data, is stored in the Google cloud. Advantages of this approach include automatic back-ups and the ability to restore a running system in minutes, if a Chrome OS computer was stolen or had to be replaced. Chrome OS is a lightweight, quick, and energy efficient operating system that provides only a web browser to access web applications. The first Chrome OS computers were introduced in mid 2011.

Although Chrome OS, since its announcement, has fueled discussions as to whether the consumers are ready for an operating system that is restricted to the execution of web applications, Chrome OS is neither an all original idea, nor was it the first web OS on the market. In November 2009, a startup company called litl LLC[26] released the *litl webbook*, which is regarded as the the first cloud-based netbook[27]. The concept of the litl webbook is remarkably similar to that of Chrome OS. The operating system keeps itself up to date automatically and all user data is stored in the cloud. Both the litl webbook and Chrome OS are examples of innovative products that have been made possible through cloud computing infrastructure.

### Data Access and Synchronization

With the appearance and ever-growing popularity of smartphones and tablets, many consumers own several Internet-enabled devices that are used to surf the Web, read e-mail, manage photographs, and to edit documents. This heterogeneity of computing devices has introduced several new challenges: How do you print documents from you mobile phone? How do you synchronize your bookmarks across your desktop computer, laptop, and tablet? How do you share photos with friends or collaborate on the same document with colleagues, making changes visible in real time? With its flexible infrastructure, virtually unlimited computing resources, and storage capacities, could computing offers the technical

---

[25] A cluster is a group of interconnected computers that appear as a single high-performance computer.
[26] http://www.litl.com, last visited on October 18, 2011.
[27] http://litl.com/meet-webbook/overview.htm, last visited on October 26, 2011.

## 4. The Web as a Platform

capabilities to converge data in the cloud — where it becomes accessible with all personal Internet-enabled devices. In this sense, the cloud is quickly becoming an extension of individual computing devices.

One example of a service that permits the synchronization and sharing of arbitrary data is *Dropbox*. Dropbox makes it possible to keep files synchronized across individual computers and mobile devices, by storing these in the cloud. Changes to files are detected automatically and pushed to other subscribing devices. Files can be shared with other users, which makes Dropbox very suitable collaboration tool. 2GB of online storage are free for registered users, whereas paying customers can acquire up to 100GB. Dropbox supports Windows, Mac, and Linux computers, as well as Android, Blackberry, iPhone, and iPad mobile devices. This makes Dropbox a valuable tool for collaboration, information exchange, backup, and data access on the go. Canonical's Ubuntu One[28] service takes a similar approach, but intends to integrate file sharing and synchronization features with its Linux operating system Ubuntu. Ubuntu One, marketed as "your personal cloud", synchronizes notes, bookmarks, and files between Ubuntu computers and the Web. In addition, in focuses on music and makes it possible to stream tracks from the Ubuntu cloud to Android or iPhone devices. Apple has recently announced a similar cloud-based storage and synchronization service called iCloud[29].

### Mobile Navigation

The Google Maps application for Android[30] is a great example of how cloud services can empower mobile devices and applications. Google Maps for Android is a full-featured turn-by-turn navigation system. The navigation, however, is not performed by the mobile device itself. Instead, the routing is performed in the cloud, based on the user's current location and the desired destination. After the route has been calculated in the cloud, it is sent to the mobile device and visualized by Google Maps. While performing the turn-by-turn navigation, Google Maps interfaces with the Street View[31] service and combines photographs of turns and buildings with the representation on the map. This unique enhancement aims to provide a better overview to the driver.

Google Maps for Android also supports speech input. Instead of typing the target address, the driver can *tell* the Android device where to navigate to. Unlike traditional speech recognition software on the PC, the translation does not happen on the mobile device. The recorded speech fragment is sent to the cloud, where it is analyzed, transformed into a destination, and returned to the mobile device. The Street View photographs, the routing, and the speech input are provided to the Android devices as a cloud service, which makes a wireless connection a prerequisite for the navigational service. Even the synthesized audio directions that guide the driver are streamed over the Internet. It is difficult to imagine how the turn-by-turn navigation system of Google Maps for Android could be implemented on a mobile device without the computational power, storage, and connectivity of the cloud.

### Productivity Applications

Cloud computing also brings innovation to established product groups, such as office productivity suites. While office suites are traditionally offered as feature-rich native applications, several products

---

[28] http://one.ubuntu.com/, last visited on September 29, 2011.
[29] www.apple.com/de/icloud/, last visited on September 29, 2011.
[30] Google Android is an operating system for mobile devices, e.g. smartphones and tablets.
[31] Google Street View provides panoramic views from varying positions along the streets of cities. The views are composed of photographic images.

have lately appeared that offer document-editing as a service, accessed with the web browser. Perhaps the most prominent example of these SaaS office suites is Google Apps. Google Apps provides much of the functionality of traditional native office suites, such as Microsoft Office or OpenOffice, in the form of a web application. In addition to the common advantages of web applications that were discussed in Section 3.3, Google Apps boasts enhanced collaboration features that surpass those of native productivity suites. Remotely displaced users can collaborate on the same document and watch as their peers make changes as well — in real time! Recently, this functionality was extended to mobile devices, making it possible to collaborate on documents on the go. Storing documents in a central repository in the cloud is the prerequisite for this level of service integration, which is one of the reasons why established native office suites struggle to match the collaboration features of Google Apps.

## 4.5. Challenges for the Web as Platform

Although cloud computing has enabled a wide range of new and innovative web services and web applications, challenges remain in the areas of security and data confidentiality, governance, data lock-in, and service availability. As illustrated in Figure 4.8, security and privacy concerns are the primary reasons for companies that are reluctant to embracing infrastructure services. Governance is an issue as cloud services may be powered by data centers around the globe. There are substantial differences in data protection regulations around the World, e.g. the European Union Directive 95/46/EC states that only transfers of "personal data from a Member State to a third country with an adequate level of protection are authorised" [EU]. This can potentially conflict with the US patriot act, which allows government agencies to demand the handover of records linked with suspects. Cloud computing APIs have not yet been subject to standardization and are essentially proprietary. This makes it difficult, if not impossible, for customers to migrate their applications and data from one cloud vendor to another. While this lock-in might seem attractive to cloud computing providers, it leaves their customers vulnerable "to price increases, to reliability problems, or even to providers going out of business" [Armbrust et al. 2010]. Service availability is a key requirement for Internet businesses. Although the availability of existing cloud services and platforms is extraordinarily high, the customers of cloud services are dependent on the abilities of their vendors to prevent and rectify service outages.

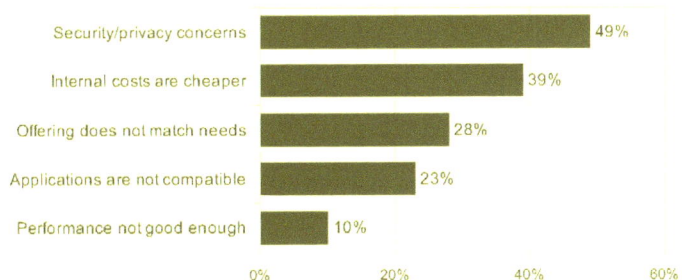

Figure 4.8.: Why companies avoid infrastructure services [Forrester Consulting 2010]

As outlined in Section 3.3.2, HTML5 brings much needed technological enhancements to the functionality of web applications. However, it "is not designed to solve discovery, distribution or monetisation problems — in other words it is not designed to change the business model" [Vision Mobile 2011]. The

## 4. The Web as a Platform

development and embracement of platforms on top of the Web as a platform and the overwhelming success of mobile platforms indicate that these non-technical aspects are key factors for economic success. A strong platform must provide the technical foundations and the tools required to create arbitrary applications, but it must also provide a way to discover, distribute, and monetize them. All of these aspects pose challenges to the Web as a platform.

The openness of the Web as a platform, one of its foremost strengths, is also one of its most crucial weaknesses: The agreement on open standards and the lack of control through a single entity with a sharp future vision is slowing down innovation and the adoption of new functionality. HTML5 is not expected before 2014 and even then it will not elevate web applications to the level of functionality of mobile and native applications (compare with Section 3.3.2). The question is whether and when HTML5/JavaScript will be able to facilitate comparable applications in the web browser, especially applications with high computational demands? The extension of web applications with compiled native code and the corresponding reuse of legacy code could become a short-term solution to the shortcomings of the Web as a platform. These hybrid native/web applications attempt to combine the strengths of native and web applications and are finally becoming technologically feasible.

# 5. Native Web Applications

The technological shortcomings of JavaScript web applications have motivated the inception of two independent projects that aim to bring the computational performance of compiled native code and the rich functionality of native desktop applications to web applications: Native Client and Xax. Both projects allow the creation and execution of *native web applications*. Native web applications are web applications that are extended with compiled native code. Although, at first glance, they share many similarities with the browser plugins that were discussed in Section 3.1, native web applications differ substantially from NPAPI and ActiveX.

This chapter provides an introduction to native web applications and outlines their central goals. The overview is followed by a detailed discussion of the motivation, architectural principles, and implementation specific details of the Native Client and Xax projects. Their core components are explained with a focus on their respective security frameworks. The chapter closes with a comparison of Native Client and Xax.

## 5.1. Goals of Native Web Applications

Native Client and Xax share four central motivations for the creation of native web applications:

1. Performance
2. Security
3. OS-independence
4. Code/functionality Reuse

Native web applications employ compiled native code to deliver the performance of native applications in the web browser. As explained in Section 3.2.4, it is highly unlikely that JavaScript will ever be able to match this level of performance. In addition, due to its nature as a high-level programming language, JavaScript does not provide low-level access to the computing hardware or extensive support for concurrent programming[1]. The ability to extend web applications with highly optimized, low-level source code in C or C++ could enable new, unprecedented, and high-performance browser applications in the fields of "simulation of Newtonian physics, computational fluid-dynamics, and high-resolution scene rendering" [Yee et al. 2009].

Native Client and Xax have learned from the security shortcomings of NPAPI and ActiveX. Instead of permitting the execution of untrusted native code without containment and with full privileges (see Sections 3.1.1 and 3.1.2), they employ effective security measures that give the web browser complete control over the execution of native application modules. The security frameworks of Native Client and Xax build on research in the area of browser security. For instance, the Tahoma research browser introduces the concept of executing web applications in virtual machines, in order to isolate them

---

[1] Concurrent programming allows the creation of computer programs that execute tasks in parallel instead of sequentially.

## 5. Native Web Applications

from another and from the rest of the system [Cox et al. 2006]. Other research projects, such as the OP web browser, apply findings from operating system research to the web browser and suggest the partitioning of the browser itself into smaller subsystems [Grier et al. 2008]. Microsoft Research has presented Gazelle, the idea of the web browser as a "multi-principal OS for web site principals", in which the browser kernel manages resource protection exclusively [Wang et al. 2009]. The use of OS process isolation for the containment of websites and web applications was suggested to enhance the robustness of the web browser — this concept has since been implemented in the Google Chrome browser [Reis and Gribble 2009]. Last but not least, sandboxing techniques (see Section 3.1.1) were evaluated in order to reduce the privileges and potential damage through "high-risk components, such as the HTML parser, the JavaScript virtual machine, and the Document Object Model (DOM)" [Barth et al. 2008].

As discussed in Section 3.3.1, one of the foremost advantages of web applications over their native counterparts is their OS-independence. The creators of Native Client and Xax realized that OS-independence is a key requirement for native web applications. Both technologies replace OS-specific system calls[2] with a custom system call interface, thus decoupling their applications from the underlying OS. This allows the development of compiled native web applications without targeting OS-specific functionality. The functionality for the custom system call interface is provided through the reuse of mechanisms already present in the web browser.

The ability to reuse legacy code was one of the most compelling drivers for the creation of native web applications. As explained in the problem statement in Chapter 2, a large number of applications and libraries were written in non type-safe programming languages such as C and C++. These software components are incompatible with JavaScript and other web programming languages. Native web applications make it possible to reuse legacy code for web development, instead of requiring the reimplementation of its functionality in JavaScript.

## 5.2. Xax

Xax is a project at Microsoft Research that enables the development of native web applications — it allows the extension of web applications with compiled native code. Xax' vision is "to deliver feature-rich, desktop-class applications on the web" [Douceur et al. 2008]. Its creators believe that the fastest way of creating richer web applications is to make the functionality encapsulated in legacy code available for web application development.

Because the development of complex software systems requires a substantial effort, the reuse of software components has long become one of the foundations of the computer industry. The fact that these software components cannot currently be employed for the development of web applications is a major problem. Companies have invested substantial amounts of time and money into the development of software components that have, with the growing importance of the Web as a platform, become legacy code. The desire to permit the reuse of legacy software components was the primary motivation for the development of Xax. However, in order to become available for the development of Xax applications, legacy code must generally be modified and adapted to the Xax platform. The Xax authors claim, however, that the porting[3] effort for many applications and libraries, even those with large code bases, is commonly low [Douceur et al. 2008]. The extension of web applications with tried and tested native

---
[2] Operating system functionality and services are provided to application processes through system calls.
[3] The porting of an application refers to its adaptation from its original computing environment to a different computing environment.

code components has another advantage: It provides moderately skilled web developers with access to powerful functionality and tools, without exposing them to the implementation specific details of native applications.

In addition to allowing the reuse of legacy code, Xax attempts to solve the performance implications of JavaScript web applications in a secure and OS-independent manner. Xax implements a security model that is far superior over those of NPAPI and ActiveX, which were discussed in Section 3.1. The Xax security model does not demand interactions or trust assumptions from its users. Instead, Xax applications are contained in a very restricted OS process and do not have direct access to OS system calls. Xax provides its own, limited system call interface for the sake of security and OS-independence. Modern web browsers support mechanisms such as memory management, Internet access, and other low-level services that are required for the execution of JavaScript web applications — and by the browser itself. This functionality is reused by Xax to support the execution of compiled native Xax applications within the web browser. While the Xax system call interface allows the development of native applications for the Xax framework, instead of a specific OS, the reuse of browser functionality turns the web browser into the runtime for Xax applications — regardless of the underlying OS. The benefit of this approach is that compiled Xax applications can run unmodified on Windows and Linux.

### 5.2.1. Architecture

The foundations of the Xax architecture are easily explained: first, contain untrusted native code in a very restricted operating system process. Second, replace these system calls with custom *xaxcalls* that provide the necessary functionality to Xax applications using the infrastructure of the web browser. The key components of the Xax architecture are, as illustrated in Figure 5.1, the picoprocess, the Xax Monitor, the xaxcall interface, and the Platform Application Layer (PAL).

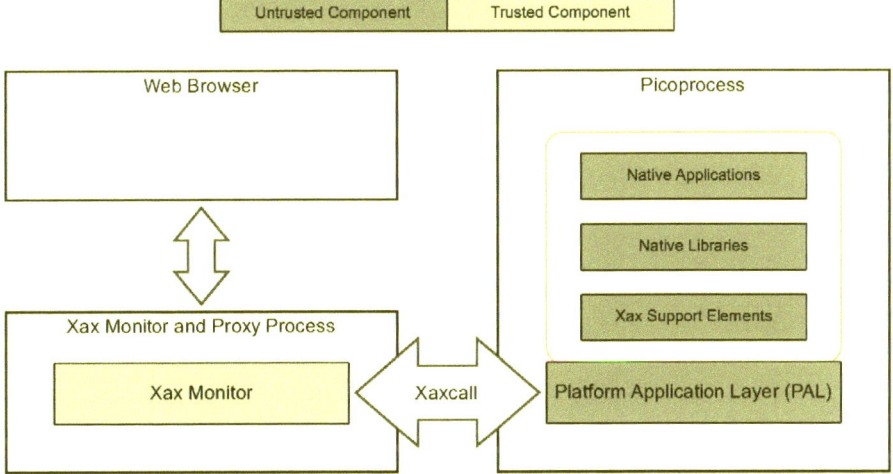

Figure 5.1.: The Xax architecture

## 5. Native Web Applications

Xax achieves its primary design goals of security, performance, OS-independence, and legacy support with four mechanisms. These mechanisms build on the components of the Xax architecture, but go beyond those by supplying best practices as well:

1. The *picoprocess*, a highly restricted execution container for native code
2. The *Platform Abstraction Layer (PAL)* that defines an OS-independent programming interface for application development
3. *Access to browser mechanisms* in order to provide application functionality such as networking, user interface, and local storage
4. *Modifications* to the source code of legacy applications and libraries in order to adapt these to the Xax framework

### Picoprocess

The primary component of the Xax security model is the picoprocess. A picoprocess is a very restricted operating system process that is deprived of the ability to make system calls. It isolates untrusted native application code from the rest of the system. Picoprocesses are created and controlled by the *Xax Monitor*. The Xax Monitor is part of the browser's trusted code base (TCB). It uses OS services to create and manage picoprocesses and therefore is OS-specific. Picoprocesses communicate with the Xax Monitor by issuing *xaxcalls*, which are analogous to system calls. They provide raw functionality such as memory allocation and deallocation, basic communication with the web browser or the origin server, access to URL query parameters, and picoprocess exit.

Together, the Xax Monitor and the xaxcall interface implement the functionality guaranteed by the Platform Application Layer. The PAL defines a concise and stable interface that describes the services available to Xax applications. The xaxcall interface, on the other hand, is kept simple and flexible — it does not even specify a mandatory set of xaxcalls. The lack of a rigid specification makes it possible to tailor the Xax Monitor and the corresponding xaxcall interface to different operating systems. The only obligation for the Xax Monitor and xaxcall implementations are that they must provide the functionality guaranteed by the PAL.

### Platform Abstraction Layer

In order to facilitate the development of cross-platform and OS-independent applications, Xax defines a consistent application binary interface (ABI)[4]. The ABI itself is operating system neutral — it defines the interface and not the implementation. Applications developed against the ABI can be executed on any operating system that implements the necessary functionality. In the Xax architecture, the component that is responsible for the implementation of the ABI is the Platform Application Layer (PAL).

The PAL runs inside the picoprocess as an untrusted component. It translates the OS-independent ABI into OS-specific xaxcalls that can be executed by the Xax Monitor. The relationship between the PAL, the Xax Monitor, and the xaxcalls is illustrated in Figure 5.1. Although the PAL is executed within the realm of a picoprocess, it is not part of a Xax application. Like the Xax Monitor, the PAL is distributed as part of the Xax framework.

---

[4]An application binary interface describes a low-level interface between applications and an operating system or other applications on a binary level.

## 5.2. Xax

### Browser Mechanisms

"A key Xax principle is that there is sufficient functionality within the browser to support the system services needed by web applications" [Douceur et al. 2008]. The Xax Monitor reuses existing browser mechanisms in order to implement the xaxcall interface, which turns the web browser, instead of the underlying OS, into the runtime for Xax applications. Since Xax applications are programmed against the xaxcall interface and do not directly make use of OS system services, they become OS-independent. Another advantage of this approach is that the Xax Monitor gains additional control over the xaxcalls issued by Xax applications. It is able to filter and disallow illegal system calls that can be exploited by malicious code.

The Xax Monitor provides the services as defined by the xaxcall interface. In addition to basic services, such as to memory allocation and deallocation, the Xax Monitor provides a communication channel between the browser and a picoprocess. In this scenario, the picoprocess appears to the web browser as a web server. Xax applications can issue `read` and `write` calls to serve HTTP content to the web browser — with the same security restrictions as applied to a *real* remote web server. The same communication channel provides access from Xax applications to JavaScript statements in order to perform user interface operations, DOM manipulations, and cookie management. Instead of relying on JavaScript to perform network operations, Xax provides the `xabi_open_url` ABI call that allows direct communication between a Xax picoprocess and its origin server.

### Code Modifications

Xax replaces OS-dependent system calls with an OS-independent ABI with limited functionality. Therefore, legacy applications and libraries must be ported to Xax — they must be adapted to the Xax framework in order to become available for the development of Xax applications. The porting process involves making modifications to the source code of legacy software components. Although this can potentially be a lot of work, the Xax authors claim that the effort of porting applications and libraries to Xax is generally low, with the process itself being straightforward. They have developed a five-step porting guide [Douceur et al. 2008]:

1. Removal of irrelevant dependencies
2. Restriction of application interface usage
3. Removal of trivial system calls
4. Internal replacement of system call functionality
5. Provision of real system call functionality via xaxcalls

In the first step, unused libraries and other irrelevant software components are removed from the build process of the application. This step reduces the size of the application and the total amount of code that must be ported to Xax. In the second step, the quantity of interfaces that are used by the application is reduced and consolidated. This can be done by setting command-line arguments or environment variables. Trivial system calls are identified and removed in the third step, for example by returning an error code that indicates that the requested functionality is not available. In the fourth step, remaining system calls are emulated within the application itself. For example, an application specific random access memory (RAM) disk could be created to hold temporary files that would usually be stored on the file system. Finally, in the fifth step, functionality provided by system calls that cannot be otherwise removed is replicated with real xaxcalls. To avoid an inflation of xaxcalls,

5. Native Web Applications

which would eventually bloat the xaxcall interface, this approach should only be pursued to implement functionality that benefits numerous applications and cannot be replaced otherwise.

### 5.2.2. Implementation

The Xax team at Microsoft Research has implemented Xax for the Windows and Linux operating systems. Both implementations are very similar, but differ in the kernel support for process isolation and communication. Unfortunately, the code is not open source and has not been made freely available.

**Xax Monitor and PAL**

The Xax Monitor is a user-mode process that is responsible for the creation and management of picoprocesses. It also provides the core functionality for xaxcalls, i.e. their implementation. A picoprocesses is realized as a child process of the Xax Monitor process. It runs in user-mode and is protected by OS hardware memory isolation. When a new picoprocess is created, it executes an OS-specific boot block that revokes its ability to issue subsequent system calls. Although the boot block is executed within the picoprocess, it is part of the Xax TCB and not part of a Xax application. With the completion of the boot block, the child process becomes an isolated picoprocess. The control flow is then passed to the PAL, which starts up and subsequently hands the execution to the actual Xax application. The PAL is responsible for the implementation of the Xax ABI by making xaxcalls to the Xax Monitor. The Windows and Linux versions of the Xax Monitor essentially handle the xaxcalls in a similar way, although their implementations differ.

**Kernel Support**

The Linux implementation of Xax does not employ a custom kernel module and makes use of the kernel's `ptrace` facility instead. `Ptrace` allows the observation and controlling of another process. When setting up a new picoprocess, the boot block calls `ptrace(TRACE_ME)`. This instructs the kernel to intercept subsequent system calls and to return the control flow to the Xax Monitor parent process instead. The Xax Monitor then replaces the system call with a harmless syscall, e.g. `getpid()`. This setup isolates the picoprocess and prevents it from issuing direct system calls altogether. The same infrastructure is employed by the PAL, which uses system calls to signal a xaxcall. `Ptrace` then notifies the Xax Monitor, which checks and executes the xaxcall operation, if it is legitimate. This procedure of system call interception and replacement is illustrated in Figure 5.2.

The advantages of the `ptrace`-approach are that it does not demand a custom kernel module or root privileges. On the other hand, it causes a performance penalty, since every xaxcall requires three system calls from the Xax Monitor: the first to replace the system call with a harmless alternative, the second to enter the kernel mode, and the third to transfer the control flow back to the originating picoprocess. Perhaps the most dangerous disadvantage is that, should the Xax Monitor exit unexpectedly and without proper signal handling, its child picoprocess may continue to run without system call interception — rendering the primary picoprocess isolation ineffective [Provos 2003]. For these reasons, the Xax team plans to implement and employ a custom kernel module in the future.

The Windows implementation of Xax already features such a custom kernel module, called *XaxDrv*. The module isolates a picoprocess by overwriting its internal system call handler table. Incoming

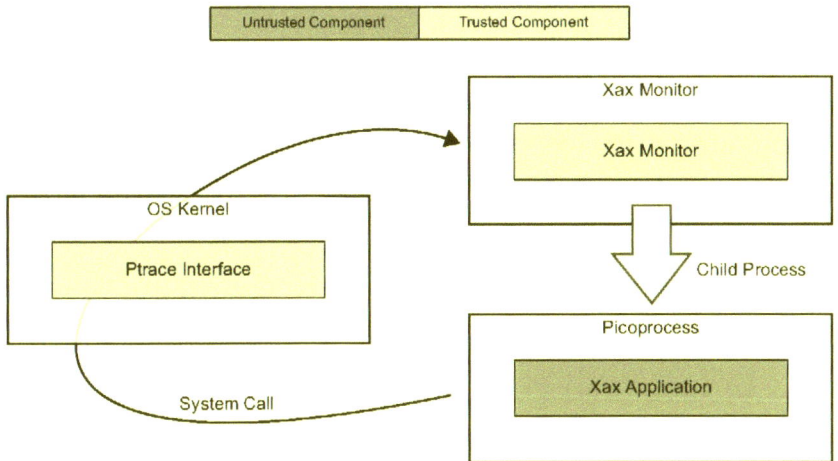

Figure 5.2.: The interception of a Xax application system call using the ptrace kernel interface

user-mode system calls are translated into inter-process calls to the Xax Monitor. Kernel mode system calls, on the other hand, are preserved. Since XaxDrv is a custom kernel module, it must be ported to every supported version of the Windows operating system. Clearly, this implies additional maintenance overhead, although the Xax authors claim that the differences between Windows versions are minimal.

**Browser Integration**

Xax applications are not hooked into the web browser as plugins. Instead, they are integrated via a proxy. This approach is feasible since Xax applications appear to the web browser as parts of their HTTP origin server. An inherent advantage of the proxy approach is that it is easily integrable with all web browsers. The proxy passes common HTTP requests unmodified to the dedicated hosts. In cases where the URL's path component begins with /_xax/, however, the proxy redirects the request to an existing picoprocess or triggers the creation of a new one. The proxy is implemented as part of the Xax Monitor process and allows the communication between picoprocesses and their origin servers through the xax_open_url call.

### 5.2.3. Capabilities

**Performance**

The authors of Xax have published the results of performance experiments that were conducted at Microsoft Research. The performance of Xax applications was found to be comparable to that of native Linux applications. Native Windows applications had a slight advantage over their Xax counterparts, which was attributed to the usage of different compilers. On the other hand, the context switching overhead of the xaxcall interface was found to be substantial — although this did not significantly

## 5. Native Web Applications

affect applications that performed little I/O. The Xax team also conducted Mandelbrot benchmarks, in which native C, Java, and Xax applications performed comparably and outperformed a JavaScript implementation of the same benchmark by magnitudes.

The context switching overhead of the xaxcall interface leaves room for optimizations, especially on the Linux platform, where a custom kernel module could provide additional performance gains. Overall, the initial benchmarks indicate that Xax applications perform favorably compared to their native counterparts.

**Legacy Support**

The Xax authors have implemented several Xax applications in order to evaluate its support for legacy code. These applications employed 15 libraries, with a total of 3.3 million lines of source code in four programming languages. "Only minimal changes were needed to compile the libraries" [Douceur et al. 2008]. In many cases the changes were trivial and merely involved the adaptation of compile settings. These results led to the conclusion that Xax is indeed well suited for the reuse of legacy code.

**OS-Independence**

The Xax framework was successfully implemented and tested on several operating systems: Linux 2.6, Windows XP, Windows Vista, and Windows Server 2008 — on the Intel x86 and the PowerPC CPU architectures. While Xax applications run unmodified on different operating systems, they are tied on the CPU architecture that they have been compiled for. The Xax ABI varies across CPU architectures, which means that Xax applications compiled for Intel x86 will not run on the PowerPC architecture and vice versa. This is a well known "limitation" of native code that is caused by its compilation for the instruction set of dedicated CPU architectures.

It is noteworthy that, in addition to achieving OS-independence, Xax also achieves browser independence through the use of a proxy. Xax has successfully been tested with several different browsers on different operating systems. The proxy approach does, on the other hand, pose several disadvantages. First, the rewriting of the origin server's namespace is not conformant with the HTTP protocol. Second, the proxy cannot reliable terminate and reclaim a picoprocess, as it is not aware if the browser has navigated away from a web page. Finally, the proxy cannot support the HTTPS protocol, which enforces authentication and encryption. These drawbacks suggest a tighter integration with the web browser, e.g. as a browser plugin.

**Security**

The Xax authors' main argument for the security of their architecture is its small trusted code base. The TCB of the Xax picoprocess consists of less than 5,000 lines of code, which is substantially less than that of (open source) Flash and Java frameworks. On of the reasons for the small code base is the use of hardware memory protection for process isolation. While a small TCB is certainly an advantage, an in depth security analysis of the Xax architecture would be desirable.

## 5.3. Native Client

Native Client (NaCl) is an open source project that was initiated by Google and that is developed under the umbrella of the Chromium[5] project. Its goal is to "give browser-based applications the computational performance of native applications without compromising safety" [Yee et al. 2009]. NaCl makes it possible to extend JavaScript web applications with compiled native code, while maintaining browser neutrality and operating system portability. Like Xax applications, NaCl applications reuse existing browser mechanisms, instead of directly accessing the underlying operating system. The web browser acts as the platform for NaCl applications, which allows compiled binaries to run unmodified on different operating systems — as long as they share the same CPU architecture. According to its developers, NaCl is intended for tasks that focus on computation, such as "simulation of Newtonian physics, computational fluid-dynamics, and high-resolution scene rendering" [Yee et al. 2009].

In addition to its focus on computational performance, NaCl was designed with an emphasis on security. This approach marks a radical departure from previous attempts to allow the execution of native code in the web browser, such as NPAPI and ActiveX. As explained in Section 3.1, these approaches circumvented the security mechanisms applied to web content in order to grant full access to OS functionality and maximum performance to plugins. NaCl, on the other hand, consists of a constrained execution environment and a runtime that executes native code modules, while isolating them from the rest of the system. Instead of placing the trust problem on the user, NaCl provides a security framework that was designed to prevent unintended side-effects and to permit allowable side effects safely. NaCl remains work in progress and has recently been integrated into the beta channel of the Google Chrome browser[6].

### 5.3.1. Architecture

NaCl permits the execution of arbitrary, untrusted native code in the web browser. Upon navigating to a website that requires the execution of a NaCl module, the web browser automatically downloads, validates, and executes the native code extensions. This process is completely transparent to end users and requires absolutely no interaction. A NaCl application generally consists of trusted and untrusted components. Core NaCl components are considered trusted, whereas NaCl modules that are downloaded from web servers are considered untrusted. All components run in their own private address space and are isolated from another. NaCl provides a reliable datagram service, the *IMC (Inter Module Communications)*, for inter-component communication. "The IMC also provides shared memory segments and shared synchronization objects, intended to avoid messaging overhead for high-volume or high-frequency communications [Yee et al. 2009]. NaCl applications do not have direct access to OS system calls. Instead, memory management, thread creation, and other system services are provided by the *service runtime*. The NaCl system architecture and its primary components are illustrated in Figure 5.3.

**Inner and Outer Sandbox**

NaCl applications are generally considered untrusted. Therefore, they are contained in a dual sandboxing environment that consists of an *inner sandbox* and an *outer sandbox*. The inner sandbox is

---

[5]The Chromium project is the open source foundation of the Google Chrome web browser.
[6]http://chrome.blogspot.com/2011/08/building-better-web-apps-with-new.html, last visited on October 18, 2011.

## 5. Native Web Applications

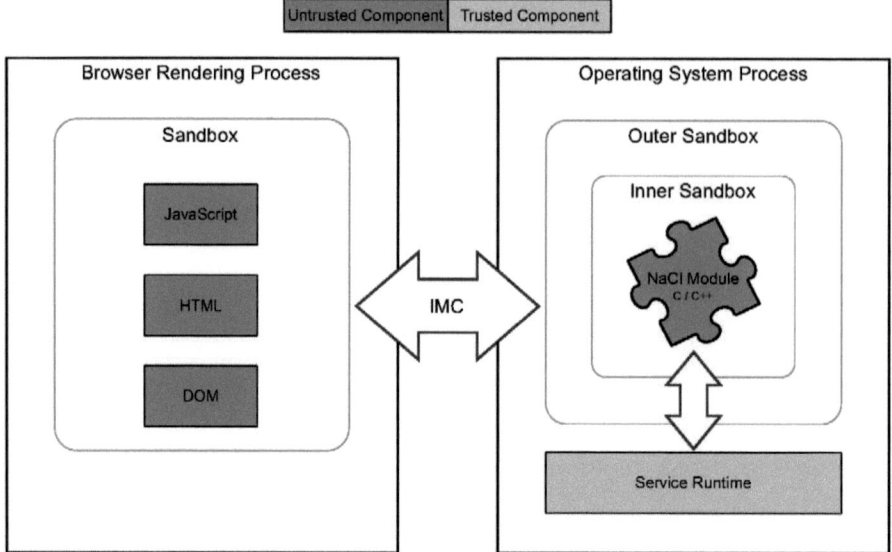

Figure 5.3.: The Native Client architecture

the primary security measure. It disassembles untrusted native code and uses static analysis to detect security defects. NaCl forbids self modifying code and overlapping instructions by imposing a set of alignment and structural rules. These rules ensure that untrusted code can be disassembled reliably. Upon disassembling the code, a validator determines that untrusted code employs only legal machine instructions. Unsafe machine instructions are disallowed. Early implementations of NaCl employed x86 segmented memory to constrain memory references. Unfortunately, x86 segmented memory is a hardware capability that is unique to the 32-bit Intel x86 processor architecture and not available for the x86-64 and ARM processor architectures. This limitation has since been overcome by the development and implementation of an innovative approach to software fault isolation (SFI) [Sehr et al. 2010]. SFI prevents the modification of trusted data by sandboxing store instructions. Its performance impact was found to be, on average, less than 5% for ARM and less than 7% for x86-64. Using software fault isolation, NaCl is able to support the x86-64 and ARM CPU architectures, for which SFI assumes the role of segmented memory, without relaxing its security model.

The inner sandbox creates an additional security subdomain inside an OS process. This extra isolation layer allows the placement of a trusted service runtime instance within the same process as untrusted native application code. A springboard/trampoline mechanism is employed to permit the secure transfer of the control flow between trusted and untrusted code. The NaCl authors believe that the inner sandbox is superior over process isolation, as its security is not reliant on the correctness of the operating system. The "inner sandbox not only isolates the system from the native module, but also helps to isolate the native module from the operating system" [Yee et al. 2009].

The outer sandbox is a secondary security measure and an additional obstruction to prevent unwanted side-effects. It examines the system calls made by the NaCl process and matches them with a white list. NaCl applications are granted access to a limited set of system calls. System calls that are not white listed are disallowed.

### Runtime Services

NaCl provides the Inter-Module Communications (IMC) service for communications between processes and modules. The IMC can be used by accessed trusted and untrusted modules and is used to share files, objects, descriptors, etc. across process boundaries. It also provides the foundation for two higher level services, the *Simple Remote Procedure Call (SRPC)* and *PPAPI* facilities. SRPC makes it possible to implement subroutines across NaCl module boundaries, facilitating, most notably, calls to NaCl from the JavaScript layer. PPAPI, the browser plugin interface (see Section 3.1.1), provides access to the browser state and makes it possible to open URLs and to access the document object model (DOM).

The NaCl service runtime is an operating system process that serves as the container for NaCl modules. It provides a reduced set of system calls and a subset of the POSIX thread interface for NaCl application development, including support for mutexes, semaphores, condition variables, and thread local storage. While the service runtime implements the POSIX file I/O interface for operations on communication channels and read-only web content, access to the local file system and sockets is unavailable to NaCl applications. Network system calls such as connect() and accept() are omitted. Therefore, NaCl web applications must access network and file resources through JavaScript.

### 5.3.2. Implementation

NaCl is implemented as a browser plugin that is available for the Windows, Mac OS, and Linux operating systems. Initially, it targeted the Netscape Plugin API (NPAPI) and a set of custom extensions that were referred to as Pepper. As the development of NaCl progressed, the NPAPI/Pepper interface was dropped in favor of an entirely new plugin API, termed Pepper 2. Pepper 2 was developed to address the shortcomings that were discovered in NPAPI/Pepper.

A typical NaCl application consists of an HTML/JavaScript part, the C/C++ NaCl module, and some C/C++ glue code to connect both parts, instantiate the module, and to grant JavaScript with access to functions provided by the NaCl module. Each NaCl module runs in a dedicated OS process in order to isolate modules from another.

### Inner Sandbox

The security model of the NaCl inner sandbox consists of three basic components [Yee et al. 2009]:

1. Structural rules for the reliable disassembly of NaCl applications
2. A modified compiler tool chain that follows these rules
3. A validator that enforces these rules

By keeping the compilation tools outside of the trusted code base (TCB), the NaCl authors were able to limit the TCB to the validator, thus reducing its size substantially. The validator was implemented with merely 500 C statements (semicolons) — its compactness allows for thorough review and testing. The validator guarantees four fundamental prerequisites of NaCl applications [Yee et al. 2009]:

## 5. Native Web Applications

- Data integrity
- Reliable disassembly
- Validation of instructions
- Control flow integrity

Data integrity is guaranteed by a combination of x86 segmented memory (32-bit Intel x86) and SFI (Intel x86-64 and ARM). It is unclear whether the x86-32 implementation of NaCl will eventually use SFI for memory segmentation as well, in order to unify the code base. Both approaches create a data sandbox that restricts a NaCl module's access to memory. Reliable disassembly is facilitated by alignment and structural rules that are imposed by the NaCl architecture and which must be followed by NaCl applications. After the application binaries have been disassembled, unsafe instructions can easily be detected and prohibited. Finally, control flow integrity is guaranteed by ensuring that "all control flow in the program text targets an instruction identified during disassembly" [Yee et al. 2009]. The entire process of the static analysis, from download to execution, is illustrated by Figure 5.4. The validator has been found to be able to check code at approximately 30 MB/second. At this speed, the time required to validate an untrusted NaCl application is not significant, especially when compared to the duration of the download.

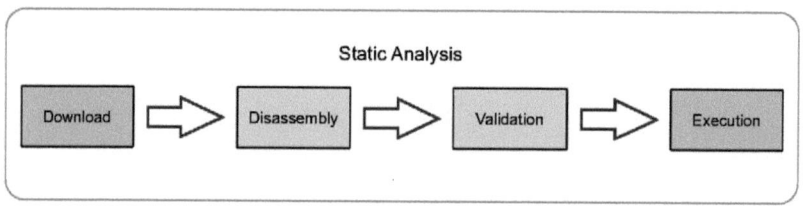

Figure 5.4.: Download, validation, and execution of an untrusted NaCl module

The inner sandbox has been tested for security defects by the NaCl authors. Among the employed tests were "random instruction generation", "exhaustive enumeration of valid x86 instructions", and "fuzzing[7] tests" [Yee et al. 2009]. These tests have exposed critical implementation defects that have subsequently been fixed. Therefore, the NaCl authors consider the inner sandbox to be extremely robust.

**Outer Sandbox**

The outer sandbox is the second level of defense in the NaCl security framework. It validates and mediates system calls from NaCl applications to the underlying operating system. Should the inner sandbox be compromised, the attacker would gain access to the service runtime, but the outer sandbox would restrict further access to the rest of system. Unfortunately, the MacOS and Windows implementations of the outer sandbox were work in progress at the time of the publication of the NaCl research paper. Therefore, only the Linux implementation is discussed in depth.

The Linux and MacOS implementations make use of the ptrace kernel interface. The Windows implementation, on the other hand, employs Windows access-control-lists. For concerns over maintenance

---
[7]Fuzzing is an approach to software testing that involves providing invalid or random input data to a computer program, in order to reveal unexpected defects.

## 5.3. Native Client

overhead, the NaCl authors deliberately avoided the use of custom kernel modules or device drivers. Instead, they implemented NaCl using standard system services that do not require adaptation to different Linux kernels or Windows operating systems. The Linux outer sandbox spawns a child process for the NaCl container and traces its system calls using `ptrace`. Every system call is matched with a white list that is maintained by the outer sandbox. The use of a disallowed system call causes the immediate termination of the NaCl module. The NaCl programming model encourages developers to limit their use of system calls and inter-module communications, as the `ptrace` approach adds computational overhead. Every system call triggers two context switches and a table lookup.

### Exceptions

NaCl does not support hardware exceptions, e.g. segmentation faults and floating point exceptions, due to incompatible exception models between supported operating systems. Therefore, NaCl applications cannot recover from hardware exceptions and must prevent their occurrence — flawed applications risk abrupt termination. On the other hand, NaCl supports C++ exceptions, which are synchronous and implemented entirely within user-space. Exception isolation is achieved through the fact that each NaCl module runs in its own OS process. Windows Structured Exception Handling is not portable to MacOS or Linux and therefore not supported.

### Service Runtime

The service runtime is an OS specific, trusted component that isolates untrusted native application code from the underlying operating system and other host resources. Technically, it is a native executable that is invoked by the NaCl browser plugin. This plugin also handles the interaction between the web browser and the service runtime. The service runtime also implements the springboard/trampoline mechanism that is used to transfer the control flow from trusted to untrusted code and vice versa. This mechanism is part of the trusted code base and is therefore granted access to instructions that are forbidden to be used by untrusted code. While trampolines permit the crossing from untrusted to trusted code, springboards enable the transfer of the control flow in the reverse direction. Both mechanisms employ the `far call` instruction to cross trust boundaries. Alignment rules ensure that the springboard cannot be invoked by untrusted code. The system calls implemented by service runtime exhibit a slight amount of overhead compared to native OS system calls. For example, the `null` NaCl system call executes in 156 ns, which is slightly slower than that Linux `getpid` OS system call time that completes in 138 ns on the same hardware.

### Communications

The communication services of the IMC are built on NaCl sockets. The NaCl socket facility provides a bi-directional, reliable, in-order datagram service that is comparable to Unix domain sockets. Every untrusted NaCl module receives a NaCl socket when it is created. This socket is available from the JavaScript layer through the DOM and is used to send messages from JavaScript application code to NaCl code. NaCl sockets can also be shared or connected to other services.

NaCl's SRPC interface is implemented in untrusted code, using the IMC framework. SRPC allows the creation of procedural interfaces between the JavaScript and NaCl application layers — or between two NaCl modules. It supports NaCl descriptors, arrays, and a few basic types (int, float, char). The PPAPI interface also builds on the IMC.

5. *Native Web Applications*

**Developer Tools**

Currently, NaCl supports the development of C and C++ applications. Application development is carried out with a modified version of the GNU tool chain, which should be familiar to most Linux and Unix developers. The gcc compiler was modified to align function entries and target branches to 32 bytes. In addition, `nacljump` was implemented for indirect control transfer. In addition to the compiler, the assembler and linker were adapted to NaCl's block alignment and address spaces requirements. The NaCl compiler creates application binaries for all three supported platforms: 32-bit and 64-bit Intel x86, as well as the ARM CPU architecture. According to the NaCl developers, the modifications were "achieved with less than 1000 lines"[Yee et al. 2009] of changed code, outlining the feasibility of porting other compiler suites to Native Client. In the future, NaCl could gain support for other programming languages.

NaCl does not yet support the debugging and profiling of applications. However, due to their roots as traditional native applications, NaCl applications can be compiled as stand-alone programs that can then be debugged with standard tools. The NaCl authors are aware of this shortcoming and hope to provide integrated support for debugging and profiling in the future.

### 5.3.3. Portable Native Client

Although NaCl applications are OS-independent, the fact that they are compiled to machine language makes them dependent on the CPU architecture. In order to overcome this dependency, the *Portable Native Client* (PNaCl, pronounced "pinnacle") project was initiated. PNaCl employs the *Low Level Virtual Machine (LLVM)*[8] bitcode format to create processor independent application binaries that follow the compile once, run everywhere mantra [Donovan et al. 2010]. Instead of compiling the source code directly into machine executable code, PNaCl introduces an additional intermediate step, called *translation*. The initial compilation step compiles the source code into LLVM bitcode, which can then be distributed. In the second stage, the bitcode is translated into the client's instruction set — a step which commonly occurs directly on the client's machine. PNaCl preserves the security characteristics of Native Client, while enhancing the portability of its executables. The project is currently in a very early stage of development.

### 5.3.4. Capabilities

**Performance**

The Native Client authors implemented a series of benchmarks to evaluate the performance of NaCl. The benchmarks focused on computational performance, a scenario for which Native Client was originally designed, and included a port of SPEC2000, thread performance tests, a H.264 decoder, an open physics simulation system, and a port of the popular Quake 3D game [Yee et al. 2009].

As CPU bound applications are most susceptible to the impacts of NaCl's alignment and sandboxing overhead, the SPEC2000 CPU benchmark suite was ported to NaCl in order to evaluate these effects. Experiments found that the performance impact of NaCl, compared to native Linux executables, was less than 5% on average and about 12% in the worst case. While NaCl's alignment rules led to a

---

[8]LLVM is a programming language and target independent compiler framework [Lattner and Adve 2004].

general increase in code size, their impact on performance varied. In some cases, the NaCl executables performed the SPEC2000 benchmarks faster than their native Linux counterparts.

In order to evaluate NaCl's multi-threading performance, three dedicated benchmarks were implemented:

1. *Earth:* a ray-tracing animation that renders the texture of Earth onto a spinning cube
2. *Voronoi*: a brute-force Voronoi tessellation[9]
3. *Life*: simulation of Conway's Game of Life[10]

Overall, NaCl's thread implementation compared favorably to native Linux thread performance. It scaled accordingly with increased thread count and managed to obtain a performance lead over the native Linux implementation of the Voronoi tessellation. In the other benchmarks, the native Linux executables ran approximately 12% to 14% faster than the NaCl applications. The H.264 decoder ported to NaCl with minimal effort. Its performance was found to be comparable with the original Linux application and limited by the video frame rate. The port of Bullet, an open physics simulation system, was considerably more work, although it was described as straightforward. The HelloWorld demo from the Bullet distribution, which simulates a large number of spheres falling to and colliding with a flat surface, showed a marginal slowdown of 2% for the NaCl application. The NaCl port of the popular Quake 3D game (using software rendering) achieved an average frame rate of 143.7 frames per second (FPS) — marginally faster than the original application with 143.3 FPS.

These benchmarks results suggest that NaCl indeed delivers a level of performance that is comparable to that of native Linux applications. The exact impact of the NaCl sandbox and its alignment restrictions depend on the application itself and can vary substantially.

**Legacy Support**

The benchmark experiments indicated that porting Linux applications and libraries to the NaCl framework is generally possible within a reasonable amount of time. Legacy Linux libraries port to NaCl with minimal effort, as long as they don't require network and disk access. The port of the H.264 decoder required about 20 lines of additional C code — more than half for the sole purpose of error checking. Even larger software projects, such as the Bullet physics library, were ported to NaCl within "a couple of hours" [Yee et al. 2009]. These results imply that existing legacy C and C++ code can be reused in many cases to build NaCl native web applications.

**OS-independence**

Although initially implemented on the Linux operating system, NaCl has since extended its support to the Microsoft Windows the Apple MacOS operating systems. When a developer compiles a NaCl application, the NaCl compiler automatically outputs three different executables: one each for Intel x86-32, x86-64, and for the ARM CPU architecture (32-bit). These application binaries are then deployed on the web server that hosts the NaCl-enabled web application. Upon accessing the web application, the Chrome browser automatically downloads, inserts, and executes the appropriate NaCl

---

[9]The Voronoi tessellation allows the decomposition of a plane into regions, according to a given set of objects, e.g. points, on the plane.
[10]Conway's Game of Life is a computer simulation of lifeforms that populate a two-dimensional, checkered plane. Depending on their neighborhood they live, die, or spawn new life.

5. Native Web Applications

module for the underlying CPU architecture. Compiled NaCl modules can run unmodified on Linux, Windows, or MacOS, yielding true OS-independence.

## 5.4. Comparison of NaCl and Xax

NaCl and Xax share many similarities in their goals and even in their architectural approaches. Both technologies aim to bring the computational power of native code execution to web applications, with Xax focusing especially on the reuse of legacy code and NaCl focusing on security. NaCl and Xax have learned from the mistakes made by NPAPI and ActiveX, namely the lack of a solid security framework and insufficient plugin control, and therefore provide containment for untrusted native code.

Table 5.1.: A comparison of NaCl and Xax

|  | NaCl | Xax |
| --- | --- | --- |
| Browser integration | plugin | proxy |
| Implemented as kernel module | no | yes, ideally |
| Intercepts OS system calls | yes | yes |
| Introduces a new tool chain | yes | no |
| Network and file access | no | yes |
| Open source | yes | no |
| OS-independent applications | yes | yes |
| Primary method of containment | dual sandboxing | process isolation |
| Requires modification to legacy code | yes | yes |
| Reuses browser functionality | yes | yes |
| Static analysis of untrusted code | yes | no |
| Support for multi-threading | yes | no |
| Supported programming languages | C, C++ | C, C++, Java, Python |

NaCl is implemented as a browser plugin, while Xax is connected to the browser using a proxy. The Xax approach has the advantage that it works with virtually all web browsers, while NaCl is, at least for the time being, limited to Google's own Chrome browser. On the other hand, from a technical standpoint, the plugin approach is clearly favorable over the proxy approach, as it provides deeper integration with the web browser and a greater level of control over native application modules.

Both Xax and NaCl use the Linux kernel's `ptrace` facility to intercept system calls that are issued by their applications — at least on the Linux OS. Xax favors the approach of employing a dedicated kernel module for this task, as is done by its Windows implementation. NaCl, on the other hand, was designed to avoid custom kernel modules. Its creators fear that the overhead of having to develop and maintain a kernel module for every version of the supported Windows, Linux, and MacOS operating systems does not justify the advantages of deeper kernel integration.

Xax and NaCl follow similar approaches to achieve OS-independence: disallow the use of OS specific system calls and provide a dedicated system call interface instead that reuses existing web browser

## 5.4. Comparison of NaCl and Xax

functionality. When applications issue these custom system calls, they are intercepted and mediated to the operating system level by a trusted component within the framework. For Xax this is done by the Xax Monitor. The corresponding NaCl component is called the service runtime. By removing the dependency on native OS system calls, Xax and NaCl are able to achieve true OS-independence.

NaCl places structural and alignment rules on its applications. These restrictions mandate the introduction of a dedicated tool chain to follow these rules. The standard GNU tool chain was modified to provide the capabilities to compile and link compliant NaCl applications. Legacy code must be ported to this tool chain in order to be made available for NaCl application development. Xax does not define any rules for the alignment of its native executables. Therefore, it does not need to introduce a new tool chain. Xax applications can be compiled and linked using standard tools.

Xax permits file system and network access to its applications. For example, the `xabi_open_url` may be used by a Xax picoprocess to communicate with its origin server. NaCl, on the other hand, disallows network and file system access from untrusted code. This means that NaCl web applications must depend on JavaScript for these tasks.

Although the development of NaCl is driven by Google, it is an open source project. Its source code is available to the general public, which allows for reviews of its implementation, especially in respect to possible security defects. Xax, on the other hand, is a closed project at Microsoft Research. Its source code is not publicly available for testing or review. While NaCl, like Xax, has started as an experiment, it has recently been included and activated by default in the beta version of the Chrome 14 web browser. While NaCl has evolved into a public framework for the development of native web applications, it is unclear whether the Xax experiments will be pursued and whether they will be turned into a product.

NaCl and Xax differ substantially in the way they contain and isolate untrusted native application code. Xax relies on process isolation for its primary security measure and introduces a picoprocess that is deprived of the ability to issue OS system calls. NaCl, on the other hand, goes at least one step further, underlining its focus on security. It employs two sandboxes to create an additional security subdomain inside an operating system process. The inner sandbox disassembles and validates untrusted application code using static analysis (see Section 5.3.1). The outer sandbox checks system calls and permits only those that are whitelisted. Invalid instructions or system calls are rejected and result in the immediate termination of the NaCl application.

The porting of legacy code to NaCl or Xax generally requires modifications. The authors of Xax have created a five-step porting guide that outlines the steps of porting a legacy application or library to Xax. The primary difficulty of this procedure lies in the removal and/or replacement of the native OS system calls. The NaCl tool chain is compatible with the standard GNU tool chain, which simplifies the porting of legacy code. Both, the Xax and NaCl creators claim that the effort of porting legacy applications and libraries to their frameworks is reasonable and generally straightforward.

The realization that the web browser provides the functionality required to execute native web applications is the foundation of Xax and NaCl. Both technologies reuse browser mechanisms to support compiled native modules. By employing the web browser as a middleware between the native OS and the native web applications, Xax and NaCl achieve a degree of OS-independence that was previously inexistent for native applications.

NaCl and Xax allow the execution of arbitrary, untrusted native code in the web browser. NaCl employs static analysis as an effective security measure to detect flaws and defects in this untrusted code. Structural and alignment rules ensure that any NaCl application can be reliably disassembled. Following the disassembly, the static analysis is straightforward, with a validator checking the instructions

## 5. Native Web Applications

for unsafe sequences. Although its creators acknowledge similar techniques in their paper, Xax does not employ static analysis. Instead, it relies on process isolation and system call interception for the containment of untrusted native code. Considering that the additional security measures employed by NaCl add little computational overhead, its approach seems vastly superior over that of Xax.

Unlike NaCl, Xax does not support the development of multi-threaded applications. Multi-threading makes it possible to distribute the workload of a computationally demanding application among several processing cores. Considering that multi-core CPUs are state of the art and widely available, this limitation is a major setback for the suitability of Xax for the development of these applications. NaCl, on the other hand, provides a subset of the POSIX threads specification that is sufficiently complete to support the Intel Thread Building Blocks[11], which is a popular framework for the development of multi-threaded applications.

As described above, native web applications allow the extension of web applications with compiled native code. They promise to bring computational performance and the ability to reuse legacy code to web application development. The foremost questions are: Can native web applications deliver their promises in terms of computational performance? Can they combine the strengths of native applications and web applications? In order to answer these questions, an analysis of the performance characteristics of native web applications is necessary. Additional factors, such as the ability to reuse legacy code, openness, maturity, and of course industry support and market penetration, must be considered to determine the potential of native web applications. In the following chapter, a performance analysis of native applications, JavaScript web applications, and NaCl native web applications is conducted. The results of the performance analysis will be complemented with an evaluation of additional factors in Chapter 7.

---

[11] Intel Thread Building Blocks is a C++ template library that simplifies the implementation of concurrent algorithms and applications.

# 6. Performance Analysis

Native web applications aim to bring the computational performance of compiled native code to web development. As described in the previous chapter, they provide additional benefits, such as OS-independence and the ability to reuse legacy code — without sacrificing security. Although the details of their implementations differ, both NaCl and Xax share many similarities in their fundamental concepts and goals. The fact that two of the leading IT companies of the world, Google and Microsoft, have independently developed similar solutions to the problem of web application performance leads to the implication that this is indeed a valid concern.

The authors of NaCl and Xax have conducted experiments comparing the computational performance of native web applications to that of traditional native applications. First of all, the results of these experiments have not yet been confirmed by independent researchers. Second, and more importantly, several central questions have not yet been addressed:

1. How does JavaScript performance compare to that of traditional native applications and native web applications?
2. Is JavaScript fast enough to enable web applications of the future or is an alternative needed?
3. What are the benefits and drawbacks of extending JavaScript web applications with compiled native code?

It is the goal of this chapter to address these questions and to provide a performance analysis and comparison of native C applications, JavaScript web applications, and NaCl native web applications. It introduces four benchmarks to evaluate several performance characteristics of each technology. The *pi-* and *pi-MT benchmarks* focus on number crunching performance. The *gears benchmark* evaluates 3D graphics performance, which is relevant for 3D games and CAD applications. Finally, the *spectral benchmark* focuses on the processing of large amounts of binary data — a subject that is relevant to video and audio editors, among other applications. Each benchmark was implemented as a native C application, a JavaScript web application, and as a NaCl native web application. During the development of the benchmark applications, the effort of porting the C implementations to NaCl was evaluated. Unfortunately, Xax is a closed research project at Microsoft and not available to independent researchers. Therefore, it could not be included in the performance analysis.

Since JavaScript web applications run in the web browser, their performance depends heavily on the browser's JavaScript engine. The JavaScript engine is a web browser component that is responsible for the execution of JavaScript programs. The leading web browsers employ different JavaScript engines and their performance can differ substantially. Therefore, the JavaScript performance analysis was extended to include the most significant web browsers, i.e. Apple Safari, Google Chrome, Mozilla Firefox, and Opera. Unfortunately, the Microsoft Internet Explorer, the leading web browser in terms of market share, could not be included in the comparison. It lacks support for several modern web technologies, e.g. Web Workers, WebGL, and typed arrays (`ArrayBuffer`), that were employed in the benchmark applications. The desktop web browser market share, as of September 2011, is illustrated in Figure 6.1.

## 6. Performance Analysis

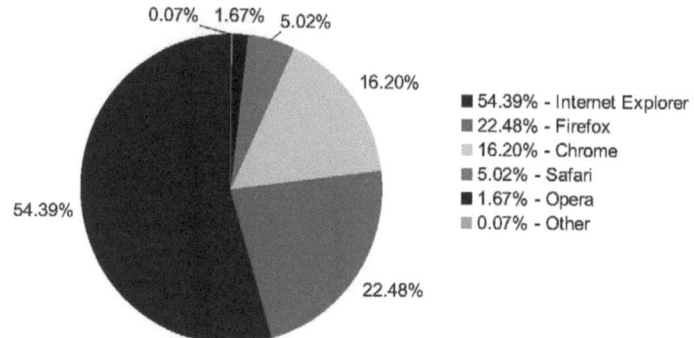

Figure 6.1.: Desktop web browser market share (Sept. 2011) [Net Applications 2011]

The source code for all benchmark implementations is available under an open source license at https://github.com/dennisjarosch/Dissertation.

### 6.1. Experimental Environment

The experiments were conducted on an Apple MacBook Pro (5,5) laptop running the 64-bit edition of Ubuntu 10.10 *Maverick Meerkat* Linux and the stock 32-bit Mac OS 10.6 Snow Leopard operating systems in a dual boot environment. During the benchmarks, the laptop was connected to power at all times.

The *gcc* compiler 4.4.5 and the C library *libc* 2.12.1 were used to compile the C benchmarks. The JavaScript benchmarks were evaluated in the Google Chrome 9, Mozilla Firefox 4, Apple Safari/Webkit[1], and Opera 11 browsers, unless otherwise stated. The JavaScript benchmarks were run without a web server, i.e. the HTML files containing the JavaScript code were loaded directly into the web browsers.

The NaCl benchmarks were compiled with the software development kit (SDK) version 0.1.507.0[2] This version of the NaCl SDK is based on the NPAPI plugin interface. As NaCl remains work in progress, the SDK was updated during the experimental process and support for NPAPI was dropped. It was replaced with the PPAPI/Pepper 2 plugin interface (see Section 3.1.1). The newer SDK, in contrast to the NPAPI release, does not support OpenGL-based 3D graphics. For this reason, and because large portions of the completed NPAPI-specific plugin interface code would have required a re-write from NPAPI to Pepper 2, the decision was made to base the benchmarks on the older Native Client SDK. Newer version of the Chrome browser no longer support NaCl with the NPAPI interface, therefore version 9 of the Google Chrome browser was employed as the reference browser for all NaCl benchmarks. NaCl automatically downloads and inserts native modules when accessing a web site. Therefore, NaCl native web applications must be run from a web server. The NaCl benchmark applications were served by the *httpd.py* Python web server that is part of the NaCl SDK.

---
[1] WebKit is an open source web browser engine that forms the basis of Apple's Safari browser.
[2] The current Native Client SDK can be obtained at http://code.google.com/chrome/nativeclient/, last visited on October 4, 2011.

## 6.2. Pi Benchmark

The pi benchmark calculates an approximation of $\pi$ using the Leibniz formula, for a given number $N$ iterations.

### 6.2.1. Problem and Objective

The purpose of the pi benchmark is to evaluate and compare the computational performance of C, NaCl, and JavaScript in the fields of number crunching and the evaluation of mathematical terms. The Leibniz formula was developed by Gottfried Wilhelm Leibniz in 1682 in order to approximate the number $\pi$. It was chosen as the basis of this computational benchmark due to its simplicity and inefficiency. While the Leibniz formula is easy to implement in multiple programming languages, it "converges so slowly that hundreds of terms would be required to compute the numerical value of $\pi$ to even two digits accuracy" [Bailey et al. 1997]. This makes it a suitable problem to test the computational performance of simple mathematical operations in conjunction with loop execution performance. While the native C implementation of the pi benchmark is expected to deliver the best results, the interesting question is how JavaScript and NaCl will complete this simple computational benchmark.

### 6.2.2. Theoretical Background

The Leibniz formula is a mathematical series that is mathematically defined as:

$$\pi = 4 \cdot \sum_{n=0}^{N-1} \frac{(-1)^n}{2n+1}. \tag{6.1}$$

### 6.2.3. Implementation Details

#### JavaScript

Since the Leibniz formula is a very simple mathematical equation, the JavaScript implementation of the pi benchmark was rather trivial. The initial version was programmed as a blocking script, i.e. long running computations with several thousands of iterations blocked the user interface of the benchmark application and triggered the infamous "script is not responding"-dialog. In order to ensure that this behavior could not affect the benchmark results, the JavaScript benchmark was rewritten to employ *Web Workers*.

Web Workers make it possible to run tasks in the background without blocking the main process, i.e. the user interface of a web application [Mozilla Developer Center 2011c]. Depending on the web browser, workers are usually implemented as operating system processes or threads[3]. A web application and its workers communicate by posting messages. The JavaScript pi benchmark automatically creates a single Web Worker upon its execution. The worker remains idle and waits for the initiation of the computation. When the *calculate* button is clicked, the web application posts a message to the worker that contains the number of iterations, thus commencing the $\pi$-approximation. After completing its task, the worker posts a return message to the web application, containing the result of the

---
[3] A thread is a lightweight process that allows computational tasks to be executed in parallel.

## 6. Performance Analysis

computation. As of this writing, Web Workers are supported by the stable versions of the Mozilla Firefox, Google Chrome, Apple Safari, and Opera web browsers. The current Microsoft Internet Explorer, version 9, on the other hand, lacks Web Worker support.

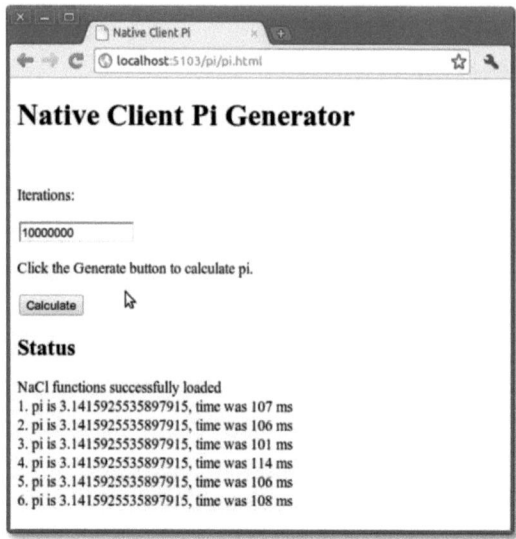

Figure 6.2.: A screenshot of the Native Client pi benchmark

The changes required to adapt the original JavaScript pi benchmark to employ Web Workers were straightforward. Unfortunately, neither Firebug[4] nor the developer tools of the Google Chrome browser allowed the debugging of the worker script. This limitation is a real disadvantage for the development of complex worker scripts and will hopefully be amended in the near future. Quick tests indicated that the Web Worker version of the benchmark is marginally faster than the blocking version — at least on Google Chrome.

## C

Due to the low complexity of the algorithm and the similarities in syntax, porting the benchmark from JavaScript to C was trivial. As the name indicates, the C version of the pi benchmark was written in plain C. It runs in a terminal, without a graphical user interface (GUI) and is executed from the command line. The program takes a single argument, which is the number of iterations $N$. In terms of the algorithm, the C program is equivalent to its JavaScript predecessor. This is desired in order to ensure a basis of comparison that is as fair a possible.

Initially, all benchmark implementations employed the pow() function to compute a single element of the Leibnitz series. Surprisingly, the NaCl implementation was much faster than the native C benchmark in early tests, which was finally attributed to type conversions prior to the function call.

---
[4]Firebug is an extension to Mozilla Firefox that provides development tools, including a debugger and a profiler.

In order to mitigate these effects on the benchmark results, the function call was replaced with a bit shifting algorithm that was suggested by Matthew Ball during a discussion in the Native-Client-Discuss group[5]. This change brought substantial performance improvements for all implementations of the pi benchmark and removed the performance penalties caused by the type conversions in the C implementation.

### Native Client

The NaCl benchmark application is a native web application that performs the approximation of $\pi$ in native code. It consists of a single HTML page that provides the same user interface as the JavaScript pi benchmark and a NaCl module that implements the pi() function in C code. The NaCl module reuses the source code of the C implementation, which did not require any noteworthy changes. The native function is called directly from the JavaScript code in the HTML page. The JavaScript portion of the NaCl benchmark does not employ Web Workers, as these are not yet supported in combination with NaCl. Therefore, the NaCl web application is implemented as a blocking script.

The NaCl pi benchmark is based on the NPAPI plugin interface. In order to expose the native pi() function to the JavaScript layer of the NaCl pi benchmark, a certain degree of *boilerplate code*[6] or glue code had to be written. This code implements mandatory plugin activation interfaces and establishes the bridge between the JavaScript and NaCl layers. This makes it possible to call the pi() function from the JavaScript layer and to deliver the result of the computation from the NaCl layer to the originating JavaScript layer. In this specific case, the amount of boilerplate code outweighs the algorithm code by a substantial amount. Therefore, most of the time porting the benchmark from C to NaCl was spent in understanding and implementing the mandatory NPAPI and NaCl interfaces. Alternatively, NaCl's remote procedure call interface (SRPC) could have been targeted instead of the NPAPI plugin interface. While the SRPC interface requires almost no boilerplate code, it also provides only basic C data types (no structs or unions). Therefore, the programming examples within the NaCl SDK generally endorse the NPAPI interface.

### 6.2.4. Experimental Setup

During the benchmarking experiments, the run times, CPU utilization, and the memory consumption of each benchmark implementation were measured. The C implementation was executed in a GNOME terminal on Ubuntu Linux 10.10. The NaCl implementation was executed on the same platform in the Google Chrome 9 browser. The JavaScript execution times were measured in the Google Chrome 9, Mozilla Firefox 4, and Opera 11 browsers on Ubuntu Linux 10.10. In addition, the pi benchmark was evaluated in Safari 5, running on Mac OS X 10.6 on the same computer.

The run times were measured with each programming language's internal timers, i.e. gettimeofday() for the C version and Date.getTime() for the NaCl and JavaScript implementations of the benchmark. The NaCl run time measurements were performed in JavaScript, with the timing code for the JavaScript and NaCl benchmark implementations being identical. The CPU utilization was measured using the top utility on both Linux and Mac OS X.

---

[5] Discussion entitled *NaCl Performance Questions*, http://groups.google.com/group/native-client-discuss/browse_thread/thread/c3f193f0130b55e8, last visited on October 13, 2011.
[6] Source code that is often repeated with little or no changes at all is referred to as boilerplate code.

*6. Performance Analysis*

The memory analysis on Linux was performed using the *smaps* kernel interface. Smaps was introduced with the 2.6.16 kernel and provides reliable information on the memory consumption of processes. It is accessible through the proc file system, under /proc/$pid/smaps, with $pid referring to the process identifier. Particularly interesting for this experiment is the amount of *private resident set size (RSS)* memory of a process, i.e. the portion its memory that is held in RAM and not shared with other processes. The output of smaps is very verbose. Therefore, the mem_usage.py smaps parser was employed to convert it into a more human-readable format [Wingo 2007]. On Mac OS X, the system profiler was employed to provide an overview of the private RSS during the benchmarking.

### 6.2.5. Execution

Prior to commencing the benchmarks, the computer was rebooted. No other applications were run during the benchmarking except a GNOME terminal on Linux and a single Finder[7] window, or a terminal window respectively for the CPU load measurements, on Mac OS.

The benchmarking process was executed as follows: the first round of the pi benchmark was executed with with 10,000,000 iterations. The second round was conducted with 20,000,000 iterations and so forth, culminating in 100,000,000 iterations in the tenth and final round. During each round, 20 running time samples were collected. After discarding both the highest and the lowest aberration, the arithmetic mean was calculated form the remaining 18 samples. This arithmetic mean determined the execution time of the pi benchmark for each round of the experiment. It should be noted that, while the arithmetic mean is not suitable for summarizing normalized benchmark results, [Smith 1988] and [Fleming and Wallace 1986], it is "the appropriate method for averaging a set running times" [Jacob and Mudge 1995]. The benchmarking process was carried out for every C, JavaScript, and NaCl implementation and for the different browsers in the experiment.

A simple shell script containing a for-loop was used to run the C benchmark and to collect the 20 samples for each round. The benchmarking of the NaCl and JavaScript applications was performed entirely manually, to ensure that compiler optimizations for the execution of 20 identical loops were impossible. Opera, Firefox, and Safari, were run without arguments. The Chrome browser was called with the following arguments, for both the NaCl and JavaScript runs, to allow the execution of the JavaScript pi benchmark from file and without a web server:

google-chrome --enable-nacl --enable-webgl --allow-file-access-from-files.

In order to determine the CPU utilization of the pi benchmark implementations during the execution of the experiments, the top utility was employed. 12 CPU utilization samples of the benchmark process were collected during dedicated benchmarking runs — these were not used to measure the run times. The default refresh time of the top utility was used, which is 3 seconds on Linux and 1 second on Mac OS X.

The memory analysis was conducted during the execution of the respective pi benchmarks with $10^9$ iterations. While the benchmark process was running, the mem_usage.py Python[8] script was executed to gather the memory status supplied by the smaps kernel interface. Unlike Firefox and Opera, the Chrome browser spawns multiple process, which all contribute to the total memory consumption. Examples include the browser kernel, Web Workers, and a separate process for each browser tab[9]. A helper shell script, which calls mem_usage.py for each Chrome process, was written to retrieve the

---

[7]The Finder is the file manager of the Mac OS operating system.
[8]Python is a high-level, object oriented, and interpreted programming language.
[9]Process isolation was introduced by Google Chrome to leave other tabs unaffected in case a single tab crashes.

smaps status of all processes during the execution of the benchmark. In addition, the `top` application was used to determine the process with the highest CPU load — which corresponds to the process that was occupied with the benchmarking itself.

When performing the memory analysis, Chrome was started with an additional argument:

```
google-chrome --enable-nacl --enable-webgl --allow-file-access-from-files
--no-sandbox.
```

Without the `--no-sandbox` flag, the kernel was unable to deliver the memory statistics for certain browser processes via smaps. The Safari memory analysis was performed on Mac OS X, with the help of the built-in activity monitor application. The activity monitor displays the amount of private memory per process.

### 6.2.6. Results

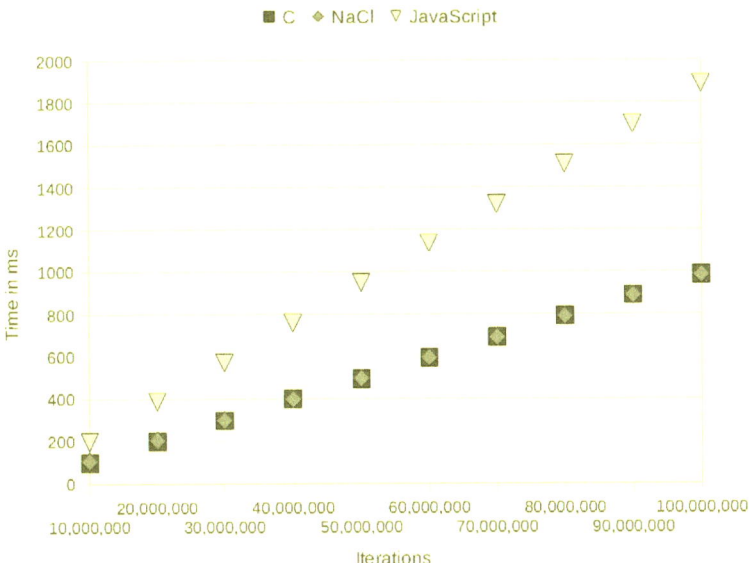

Figure 6.3.: Pi benchmark: running times of C, NaCl, and JavaScript

The benchmark results confirm the linear complexity of the Leibnitz algorithm that is being used to approximate $\pi$. Figure 6.3 compares the results of the C, Native Client, and JavaScript benchmark implementations on the Linux platform, using the Chrome 9 web browser. As expected, the C implementation of the pi benchmark consistently delivered the fastest results. The performance of NaCl was excellent and on par with C. The advantages of the C implementation was measurable but amounted to less than 1%. The JavaScript engine of the Chrome browser was unable to match the speed of the compiled native code. Both C and NaCl performed the benchmarks approximately 200% as fast as JavaScript in the Chrome web browser.

## 6. Performance Analysis

The C, JavaScript, and NaCl implementations achieved a degree of CPU utilization during the benchmarking sessions that was consistently around 100%. In other words, one of the two processing cores of the Apple MacBook Pro was occupied with the execution of a benchmark process. The CPU utilization during the pi benchmark is illustrated in Figure 6.4.

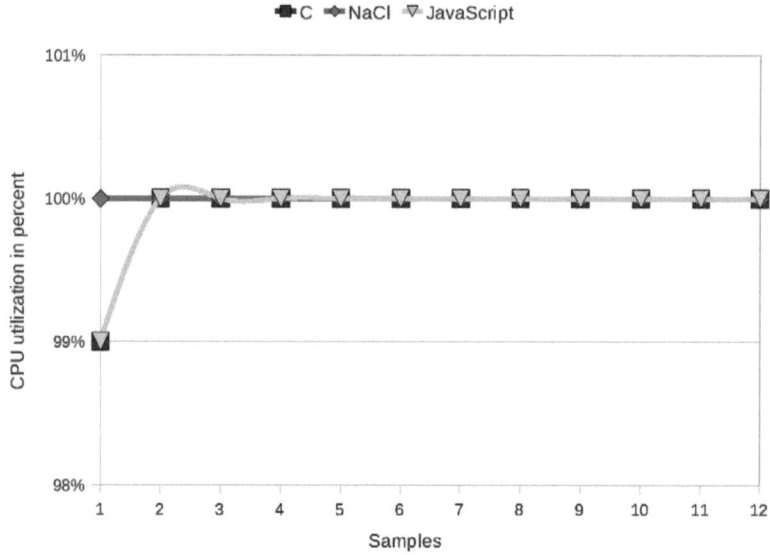

Figure 6.4.: Pi benchmark: CPU utilization of C, NaCl, and JavaScript

Unlike the CPU utilization, the results of the memory analysis varied greatly between C, JavaScript, and NaCl. According to the Linux kernel, the C benchmark merely consumed 88 KB of private RSS memory during the execution of $10^9$ iterations. This is, of course, due to the simplicity of the algorithm, the efficiency of the manual memory management, and the lack of an additional runtime, e.g. the web browser. Recall that Chrome is a multi-process web browser. As presented in Figure 6.5, the NaCl process occupied 2,408 KB of private RSS memory — about half of the JavaScript benchmark process running in the same web browser. The total private RSS memory consumed by all Chrome processes during the pi benchmark was similar between NaCl and JavaScript, with 22,056 KB and 23,780 KB respectively.

The results of the web browser comparison put the performance of Google Chrome's JavaScript engine into perspective. As illustrated in Figure 6.6, it was outperformed by all competing browsers in the pi benchmark.

Mozilla Firefox 4 completed the benchmarks in the least time, followed by Opera 11, Safari 5, and Chrome 9. Please note that the benchmark results of Safari are not directly comparable, as they were conducted on a different operating system — although on the same computer. It should also be pointed out that, at the time of this writing, version 9 was no longer the current stable release of the Chrome browser, although quick experiments with Chrome 10 and the Chrome 11 beta did not promise any substantial performance improvements. Therefore, the experiments were completed with

## 6.2. Pi Benchmark

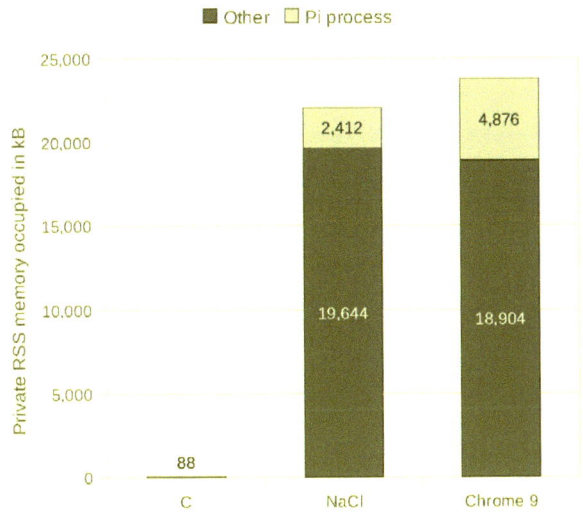

Figure 6.5.: Pi benchmark: memory consumption of C, NaCl, and JavaScript

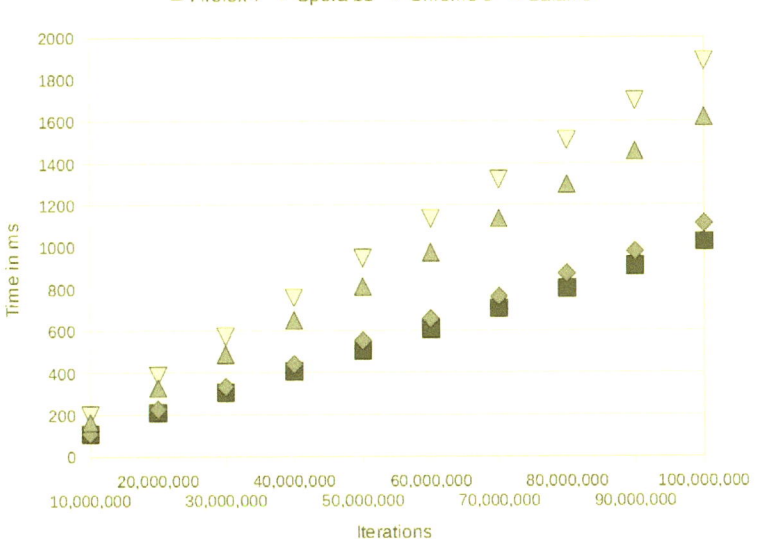

Figure 6.6.: Pi benchmark: web browser comparison

## 6. Performance Analysis

Chrome 9, which, due to changes in the Chrome 10 Native Client implementation, was the only version of the browser that permitted direct comparability between NaCl and JavaScript performance.

The fastest web browser, Firefox 4, completed the pi benchmark almost 200% as fast as the Chrome browser — and only marginally slower than C or NaCl. C completed the benchmark with 100,000,000 iterations in 986 ms, NaCl in 988 ms, and Firefox/JavaScript in 1,025 ms. In other words, the JavaScript engine of the Mozilla Firefox 4 browser was roughly 4% slower than the C native application in the pi benchmark. This is an excellent and unexpected result that leads to the implication that JavaScript web applications are capable of computing simple mathematical algorithms almost as fast as native code written in C or NaCl — although the performance depends heavily on the browser's JavaScript engine.

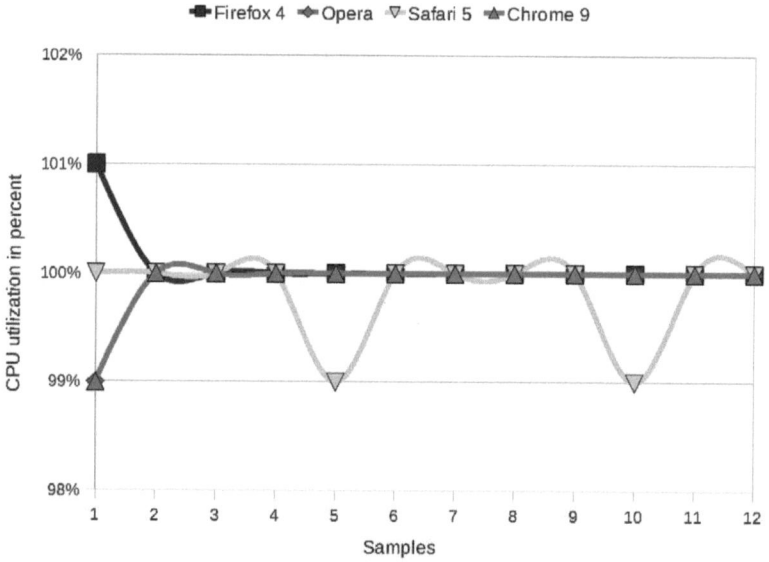

Figure 6.7.: Pi benchmark: web browser CPU utilization

All browsers managed to achieve a constantly high CPU utilization of 99% to 100% during the pi benchmark. These results are ideal for a computational benchmark, as they confirm that the majority of CPU cycles were indeed spent on the benchmarking process. Figure 6.7 depicts the CPU utilization of the web browsers during the execution of the JavaScript pi benchmark.

Although the smaps interface of the Linux kernel provides access to very detailed memory statistics, the memory consumption of the web browsers in the benchmarking sessions deviated between measurements — the exact memory consumption was inconsistent and difficult to determine. Having said this, the results of the memory analysis provide a valid overview of the memory consumption of the web browsers in the experiments. The results of the browser memory analysis are in favor of the Chrome browser, which consumed substantially less private RSS memory than its competitors on the Linux platform. The memory consumption of web browsers during the execution of $10^9$ iterations of the pi benchmark is compared by Figure 6.8. Chrome consumed 23,780 KB of private RSS memory.

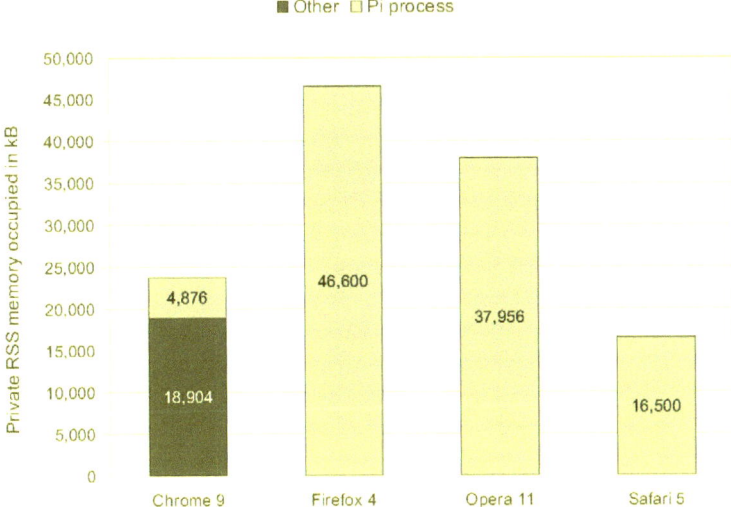

Figure 6.8.: Pi benchmark: web browser memory consumption

Firefox 4 showed its peak memory usage at 46,600 KB, which makes it the least memory efficient web browser in the benchmarking process. Opera consumed 37,956 KB of private RSS memory — approximately 15,000 KB more than the Chrome browser. Although Figure 6.8 implies that Safari 5 is the most memory efficient browser during the experiments, having consumed only 16,500 KB, the results cannot be directly compared to those of the other web browsers. Not only were they measured on a different operating system, but also using a different method. Therefore, the memory consumption of the Safari browser should be perceived as an interesting amendment to the Linux memory analysis.

## 6.3. Pi-MT Benchmark

The pi-MT Benchmark is an evolution of the pi benchmark. It employs concurrent programming[10] in order to utilize multiple CPUs for the calculation of $\pi$.

### 6.3.1. Problem and Objective

The original pi benchmark is a sequential computer program. It was not designed to take advantage of multiple CPUs. Instead, the entire computation is performed on a single computing core, leaving additional cores idle (if present). Parallel programming, a key instrument in the fields of scientific simulations and other high-performance computing areas, is able to efficiently utilize multiple CPUs, which can drastically shorten the duration of expensive computations. Multicore computers, once

---

[10] Concurrent programming allows the creation of computer programs that execute tasks in parallel instead of sequentially.

unaffordable and limited to science and the military, have become mainstream, inexpensive, and available to the general public. Most modern desktop and laptop computers are equipped with at least two processing cores — with mobile devices gradually following. Therefore, the utilization of multiple cores for performance and efficiency reasons is steadily gaining traction in the consumer space. In order to take advantage of multiple CPUs, computer programs must be designed to consist of several processes or threads that can be distributed among the processing cores individually. The operating system then schedules these tasks and executes them in parallel on multiple CPUs, if available.

As opposed to JavaScript, NaCl supports low-level parallel programming with threads. This is a substantial advantage over JavaScript, as NaCl allows developers to take full advantage of the underlying processing cores, using concurrency frameworks they already know. Not only does this facilitate the development of new parallel applications, it also simplifies the porting of legacy code to native web applications. JavaScript does not directly support threads, but provides simple concurrent programming capabilities via Web Workers. Web Workers, however, lack the flexibility that threads provide. The objective of the pi-MT Benchmark is to evaluate NaCl's threading capabilities and to compare its performance to that of native C threads and JavaScript Web Workers. In order to achieve these goals, the original pi benchmark was modified to distribute the workload of the $\pi$ computation among multiple CPUs.

### 6.3.2. Theoretical Background

Recall that the Leibniz formula describes a mathematical series that approximates the number $\pi$:

$$\sum_{n=0}^{N-1} \frac{(-1)^n}{2n+1} = 1 - \frac{1}{3} + \frac{1}{5} - \frac{1}{7} + \frac{1}{9} - \ldots = \frac{\pi}{4}. \tag{6.2}$$

The Leibniz formula consists of a series of additions. Fortunately, addition is a mathematical operation that fulfills the property of associativity: The order in which terms are evaluated does not affect the result. Addition also allows the creation of subtotals, which, together with associativity, makes it possible to implement the Leibniz formula as a parallel algorithm. In order to parallelize the computation of the Leibniz series, it is partitioned into a number of fragments that can be computed individually as tasks on dedicated CPUs. Each task computes a fragment of the series and returns the subtotal to the main benchmark process. The sum of all subtotals multiplied by 4 equals the approximation of the number $\pi$. Although the number of tasks must not necessarily coincide with the number of physical processing cores, this will be the case throughout these experiments.

### 6.3.3. Implementation Details

#### C

The original C implementation of the pi benchmark was rewritten to employ multiple processing cores using multithreading. With the help of the POSIX threading library (`pthreads`), the C implementation of the pi-MT Benchmark is able to distribute the computational workload among an arbitrary number of threads. All threads compute their subtotals locally and then add their results to a shared `pi` variable. This is possible because threads share a single address space with their creator process, i.e. all child threads have access to the variables of the parent process. In order to avoid race conditions and other unpredictable effects, writes to the shared **pi** variable must be synchronized. Since threads can be interrupted by the underlying operating system at virtually any time, explicitly in between reads and writes, the programmer must ensure that no thread can write data to a shared variable that is currently being accessed by another thread. In the C implementation of the pi-MT Benchmark, this is ensured by guarding the shared **pi** variable with a **mutex**[11]. The synchronization functions as follows: A thread acquires the **mutex**, modifies the shared **pi** variable, and releases the **mutex**. While a thread owns the **mutex**, all other threads will block trying to acquire it — until the **mutex** is released.

With the computation being performed in the threads, the main process remains responsible for the initial partitioning of the Leibnitz series and the synchronization of its threads. Upon launching the benchmark application, the iterations for each thread are calculated according to the number of total iterations and the number of worker threads. In the next step, the threads are created and then executed immediately. Their computational space, consisting of the iterations, is passed as arguments. The main process then waits for all threads to complete their computations and finally multiplies the value of the shared **pi** variable by 4 in order to yield the final result. The number of active worker threads throughout the experiments of the pi-MT Benchmark was set to two, which matches the number of CPUs of the MacBook Pro.

### NaCl

NaCl provides support for the development of multithreaded applications using the **pthread** library. Therefore, the port of the C implementation to NaCl was completely straightforward. The plugin activation and JavaScript/NaCl glue code was reused from the original NaCl pi benchmark and merged with the algorithmic source code from the C implementation of the pi-MT Benchmark. The implementation of the NaCl benchmark is widely analogous to the C implementation, including the basic principles of the shared **pi** variable and its protection with a **mutex**. The amount of code changes were minimal and related to the nature of the benchmark as a native web application. Overall, the NaCl implementation of the pi-MT Benchmark was completed in less than an hour.

### JavaScript

JavaScript does not offer parallel programming models that are comparable to those of C and NaCl. It does, however, support basic concurrency programming through Web Workers. Web Workers were devised as a simple mechanism to allow the execution of worker tasks in the background. Unlike threads, workers do not have access to shared variables and thus do not require synchronization to avoid race conditions and data consistency issues. The basic programming model for Web Workers is simple: A worker is created, commissioned with a certain task, and returns the corresponding result to the main process upon completion. The fact that workers do not share a common address space (and therefore variables) with their creator process simplifies this programming model, but also limits the applications that can be realized with this restriction.

The JavaScript implementation of the pi-MT Benchmark is an evolution of the original pi benchmark, which, as described in Section 6.2.3, employs a Web Worker to perform the computation in the background. Instead of creating a single worker, the pi-MT Benchmark creates two workers and

---

[11] A mutual exclusion (or mutex) is a programming mechanism that avoids simultaneous access to a common resource.

## 6. Performance Analysis

partitions the Leibnitz series among them. Whereas the API of the `pthread` library promotes the creation of a thread and the immediate execution of its computational task, the worker model promotes a different approach. Since the message passing approach greatly simplifies the communication between workers and the parent process, the workers can easily be created at the start of the web application. They then remain idle until a benchmarking session is commenced by the user, which is signaled through the posting of a message to the workers. Of course, this approach puts the JavaScript implementation of the benchmark at an advantage over C and NaCl, because the creation of the workers does not contribute to the measurement of the run times. Yet, it seemed ignorant to force the `pthread` programming model on the creation of the JavaScript Web Workers. With the workers performing the actual computations, the parent process is responsible for their creation and synchronization, as well as the handling of the user interaction.

### 6.3.4. Experimental Setup

The experimental setup of the pi-MT Benchmarks was equivalent to that of the the original pi benchmark. All benchmarking was conducted on Ubuntu Linux 10.10, with the exception of the run time, CPU utilization and memory involving the Safari 5 browser. These were conducted on Mac OS 10.6. The JavaScript benchmarks were executed in the Chrome 9, Firefox 4, Opera 11.50, and Safari 5 browsers, while the NaCl benchmarks were run in the Google Chrome browser.

During the benchmarking process, the `top` utility was used to gather information on the CPU utilization, while the memory analysis on Linux was performed using the `smaps` kernel interface. The Safari 5 memory consumption on Mac OS was measured using the Activity Monitor. The C and NaCl benchmark implementations were configured to create two threads for the approximation of $\pi$. The JavaScript implementation of the pi-MT Benchmark was set up to utilize two Web Workers for the computation.

### 6.3.5. Execution

The computer was rebooted before the benchmarks were run. These were executed from a GNOME terminal on Linux and a single Finder window on Mac OS X. The CPU utilization was measured from a terminal on Linux and Mac OS. No other applications were run during the benchmarking process.

The execution of the pi-MT Benchmarking process closely resembled that of the original pi benchmarking process. In order to determine the average run times, ten benchmarking rounds were conducted. The first round commenced with 10,000,000 iterations and the final round was conducted with 100,000,000 iterations. The number of iterations was increased linearly in every round by 10,000,000 iterations. 20 run time samples were collected during each round. After discarding the highest and the lowest aberrations, the remaining 18 samples were arithmetically averaged to form the final run time per benchmarking round.

The C benchmark was executed with a simple shell script that conducted 20 individual runs, while the JavaScript and NaCl benchmarks were executed manually. The Chrome browser was executed with the same arguments as in the previous benchmark, while all other web browsers were executed without arguments:

`google-chrome --enable-nacl --enable-webgl --allow-file-access-from-files`.

## 6.3. Pi-MT Benchmark

The top utility was employed on Linux and on Mac OS in order to determine the CPU utilization during the benchmarking procedure. For this sake, 12 samples were collected. For the memory analysis, the sandbox of the Chrome browser had to be disabled in order for the Linux kernel to be able to correctly determine the memory consumption. Therefore Chrome was executed with an additional argument:

```
google-chrome --enable-nacl --enable-webgl --allow-file-access-from-files
--no-sandbox.
```

Analogous to the previous benchmark, the memory analysis was performed on Linux using the smaps kernel interface. The mem_usage.py python script was extended to collect memory statistics for an arbitrary list of processes that are passed as arguments on the command line. This was necessary, since the Chrome 9 browser implements Web Workers as processes, thus increasing the number of processes to monitor from five to six. The Safari memory analysis was undertaken on Mac OS using the built-in Activity Monitor.

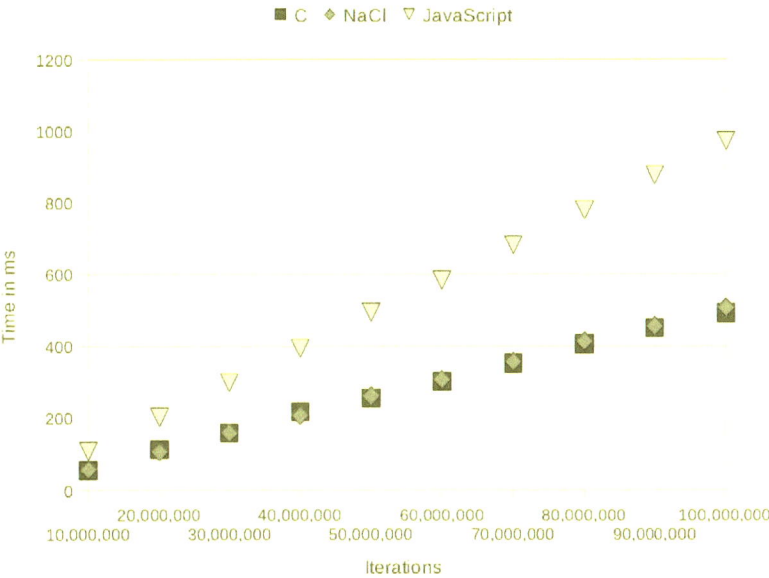

Figure 6.9.: Pi-MT benchmark: running times of C, NaCl, and JavaScript

### 6.3.6. Results

The results of the pi-MT Benchmark show substantial performance gains for the parallel implementations over their sequential counterparts. C, NaCl, and JavaScript performed the computations almost twice as fast as the original pi benchmark. In this experiment, NaCl actually completed some of the benchmark runs faster than C, although both technologies performed comparably overall. The performance relations between C, NaCl, and JavaScript remained stable. As illustrated in Figure 6.9,

## 6. Performance Analysis

NaCl and C were able to maintain their performance lead over JavaScript, outperforming the latter by factor two. JavaScript, however, did not lose additional ground to the multithreaded implementations of C and NaCl. These results indicate that, at least for simple computations, JavaScript Web Workers are able to provide a decent level of performance.

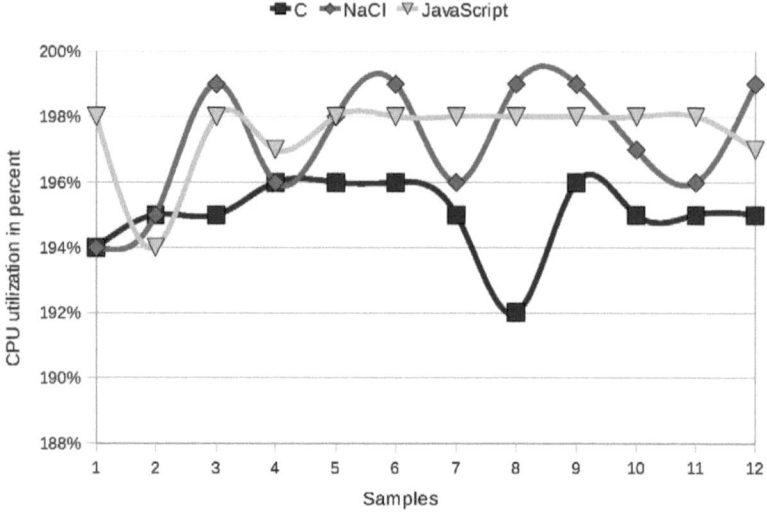

Figure 6.10.: Pi-MT benchmark: CPU utilization of C, NaCl, and JavaScript

Figure 6.10 depicts the CPU utilization of the benchmark processes, which was very similar between C, NaCl, and JavaScript. All three implementations managed to achieve utilizations between 195% and 198% on two processing cores. These results indicate that the vast majority of the CPU cycles were indeed, as intended, spent on the benchmarking task.

As compared in Figure 6.11, the results of the memory analysis resemble those of the original pi benchmark. C consumed the least private RSS memory, although its usage did increase from 88 KB to 132 KB. This increase must be attributed to the overhead of employing two additional threads to perform the computation of $\pi$. The NaCl implementation was marginally more memory efficient than JavaScript and consumed 27,832 KB, compared to 22,056 KB in the first benchmark. The multicore JavaScript pi-MT benchmark implementation saw approximately the same increase and occupied 28,628 KB of private RSS memory in the pi-MT Benchmark.

In the browser comparison, the JavaScript engine of the Firefox browser again showed the strongest computational performance and took the lead in the pi-MT Benchmark. Its advantage over the second fastest web browser, Safari on Mac OS, was considerable: Firefox was approximately 66% faster. Not only did Firefox outperform the other web browsers, its performance also rivaled that of C and NaCl. Its JavaScript engine completed all benchmarking runs only marginally slower than C and NaCl — the difference between NaCl and Firefox was usually less than 1%. This mandates the conclusion that the performance of Firefox for simple, parallel computations using Web Workers is truly excellent. As illustrated in Figure 6.12, the Chrome browser was able to take the third position, leaving the Opera browser behind as the slowest browser in the competition.

## 6.3. Pi-MT Benchmark

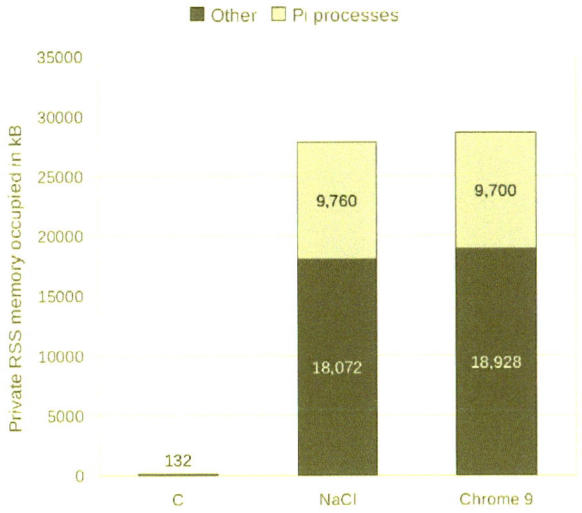

Figure 6.11.: Pi-MT benchmark: memory consumption C, NaCl, and JavaScript

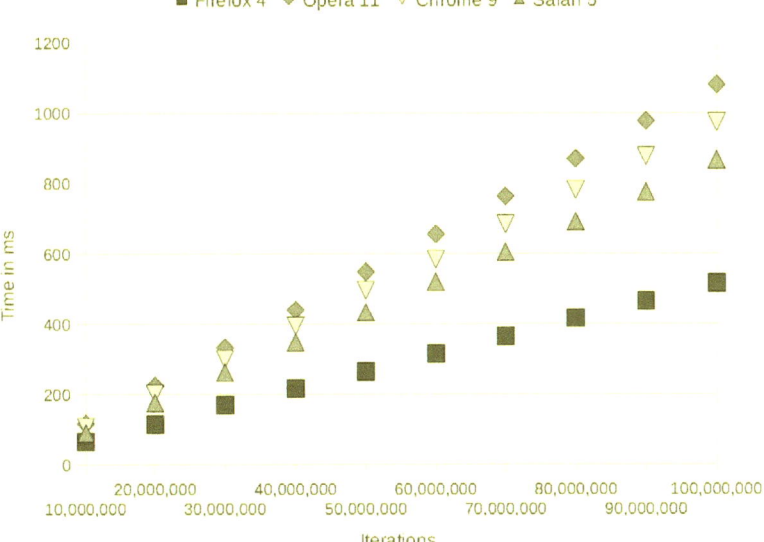

Figure 6.12.: Pi-MT benchmark: web browser comparison

## 6. Performance Analysis

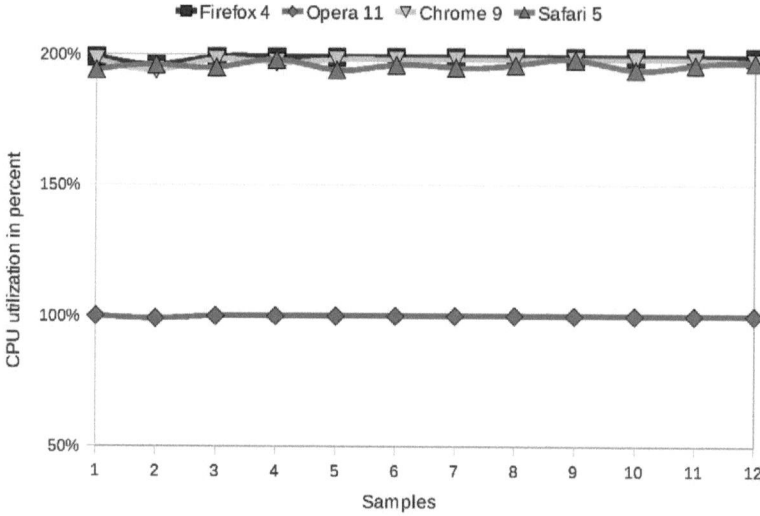

Figure 6.13.: Pi-MT benchmark: web browser CPU utilization

A closer look at Opera's run times indicates that the browser was not able to benefit from the parallel implementation of the pi-MT benchmark and its additional worker. This impression is substantiated by the results of the CPU utilization, which showed an average utilization of 100% for the Opera browser, while all other browsers achieved almost twice as much (see Figure 6.13). Although Opera supports Web Workers, it was not able to take advantage of the second CPU in the MacBook Pro and apparently executed both workers sequentially. Therefore its run times were comparable to those of the original pi benchmark. The other web browsers saw considerable performance improvements due to the additional Web Worker. Firefox, Chrome, and Safari consistently achieved CPU utilizations above 195% on two processing cores.

The results of the browser memory analysis were interesting for several reasons. Generally, all browsers consumed more private RSS memory than in the original pi benchmark, which is not surprising due to the additional Web Worker. As illustrated in Figure 6.14, Safari 5 on Mac OS consumed the least private RSS memory — although these results cannot be directly compared to those of the other browser due to the differences in operating systems and analysis methods. On Linux, Chrome was the most efficient web browser occupying 28,628 KB of private RSS memory. Opera 11 consumed 38,660 KB during $10^9$ iterations of the benchmark, while Firefox consumed the most private RSS memory: 56,912 KB.

The memory analysis revealed substantial differences between the browsers' Web Worker implementations. Chrome, for example, implements workers as processes, which became evident through the existence of an additional browser process. Firefox, on the other hand, implements Web Workers as OS threads, very much like C and NaCl do. Opera was unable to take advantage of the second Web Worker, but consumed more memory than in the first benchmark. Like Firefox, Safari implements Web Workers as threads. It did not create an additional process for the second worker and saw a very moderate increase in memory consumption, while performing the pi-MT Benchmark twice as fast as

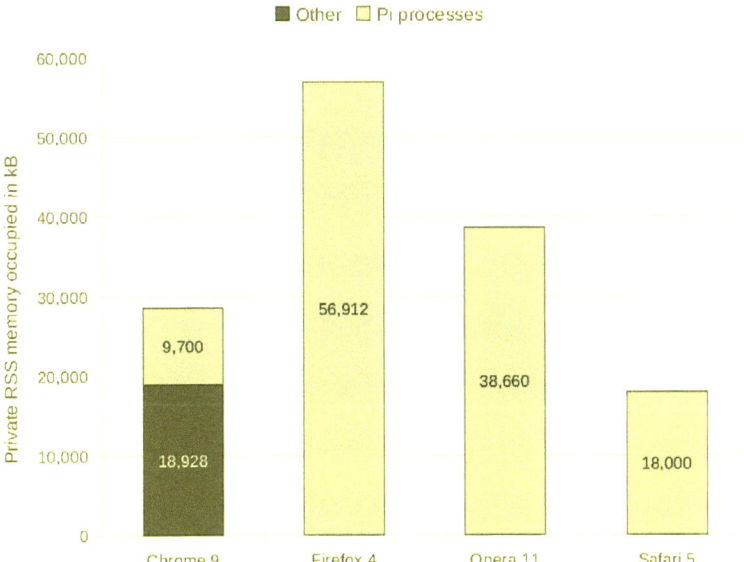

Figure 6.14.: Pi-MT benchmark: web browser memory consumption

the initial benchmark.

## 6.4. Gears Benchmark

The gears benchmark is a port of the infamous *glxgears* application that renders three animated mechanical gears in different colors, using the Open Graphics Library (OpenGL). OpenGL is a cross-platform computer graphics library that makes it possible to draw complex three-dimensional objects and scenes [Khronos Group 2011a]. It is widely used in the fields of computer aided design (CAD), virtual reality, flight simulation, and computer games. OpenGL was originally developed by Silicon Graphics Inc. and is now governed by the non-profit Khronos Group.

### 6.4.1. Problem and Objective

OpenGL has only recently become available to web developers in form of the Web Graphics Library (WebGL). WebGL is an attempt to bring hardware accelerated 3D graphics to the web browser. Version 1.0 of the WebGL specification, which is based on OpenGL ES 2.0[12], was released by the WebGL Working Group (under the umbrella of the Khronos Group) on February 10, 2011 [Khronos Group 2011b]. WebGL is available in several browsers, including Mozilla Firefox 4, Google Chrome, and the

---

[12] OpenGL ES is a subset of the large and complex original OpenGL API that is targeted at embedded systems, such as mobile phones.

development versions of Apple Safari and Opera. The Microsoft Internet Explorer 9 does not support WebGL.

While WebGL essentially provides JavaScript bindings to OpenGL ES 2.0, Native Client takes an alternative route and provides OpenGL access to C/C++ applications within the web browser. Like WebGL, NaCl targets the OpenGL ES 2.0 specification. This makes it possible to port existing 3D applications to NaCl, e.g. several classic games have already been ported to run in the web browser[13].

The objective of the gears benchmark is to evaluate and compare the performance of WebGL and NaCl, as a means of creating 3D applications that run in the web browser. In this context, the C-based glxgears applications will serve as the reference implementation. While it is worth pointing out that glxgears was not designed as a 3D benchmark, it does suffice as a tool to perform basic rendering comparisons.

### 6.4.2. Theoretical Background

**Primitives**

In three-dimensional computer graphics, complex objects are composed of primitives. Primitives are geometrical objects that are described by an arrangement of vertices. The support of primitives differs between OpenGL and OpenGL ES 2.0. Table 6.1 provides a comparison of these differences.

Table 6.1.: Primitives supported by OpenGL and OpenGL ES 2.0

| Primitive Group | OpenGL Primitives | OpenGL | OpenGL ES 2.0 |
|---|---|---|---|
| Point Sprites | GL_POINT | x | x |
| Lines | GL_LINES<br>GL_LINE_STRIP<br>GL_LINE_LOOP | x | x |
| Triangles | GL_TRIANGLES<br>GL_TRIANGLE_STRIP<br>GL_TRIANGLE_FAN | x | x |
| Quads | GL_QUADS<br>GL_QUAD_STRIP | x | |
| Polygons | GL_POLYGON | x | |

**Point Sprites** GL_POINT draws a simple point sprite for each vertex that is specified. Point sprites are commonly used for particle effects, which are rendered more efficiently with points than with quads. [Munshi et al. 2008].

**Lines** OpenGL supports three different line primitives. GL_LINES draws lines that consist of exactly two vertices, whereas GL_LINE_STRIP and GL_LINE_LOOP draw a consecutive series of connected line segments. Figure 6.15 provides examples of the different line drawing primitives. The key difference between the latter two primitives is that GL_LINE_LOOP draws a final line segment between the starting the end vertex.

---
[13]http://www.naclbox.com, last visited on September 9, 2011.

## 6.4. Gears Benchmark

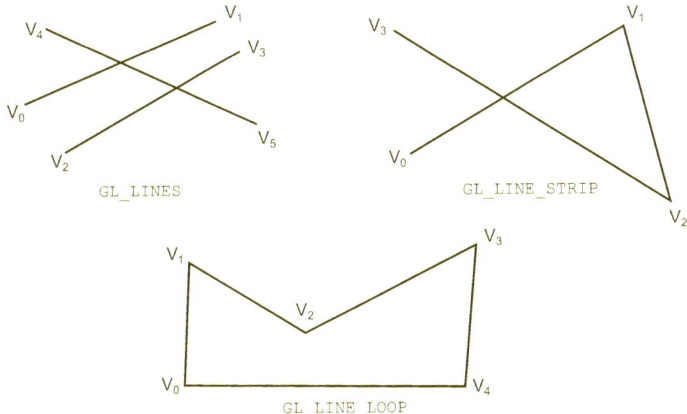

Figure 6.15.: OpenGL line primitive types

**Triangles**  Triangles are the most common method of describing geometrical objects that are rendered by a 3D application. Modern graphics hardware is heavily optimized for triangle drawing. The OpenGL API supports three different triangle primitives. `GL_TRIANGLES` draws separate triangles with exactly three vertices per triangle. Analogous to the line primitives, `GL_TRIANGLE_STRIP` draws a series of connected triangles that share edges. Figure 6.16, displays how five vertices can be used to draw three triangles with `GL_TRIANGLE_STRIP`. `GL_TRIANGLE_FAN` also draws $n-2$ connected triangles (where $n$ is the number of vertices), but in this case triangles not only share edges, they also share a common vertex. In the example presented in Figure 6.16, the vertex $V_0$ is shared by all triangles.

`GL_TRIANGLE_STRIP` and `GL_TRIANGLE_FAN` are very efficient, because they reduce the amount of vertices that are necessary to describe and draw complex objects.

**Quads**  The original OpenGL API provides two quad primitives that have not been included in the OpenGL ES 2.0 specification. As displayed in Figure 6.17, `GL_QUADS` draws a quad consisting of four vertices, while `GL_QUAD_STRIP` draws a series of connected quads that share edges.

**Polygons**  Figure 6.18 depicts the `GL_POLYGON` primitive. It draws an $n$-sided filled convex polygon, where $n$ is the number of vertices. This primitive is not available in OpenGL ES 2.0.

### Shaders

In 3D programming, a rendering pipeline specifies a sequential chain of processes, where the output of the one process forms the input of another process. The advantages of a rendering pipeline are that it can be efficiently implemented in hardware, yielding a high degree of parallelization and performance. Early OpenGL versions (prior to v2.0) relied on the fixed function pipeline, which proved to be too static and inflexible and was thus superseded by *shaders*. Shaders are small programs that run directly on the graphics processor(s), relieving the central processing unit and freeing up performance for other tasks. In the case of OpenGL, they are programmed using the OpenGL Shading Language (GLSL),

## 6. Performance Analysis

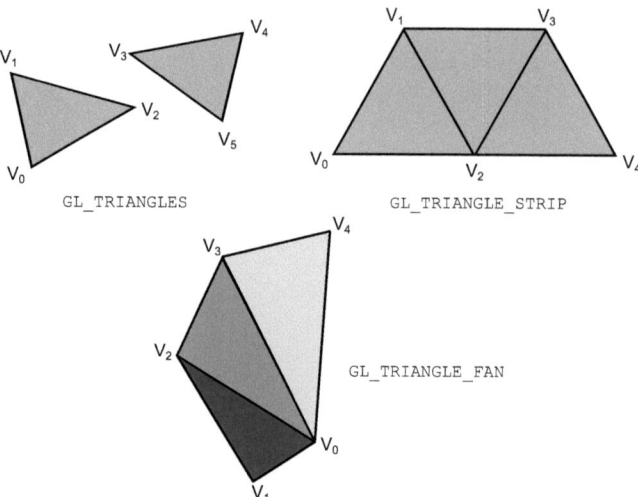

Figure 6.16.: OpenGL triangle primitive types

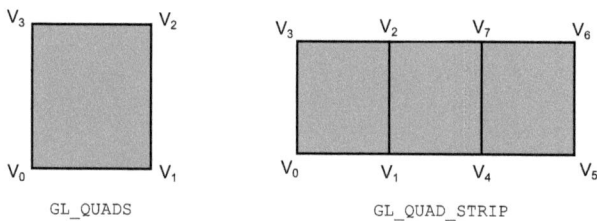

Figure 6.17.: OpenGL quad primitive types

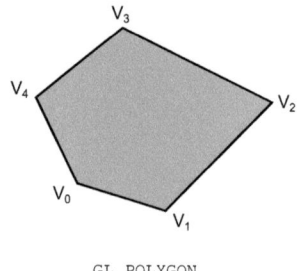

Figure 6.18.: The OpenGL polygon primitive type

which shares many similarities in terms of syntax with the C programming language. OpenGL Shaders are distinguished between fragment[14] and vertex shaders. Vertex shaders process the vertices of all objects in a scene and transform these into the three-dimensional space. Fragment shaders apply color and lighting effects to the surfaces of these objects, yielding translucency, bump mapping, and specular highlight effects, among others.

### 6.4.3. Implementation Details

#### C

The glxgears application was written by Brian Paul in the C programming language. The program is open source, meaning that its source code is freely available to the general public. The source code of glxgears was left untouched, but was used as a reference to port the application to JavaScript/WebGL and NaCl.

#### JavaScript

Since glxgears is an older application that targets the original OpenGL API, its port to a JavaScript/WebGL web application revealed two key challenges:

1. The removal of the fixed function pipeline
2. The replacement of the GL_QUADS and GL_QUAD_STRIP primitives

WebGL does not support the fixed function pipeline used in the glxgears application. Instead, it requires the use of pixel and vertex shaders. During the port of glxgears to WebGL, the drawing routines had to be completely re-written to target the OpenGL ES 2.0 API[15] — the pixel and vertex shaders were written from scratch. Unfortunately, debugging shaders in WebGL is tedious and leaves a lot to be desired. Although the shader code of the gear benchmark is certainly not very complex, it took several iterations of trial and error to get it right.

The drawing code required significant modifications, because glxgears makes heavy use of GL_QUADS and GL_QUAD_STRIP. These primitives are not supported by WebGL and had to be replaced by GL_TRIANGLES and GL_TRANGLE_STRIP respectively. While this means that the drawing code in the WebGL application differs greatly from the reference implementation, potentially distorting the performance measurements, this holds true for applications based on older OpenGL specifications that are to be ported to WebGL. Overall, the modifications and testing of the drawing code took almost a full week alone.

WebGL extends the 2D canvas element that was introduced as part of the HTML5 initiative. After declaring the canvas object, a 3D context is obtained by calling canvas.getContext("experimental-webgl").

#### NaCl

Like WebGL, NaCl targets OpenGL ES 2.0, which means that the drawing code differs substantially from the C reference implementation. Unlike in the case of the pi and pi-MT benchmarks, few elements

---
[14]Fragment shaders are frequently referred to as pixel shaders.
[15]The tutorials at http://learningwebgl.com/ provided valuable insight into the basics of WebGL: last visited on October 18, 2011.

6. *Performance Analysis*

Figure 6.19.: A screenshot of the WebGLGears application

of the original glxgears C code could be reused. It should be noted, however, that this is not the fault of NaCl. It rightfully targets a modern drawing library that has removed the fixed function pipeline altogether.

On the other hand, the port from JavaScript to NaCl was straightforward, which is not surprising due to the similarities of their respective OpenGL libraries. The shader programs were inherited from JavaScript without modifications. The drawing code itself required only subtle syntax changes. It was the boilerplate NPAPI glue code and the initialization of the 3D libraries that required the most work. In order to activate the NaCl 3D libraries, it is necessary to initialize the Pepper GL extensions and to create a PGL context. While these steps can be traced in the tumbler demo that ships with NaCl, it took a more time than was expected to figure them out and to implement them.

### 6.4.4. Experimental Setup

The gears experiments were carried out on the Ubuntu Linux 10.10 and Mac OS 10.6 operating systems, with the goal of comparing the 3D graphics performance of C, NaCl, and JavaScript. The frames per second (FPS) metric was chosen as the primary performance indicator. In addition, the CPU utilization in percent and the memory usage in KB were measured during the experiments.

Glxgears, the C reference implementation of the gears benchmark, was executed from a terminal window on Ubuntu Linux 10.10. The application outputs the frames rendered and the corresponding average frame rate to the terminal every five seconds. The NaCl and JavaScript experiments were conducted in the Chrome 9 web browser on Ubuntu Linux 10.10. All applications implement the FPS counting algorithm introduced by glxgears. For every completed render process, the number of rendered frames is incremented and every five seconds the average frames per seconds are calculated, by dividing the number of frames by the number of seconds. NaCl outputs the frames and FPS to the terminal, while the JavaScript gears benchmark lists the benchmark results directly in the web application.

The Google Chrome 9, Mozilla Firefox 4, and Apple Safari browsers were tested with the JavaScript gears benchmark to provide insight into their respective WebGL JavaScript performance. The Opera 11 browser was omitted from the comparison, because a Linux release with WebGL support was unavailable[16]. A nightly build (release 83161) of Safari with WebGL support was employed for the benchmarking on Mac OS 10.6, due to the lack of WebGL support in the current stable version. The nightly build Safari[17] does not support WebGL by default. It must be enabled by executing the following command in a terminal window:

`defaults write com.apple.Safari WebKitWebGLEnabled -bool YES.`

Firefox 4 provides an option to force software rendering, instead of hardware accelerated rendering, which was benchmarked as well to provide an overview of its performance impact. The drawback of software rendering is that, instead of outsourcing the drawing of the OpenGL primitives to the graphics processing unit (GPU), the CPU handles these tasks as well. This places additional work on the CPU and results in lower graphics performance. Software rendering can easily be enabled by entering about:config instead of a regular URL and by setting the key webgl.force_osmesa to true. In addition, the location of the Mesa library[18], e.g. /usr/lib/libOSMesa.so.6, must be provided within the webgl.osmesalib key.

The top utility was used on Ubuntu Linux and Mac OS X to gather information regarding the CPU utilization of the applications during the benchmarking. The smaps kernel interface was used for the memory analysis on Linux. On Mac OS X, the Activity Monitor was employed to collect the memory statistics of Safari.

### 6.4.5. Execution

In preparation for the experiments, the computer was rebooted. No other applications were run during the benchmarking process except for a GNOME terminal window with three tabs on Linux and a single Finder window on Mac OS, plus a terminal window during the CPU utilization measurements.

The FPS benchmarking was conducted in five rounds, in which the drawing area of the gears benchmark was increased from initially 300 x 300 pixels to 700 x 700 pixels. 12 samples were taken in five-second intervals, amounting to a total running time of one minute per round. The highest and the lowest aberrations were discarded, resulting in 10 valid samples which were arithmetically averaged to yield a single average FPS number for each round.

The benchmark applications were started from the terminal (with the exception of Safari, which was started through the finder) and run for at least 60 seconds. The resulting 12 samples were stored in text files. The text editor was closed before commencing the next round of benchmarking. Due to a known rendering bug, the NaCl benchmark sometimes did not display the animated gears upon

---
[16] At the time of this writing, a preview of Opera 11 with WebGL support was available for Microsoft Windows exclusively.
[17] Apple advertises the Safari nightly builds as WebKit nightly builds.
[18] Mesa 3D is an open source computer graphics library that implements the OpenGL specification.

## 6. Performance Analysis

launching the application in the Chrome browser. When clicking the drawing area, the animation suddenly appeared. This bug affected the first sample and rendered it useless. Therefore, it was made a procedure to generally discard the initial sample throughout the NaCl gears benchmarking process.

The glxgears application was launched with the geometry as an argument, e.g.:

`glxgears -geometry 300x300.`

The browsers were launched without arguments, except for Google Chrome, which was launched as follows during the FPS and CPU utilization performance benchmarks:

`google-chrome --enable-nacl --enable-webgl --allow-file-access-from-files.`

Before each round, the geometry of the JavaScript and NaCl web applications was set by editing the JavaScript/HTML code. For the FPS, CPU utilization, and memory measurements, the browser window was generally kept at the same size, which was large enough to view the contents of the web application at a drawing area size of 500 x 500 pixels. The benchmarks at 600 x 600 and 700 x 700 pixels were performed with the browser window maximized and taking up the full screen. Generally, the drawing area was kept visible in the browsers throughout the benchmarks, in order to minimize effects on the drawing performance.

In order to determine the CPU utilization of each benchmark implementation, the `top` application was run in parallel with the benchmark applications. 12 samples of the CPU load in percent of the benchmark process were recorded for each drawing area size, from 300 x 300 to 700 x 700 pixels. The highest and lowest aberrations were discarded and the remaining samples were arithmetically averaged to yield a single CPU utilization percentage per drawing area size. The data collection of the FPS and the CPU utilization metrics was performed subsequently and not at the same time.

The memory analysis on Linux was conducted with the help of the smaps kernel interface and the `mem_usage.py` application. In case of Google Chrome, which consists of multiple processes, a simple shell script was used to retrieve the memory information for all processes during the benchmarking. On Mac OS X, the built-in Activity Monitor was employed to determine the memory usage of the Safari browser during the JavaScript gears benchmark. For all gears benchmark applications and browsers the memory analysis was performed with a drawing area geometry of 500 x 500 pixels. The memory statistics were gathered while the corresponding gears benchmark was running. During the memory analysis, the Google Chrome browser was executed with the following arguments:

`google-chrome --enable-nacl --enable-webgl --allow-file-access-from-files --no-sandbox.`

One benchmarking run was conducted for the C and NaCl implementations of the gears benchmark. The WebGL based JavaScript implementation was executed once in each web browser, except for Mozilla Firefox, which was benchmarked twice — once each with hardware acceleration and software acceleration enabled.

### 6.4.6. Results

The gears benchmark shows a considerable advantage in terms of 3D performance for both C and NaCl over JavaScript/WebGL. As shown in Figure 6.20, glxgears, the original C implementation of the gears benchmark, yields an average frame rate of 3,195 FPS at the smallest drawing area size of 300 x 300 pixels. NaCl achieves an average frame rate of 2,736 FPS under the same conditions, while

## 6.4. Gears Benchmark

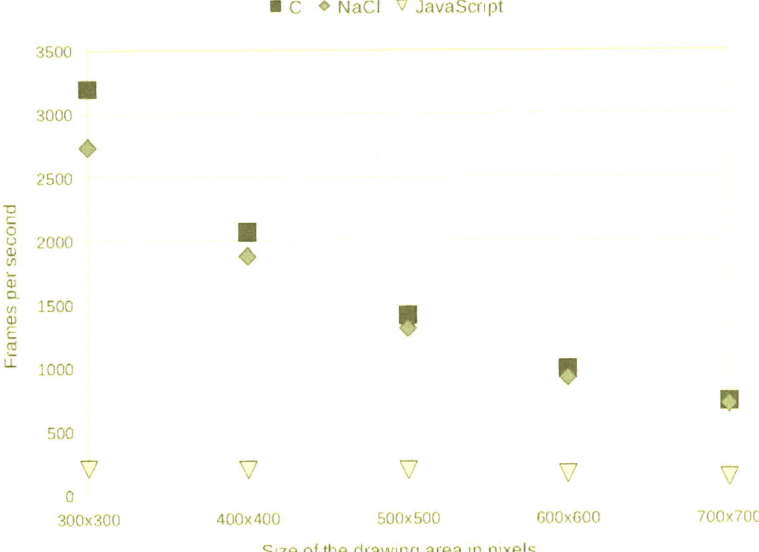

Figure 6.20.: Gears benchmark: FPS of C, NaCl, and JavaScript

JavaScript delivers an average frame rate of 208 FPS. When compared to the frame rates that are used in motion pictures and videos, which are commonly between 25 and 30 FPS, JavaScript/WebGL performs reasonably well. Still, both NaCl and C offer more than ten times the performance in the gears benchmark.

As the workload for the graphics processing unit (GPU) increases with the size of the drawing area, the performance of C and NaCl is affected to a much greater extent than that of JavaScript and WebGL. At 500 x 500 pixels, C achieves 1,413 FPS and NaCl yields 1,309 FPS — both measurements mark a considerable drop in performance. JavaScript/WebGL, on the other hand, stands its ground at an average frame rate of 192 FPS. At the maximum geometry of 700 x 700 pixels, C and NaCl still outperform JavaScript/WebGL. With a frame rate of 730 FPS, C remains roughly 5.5 times as fast as JavaScript/WebGL. NaCl's performance remains outstanding with a frame rate of 710 FPS, closing the gap to C to merely 20 FPS.

Figure 6.21 depicts the CPU utilization of the different gears implementations during the benchmarking process. These results are interesting because only glxgears managed to obtained a CPU utilization of 100% on average, which is usually desirable and distinctive for benchmarks. Although NaCl achieved competitive frame rates, its CPU utilization was substantially lower than that of C and varied between 40% and 77%. The CPU utilization of JavaScript ranged between 35% and 89% and, like that of NaCl, generally increased with the size of the drawing area.

The results of the memory analysis are illustrated in Figure 6.22. C used the least private RSS memory, 9,740 KB in total. NaCl consumed a total of 36,632 KB during the benchmarking process, with 19,460 KB amounting to the OpenGL process. JavaScript/WebGL consumed the most memory, 94,568 KB in

## 6. Performance Analysis

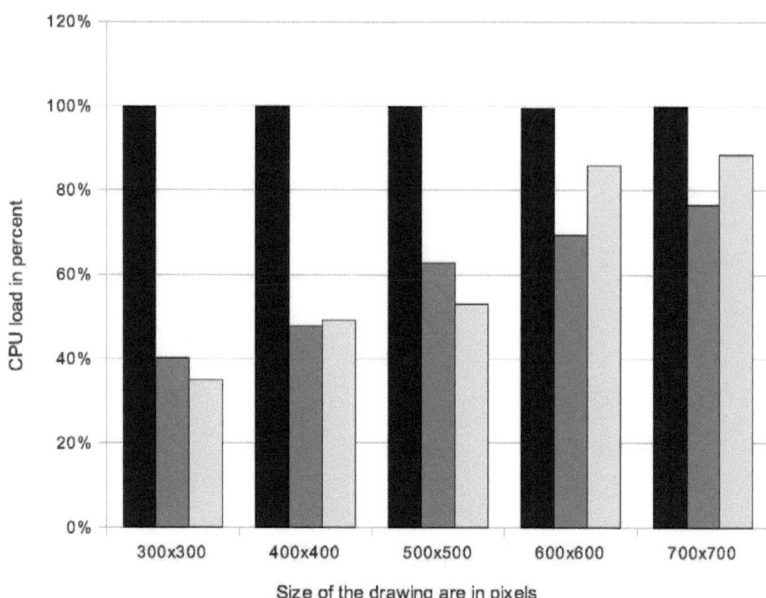

Figure 6.21.: Gears benchmark: CPU utilization of C, NaCl, and JavaScript

total with 35,668 KB being used exclusively by the OpenGL process. The NaCl OpenGL application consumed less than half the private RSS memory of its JavaScript/WebGL equivalent, both in terms of OpenGL rendering and general browser processes.

The JavaScript/WebGL performance of the web browsers tested in this experiment is compared in Figure 6.23. Google Chrome 9 consistently delivered the highest frame rates, scoring between 207 FPS (at 300 x 300 pixels) and 132 FPS (at 700 x 700 pixels). Mozilla Firefox 4 with hardware acceleration achieved very consistent frame rates between 96 FPS and 99 FPS and generally delivered the second highest frame rates, with the exception of 300 x 300 pixels, where Safari on Mac OS 10.6 took second place. The performance of the Safari nightly build dropped considerably from 118 FPS (at 300 x 300 pixels) to approximately 60 FPS for the larger drawing area sizes. As expected, all browsers with hardware acceleration performed better than Mozilla Firefox with Mesa software acceleration enabled. Firefox Mesa achieved 118 FPS at 300 x 300 pixels and dropped considerably to 22 FPS at 700 x 700 pixels.

The degree of CPU utilization achieved by the web browsers during the benchmarking process varied substantially (see Figure 6.24). Since Firefox Mesa performed the rendering on the CPU instead of the GPU, as it would with hardware acceleration enabled, the CPU utilization during the benchmark was expected to be close to 100%. However, this was not the case. Firefox Mesa employed between 81% and 93% of CPU the cycles during the benchmarking process. The utilization at 700 x 700 pixels was the lowest of all rounds — as was the corresponding frame rate.

## 6.4. Gears Benchmark

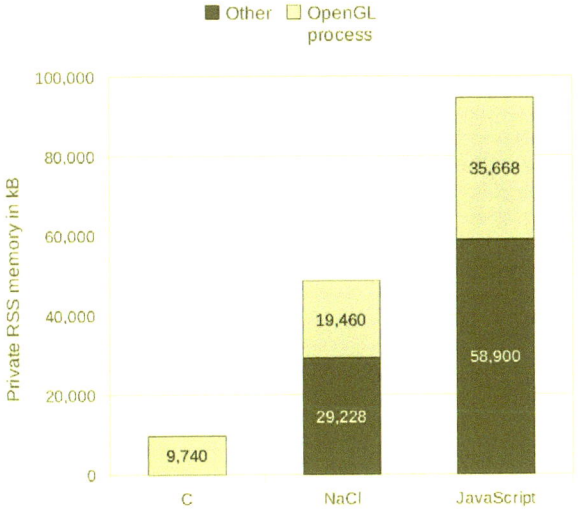

Figure 6.22.: Gears benchmark: memory consumption of C, NaCl, and JavaScript

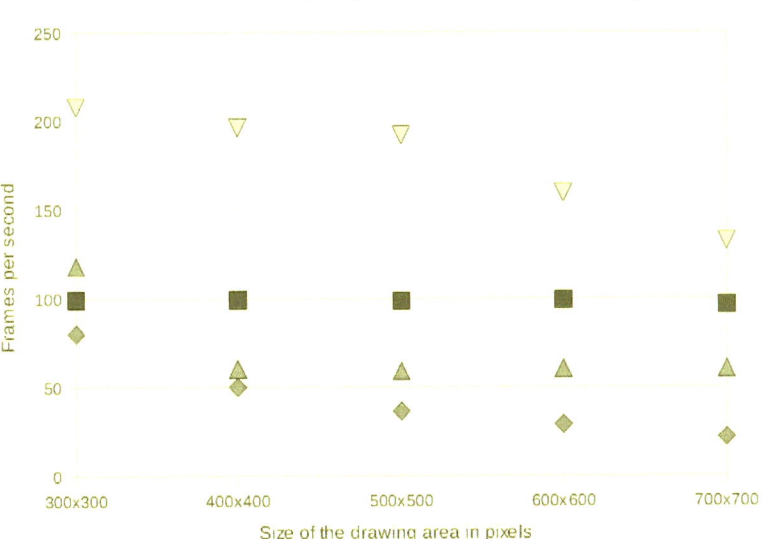

Figure 6.23.: Gears benchmark: web browser comparison

## 6. Performance Analysis

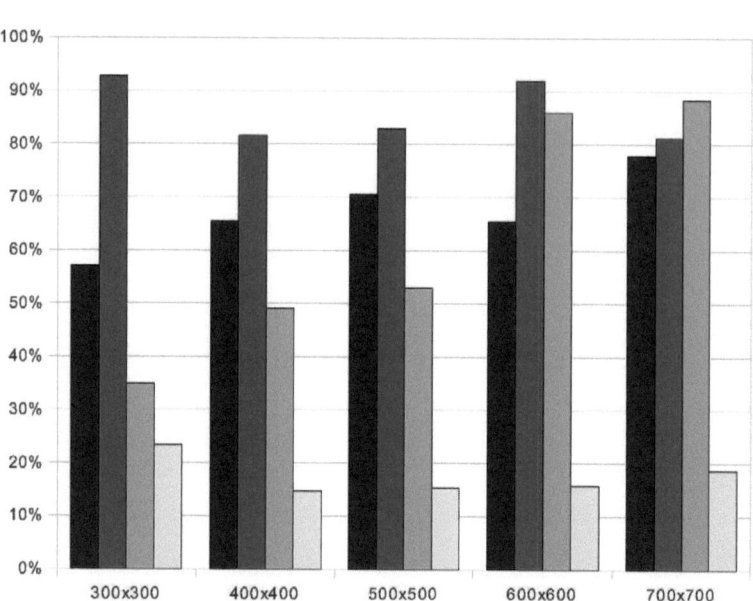

Figure 6.24.: Gears benchmark: web browser CPU utilization

The results of the Safari CPU utilization on Mac OS 10.6 were very surprising. Safari merely used between 15% and 23% of the CPU during the benchmarking process. This is by far the least CPU utilization of all browsers in the experiment and also much less than C or NaCl achieved. The results for Chrome and Firefox with hardware acceleration were less surprising. Chrome achieved a CPU utilization between 35% and 89%, which generally increased with the size of the drawing area. The results of Firefox 4 were less consistent. Its CPU utilization ranged between 57% and 78%, whereas Firefox achieved a higher CPU utilization than Chrome at drawing area sizes below 500 x 500 pixels and a lower utilization at greater sizes.

In terms of memory consumption, Safari on Mac OS was by far the most memory efficient browser in the gears benchmark. On the Linux platform, Chrome 9 consumed slightly less memory than Firefox 4. As illustrated in Figure 6.25, Chrome consumed a total of 94,568 KB, with 35,668 KB amounting to the OpenGL process alone. Firefox consumed 103,860 KB of memory with hardware rendering enabled and 103,696 KB with software rendering enabled. This leaves Chrome as the fastest and most memory efficient web browser in terms of the gears benchmark on Linux.

### 6.5. Spectral Benchmark

The spectral benchmark implements a spectral analysis of audio samples, using a short-time Fourier transform (STFT). Its output can be used to display a spectrogram of the audio data, i.e. the spectral

## 6.5. Spectral Benchmark

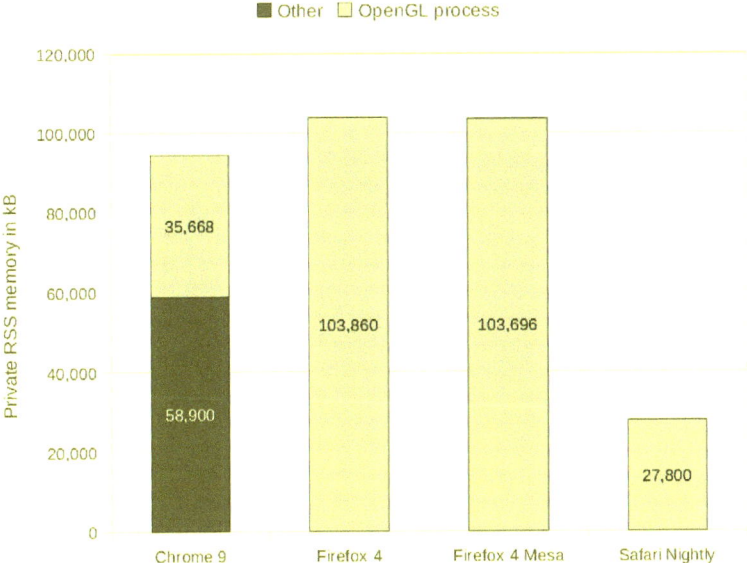

Figure 6.25.: Gears benchmark: web browser memory consumption

density of the signal at a certain time. Spectrograms are commonly used in the fields of signal processing, audio analysis, and image processing. Figure 6.26 and 6.27 display spectrograms of audio samples.

### 6.5.1. Problem and Objective

The spectral analysis employs the Fourier transform, which is not only commonplace in the field of signal processing, but also in numerical analysis. "Fourier methods have revolutionized fields of science and engineering, from astronomy to medical imaging, from seismology to spectroscopy" [Press et al. 2007]. The Fourier transform has a high practical relevance and therefore provides a solid context for a benchmarking application.

The spectral benchmark focuses on the processing of large amounts of binary data. As web applications seek to replace native applications in the areas of image manipulation, video, and audio processing, they will have to be able to obtain and process binary data at a performance that is comparable to that of native applications. Historically, JavaScript's support for binary data streams has been rather weak and inflexible. The objective of this benchmark is to evaluate and compare the current state of C, JavaScript, and NaCl applications, in the area of data processing.

## 6. Performance Analysis

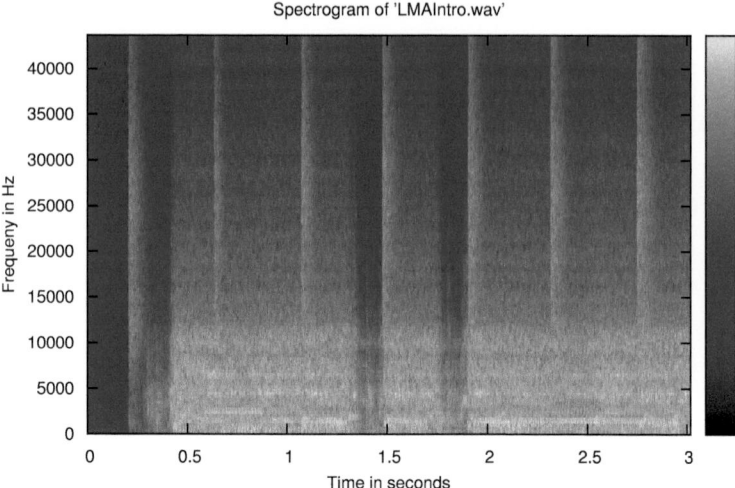

Figure 6.26.: Spectrogram of the *LMAIntro.wav* audio sample

### 6.5.2. Theoretical Background

A spectral analysis consists of several steps. After loading the audio data from the sound file, a discrete Fourier transform (DFT) is used to transform the samples from the time domain[19], into the frequency domain. Because the DFT algorithm is very inefficient, it is implemented as a fast Fourier transform (FFT). The FFT provides information about the frequency components of a signal, but it does not provide insight into how the frequency components change over time. This is the purpose of the short-time Fourier transform (STFT), which breaks up the time signal into segments of data that are independently Fourier transformed. Every segment is multiplied with a window function prior to the FFT, in order to transform the digital audio samples into a periodic input sequence — a prerequisite for the FFT.

**Extracting the Audio Data**

The initial step of the spectral analysis, as implemented in the spectral benchmark, consists of loading the audio data from the sound file. To limit the complexity of the benchmark and the work required for the implementation, only a single sound file format is supported. The *Microsoft Waveform Audio File Format (WAVE)* was chosen due to its widespread use, relatively simple basic structure, little-endian byte ordering, and multi operating system support, which includes Microsoft Windows, Apple Mac OS, and Linux operating systems, among others.

The WAVE file format is based on *RIFF, the Resource Interchange File Format*, which is a generic container format that stores data in tagged chunks. RIFF was developed by Microsoft and IBM and is in turn based on the *Interchangeable File Format (IFF)*, which was popular on the Commodore

---
[19]The time domain indicates how a signal changes over time.

## 6.5. Spectral Benchmark

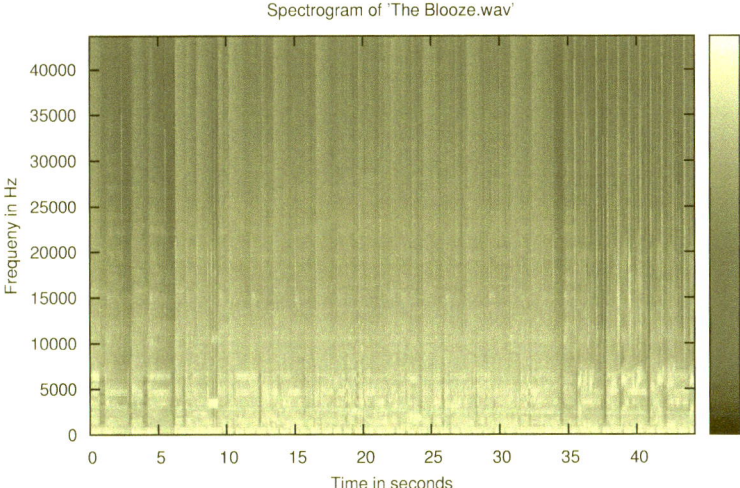

Figure 6.27.: Spectrogram of the *The Blooze.wav* audio sample

Amiga platform. The key difference lies in the byte ordering, i.e. in the representation of bytes in the computer's random access memory (RAM). For example, consider an integer number that is stored as 4 bytes in a register[20]. When this number is loaded into RAM, these 4 bytes can either be ordered with the least significant byte first (*little-endian*) or with the most significant byte first (*big-endian*). The IFF file format defines the byte order as big-endian, according to the underlying processor architecture of the Commodore Amiga. The RIFF file format, in contrast, defines the byte-ordering as little-endian, corresponding to the Intel x86 processor architecture, which is the primary hardware platform of the Microsoft Windows operating system. Figure 6.28 illustrates the differences between the little- and big-endian byte ordering schemes. By choosing a little-endian audio file format on a little-endian hardware platform (Ubuntu Linux on Intel x86 hardware), the spectral benchmark can omit byte ordering conversions altogether. Please note for completeness that the byte ordering of network protocols, such as TCP/IP, is generally defined as big-endian.

In the WAVE file format, data is stored in chunks. Each chunk begins with a 4-byte identifier, followed by a 4-byte size descriptor that indicates the amount of data that is to follow [Sapp 2003] and [Kabal 2011]. This organization into chunks makes the WAVE file format flexible and easily extensible — at least in theory. The initial chunk is always the master *RIFF* chunk, which can be followed by several sub-chunks. Of these sub-chunks, the *fmt* chunk and the *data* chunk are mandatory. The fmt or format chunk defines the format of the data, while the data chunk actually contains the audio samples. Even though the spectral benchmark only supports uncompressed PCM[21] data, it is worth mentioning that compressed non-PCM WAVE audio files are required to have a *fact* chunk, which defines at least the number of samples per channel. Figure 6.29 outlines the organization of the WAVE file format into chunks.

---
[20]Registers are memory areas inside the processor that store operands and results of calculations.
[21]Pulse-code modulation (PCM) is a method of representing analog signals as digital samples.

## 6. Performance Analysis

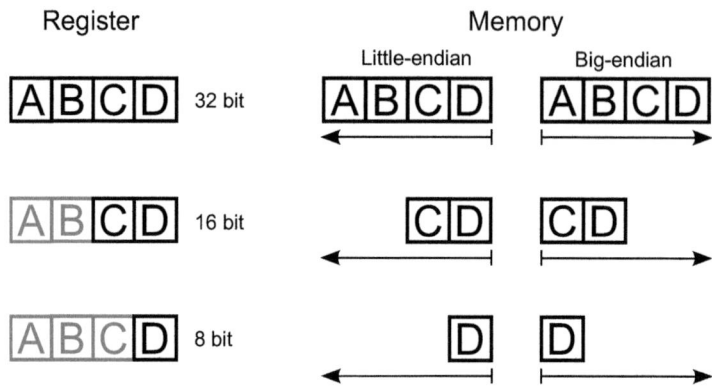

Figure 6.28.: Little-endian vs. big-endian byte ordering

The samples in the data chunk are arranged depending on the number of channels and the bits per sample. Generally, one sample for each channel is stored after the other. For example, in a stereo WAVE file with two channels, the initial sample will be the first sample of the left channel, followed by the first sample of the right channel, followed by the second sample of the left channel, etc. Depending on the bits per sample, a sample can consist either of 8 bits, 16 bits, 24 bits, or 32 bits, meaning that 1 byte, 2 bytes, 3 bytes, or 4 bytes will be stored in the file stream consecutively, which must be interpreted as a single sample. The audio samples form the input of the STFT.

**Discrete Fourier Transform**

The discrete Fourier transform (DFT) is applied to the audio samples that were extracted from the WAVE sound file. Its purpose is to transform the audio samples from the time domain into the frequency domain. The result is a frequency-domain graph that displays the frequencies (in frequency bands, depending on the resolution, i.e. the number of samples) of which the signal is composed of. Formally, the DFT can be defined as [Lyons 2004]:

$$X(m) = \sum_{n=0}^{N-1} x(n)e^{-j2\pi nm/N} \qquad (6.3)$$

$x_n$ represents a discrete sequence of audio samples in the time-domain, $e$ is the base of the natural logarithm, and $j = \sqrt{-1}$.

Unfortunately, the DFT is very inefficient and slow. In 1965, James W. Cooley and John W. Tukey presented the *Cooley-Tukey algorithm*, a very efficient algorithm to implement the DFT. The Cooley-Tukey algorithm was considered a major breakthrough in digital signal processing. It quickly became known as the fast Fourier transform (FFT) and remains the basis of most popular FFT algorithms to date. The Cooley-Tukey algorithm employs a divide and conquer strategy that implements the DFT recursively, i.e. by breaking it down into several smaller DFTs, yielding the result in less than $2N \log_2 N$ operations [Cooley and Tukey 1965]. In order to be able to break down the input sequence, the algorithm requires that its length $N$ is a composite, i.e. $N = r_1 \cdot r_2$.

## 6.5. Spectral Benchmark

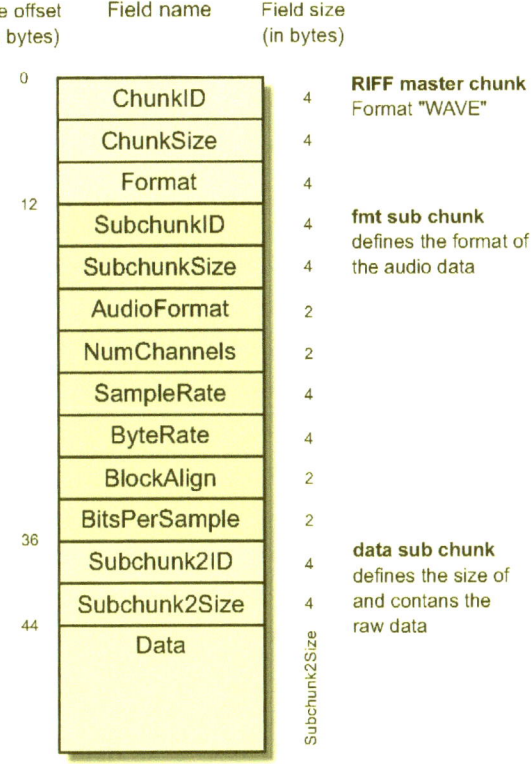

Figure 6.29.: The canonical WAVE file format [Sapp 2003]

The spectral benchmark implements the *radix-2 decimation in time* FFT, a form of the Cooley-Tukey algorithm, that assumes $r_1 = 2$ as the radix of the composite $N$. The radix-2 decimation in time algorithm is relatively simple, highly efficient, and very popular. It does, however, require that the size of the DFT is an integral power of two, i.e. $N = 2^k$, where $k$ is a positive integer. The radix-2 decimation algorithm is mathematically defined as

$$X(m + N/2) = \sum_{n=0}^{(N/2)-1} x(2n)W_{N/2}^{nm} - W_N^m \sum_{n=0}^{(N/2)-1} x(2n+1)W_{N/2}^{nm} \qquad (6.4)$$

whereas $W_N = e^{-j2\pi m/N}$ to simplify the equation [Lyons 2004]. The key expression of the mathematical equation is that the algorithm separates the input sequence $x(n)$ into two parts: the odd indexed and the even indexed elements.

## 6. Performance Analysis

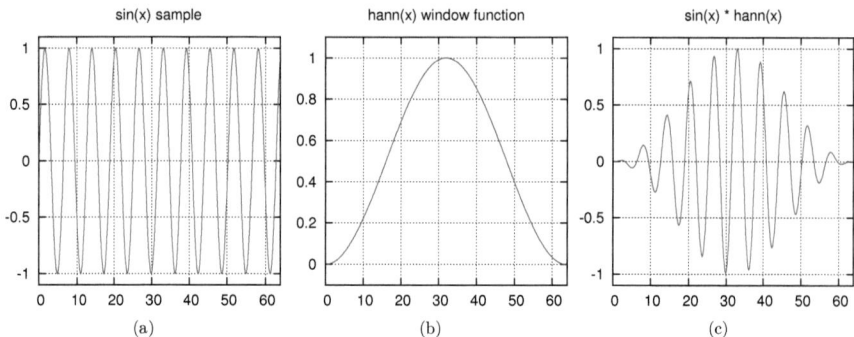

Figure 6.30.: Operation of a window function

**Hann Window Function**

The DFT implies that the input sequence $x(n)$ is periodic and could be extended infinitely by adding identical chunks of data. This is, of course, rarely the case with real-world audio samples. The DFT to these samples provides frequency-domain results that are misleading, i.e. only an approximation of the true spectra. This characteristic is referred to as *leakage*.

In order to minimize leakage, the input sequence is multiplied with a window function before the DFT. The window function modifies the amplitude of the input sequence at both the beginning and the end to go smoothly towards an identical value. In other words, it transforms the input data into a periodic sequence. The operation of the window function is illustrated in Figure 6.30. The DFT $X_w(m)$ of the input sequence $x(n)$, windowed by the function $w(n)$, is defined as:

$$X_w(m) = \sum_{n=0}^{N-1} w(n) \cdot x(n) e^{-j2\pi nm/N}. \tag{6.5}$$

The spectral benchmark implementations employ a *Hann window* function[22], which is defined as [Lyons 2004]:

$$w(n) = 0.5 - 0.5 \cos\left(2\pi \frac{n}{N}\right), \quad for \ n = 0, 1, 2, ..., N-1. \tag{6.6}$$

**Short-Time Fourier Transformation**

The short-time Fourier transform (STFT) employs the FFT to determine how the frequency components of a signal change over time. During the STFT, The time signal is broken up into segments of data, which are independently Fourier transformed. Every segment is multiplied with a window function prior to the FFT. While this minimizes leakage, the application of the window function also

---

[22] the *Hann* function is named after Austrian meteorologist Julius von Hann and frequently referred to as *Hanning* or *von Hann* function.

## 6.5. Spectral Benchmark

has the effect that valid signals are discarded. This problem can be addressed by overlapping the segments, ideally by one-half of their length [Press et al. 2007].

Assuming that $x(n)$ is the input signal and $w(n)$ is the window function, the short-time Fourier transform $X_n(e^{j\omega_k})$ evaluated at time $n$ and frequency $\omega_k$ may be defined as [Allen and Rabiner 1977]:

$$X_n(e^{j\omega_k}) = \sum_{n=-\infty}^{\infty} w(n-m)X(m)e^{-j\omega_k m}. \tag{6.7}$$

The STFT employs a fixed resolution, i.e. the size of the data segments is always of the same length. The choice of this segment length has an impact on the results of the STFT. A wide data segment leads to a more exact frequency resolution, but provides less accurate information of when the frequencies change over time. On the contrary, a narrow data segment increases the time resolution, at the cost of frequency resolution.

### Spectrum and Magnitude

The result of the STFT is a two-sided spectrum in complex form, i.e. with real and imaginary parts:

$$X(m) = X_{real}(m) + jX_{imag}(m). \tag{6.8}$$

If, as in this case, the input samples are real, only the results of the first half are independent [Lyons 2004]. The two-sided spectrum contains a positive and a negative half of the spectrum, "half the energy is displayed at the positive frequency, and half the energy is displayed at the negative frequency" [Cerna and Harvey 2009]. Since the spectrum of a real-world signal is symmetrical around DC[23], it is common that only the positive half of the spectrum is considered in practice. In this case, the negative half of the spectrum is redundant. In order to convert a two-sided spectrum to a single-sided spectrum, every data point the first half of the data array must be multiplied by two, except for DC. The second half of the array, containing the negative spectrum, is discarded.

The true amplitude results can be determined from the spectral results, by first calculating the magnitudes

$$X_{mag}(m) = |X(m)| = \sqrt{X_{real}(m)^2 + X_{imag}(m)^2}. \tag{6.9}$$

For complex inputs, the FFT magnitudes must be divided by $N$, whereas for real inputs, as in this case, they must be divided by $N/2$, to determine the correct amplitudes of the time-domain sinusoidal components [Lyons 2004].

For the sake of completeness, it should be added that the power spectrum can be calculated using

$$X_{PS}(m) = |X(m)|^2 = X_{real}(m)^2 + X_{imag}(m)^2 \tag{6.10}$$

and likewise the power spectrum in decibels (dB) can be computed with

$$X_{dB}(m) = 10 \cdot log_{10}(|X(m)|^2) \; dB. \tag{6.11}$$

---

[23]DC is the first frequency line at 0 Hz.

## 6. Performance Analysis

### 6.5.3. Implementation Details

**C**

The initial version of the spectral benchmark was implemented in plain C. It is executed from the command line, runs in a terminal, and does not feature a graphical user interface. The application takes a single argument, which is the path to the audio file that is to be analyzed. It features two modes of operation. If the option flags --info or -i are passed during execution, the spectral application will print the contents of the main RIFF chunk and the fmt, data, and fact sub-chunks to the terminal and then exit without processing the audio file. In regular operation, i.e. if these option flags are omitted, the application will process and benchmark the spectral analysis of the digital audio file. The results will not be printed to the terminal unless the --print or -p options are set.

The C programming language does not natively provide data types and arithmetic operations for complex numbers, which are required for the FFT. This functionality and the code for the FFT algorithm were taken from [LiteratePrograms 2008] and modified as required. To reduce the complexity of the spectral benchmark implementation, it is only able to process two-channel (stereo) audio files with either 16-bit or 24-bit sample rates. Other audio files will not be used during the benchmarking process.

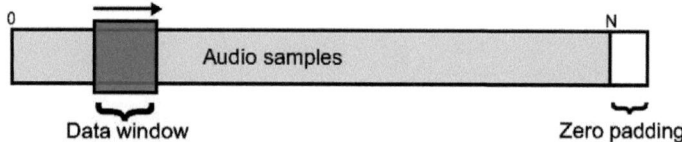

Figure 6.31.: Schematic depiction of the STFT algorithm

Before the audio samples can be processed, they need to be read from the audio file. C is a very low-level programming language and perfectly suited to parse files with binary data, as in this case. The main RIFF chunk and the sub-chunks describe the format of the sound samples, so these are extracted first and mapped to the internal data structures of the spectral application. Finally, the sample data is loaded into memory in a single step.

The STFT algorithm itself is implemented as two nested for loops. The first loop iterates over the digital audio samples, taking into account the width of the data window and the overlap. It can be imagined as sliding the data window over the audio samples from the beginning to the end. This process is visualized in Figure 6.31. The second for loop prepares the samples of the data window for the FFT and stores them in two arrays of complex numbers, one each for the left and the right channel samples. A single sample consists of either 16 or 24 bits (2 or 3 bytes) and is stored in the *two's-complement system*. The two's-complement system is commonly employed in computing to represent signed numbers. Recall that binary numbers consist of sequences (bits) of either zeros or ones. The most significant bit determines the sign of the number — a 0 indicates that the number is positive, whereas a 1 indicates that the number is negative. In order to negate a number in the two's complement system, all bits are inverted and 1 is added to the result. This conversion works both ways. An example of the two's complement system is presented in Figure 6.32.

In order to support 16-bit, 24-bit, (and theoretically also 32-bit) samples, the C implementation of the spectral benchmark treats each sample as a 32-bit integer, removes the unwanted bits, and converts the data to the two's-complement system. The result is stored in the real part of the complex number.

## 6.5. Spectral Benchmark

| Most significant bit | | | | | | | | Corresponding number |
|---|---|---|---|---|---|---|---|---|
| 0 | 1 | 1 | 1 | 1 | 1 | 1 | 1 | 127 |
| 0 | 1 | 1 | 1 | 1 | 1 | 1 | 0 | 126 |
| 0 | 0 | 0 | 0 | 0 | 0 | 0 | 1 | 1 |
| 0 | 0 | 0 | 0 | 0 | 0 | 0 | 0 | 0 |
| 1 | 1 | 1 | 1 | 1 | 1 | 1 | 1 | -1 |
| 1 | 0 | 0 | 0 | 0 | 0 | 0 | 1 | -127 |
| 1 | 0 | 0 | 0 | 0 | 0 | 0 | 0 | -128 |

Figure 6.32.: Examples of 8-bit numbers in the two's complement system

The imaginary part is set to zero. This procedure is repeated for all samples in the data window. The left and right channel arrays of complex numbers form the input of the FFT. One FFT is performed for each complex array, i.e. separately for the left and right channels. The FFT returns a two-sided spectrum of magnitudes for each channel that is converted to a single-sided spectrum and then further processed to determine the true amplitudes.

In most cases, the size of the data window and the data overlap will not match perfectly with the size of the audio file. To prevent the final iteration from attempting to read past the end of the audio samples, the memory buffer holding the samples is calculated beforehand and adds padding samples after the end of the audio samples. These padding samples are zeroed and do not affect the spectral analysis. The calloc() function is used to conveniently reserve and zero the memory prior to loading the data samples from disk. The timing is performed with the gettimeofday() function and outputted in milliseconds.

### JavaScript

Porting the data types and algorithms for the STFT from C to JavaScript was a straightforward task. Merely the fact that JavaScript generally passes objects by reference, whereas C provides a much more fine grained control over this matter, required some extra dedication — especially in respect to the recursive FFT algorithm.

The major challenge for the JavaScript implementation of the spectral benchmark was to effectively access and extract the binary data from the digital audio file. Modern browsers provide direct access to files via the XMLHttpRequest API. XMLHttpRequest was designed to request text files from a remote server. Thus the web browser parses the response data sequence as a Unicode[24] string. When requesting binary data, this causes a severe mangling of the data elements, which are erroneously treated as Unicode characters by the web browser. While it is possible to suppress the parsing of the response string by overriding the mime type of the XMLHttpRequest object[25], the preferred method is to use either the ArrayBuffer [Mozilla Developer Center 2011a] or DataView APIs [Mozilla Developer Center 2011b].

---
[24] Unicode is a standard for the encoding and representation of text in various written languages.
[25] https://developer.mozilla.org/En/Using_XMLHttpRequest#Receiving_binary_data contains more information on requesting binary data through XMLHttpRequest, last visited on October 5, 2011.

## 6. Performance Analysis

Both `ArrayBuffer` and `DataView` provide a means of accessing arbitrary buffers that contain binary data. There are, however, several differences in their implementations and applications. The binary data represented by an `ArrayBuffer` object cannot be accessed directly. Instead, an `ArrayBufferView` object must be created that provides a view to the binary data. The problem with the `ArrayBufferView` approach is that it provides a view to *either* an 8-bit, 16-bit, or 32-bit signed or unsigned integer number representation of the data[26]. In other words, `ArrayBufferView` assumes that all data in the buffer is homogeneous and follows the same number format and representation. This is, however, rarely the case in real-world scenarios with complex binary file formats, such as the RIFF Wave file format that was described in Section 6.5.2. This restriction makes it very inconvenient to parse binary data buffers with `ArrayBufferView`.

The `DataView` API solves this problem by providing a low-level interface for reading data from an `ArrayBuffer`, without the alignment restrictions imposed by `ArrayBufferView`. Unfortunately, at the time of this writing, Google Chrome is the only web browser that supports the `DataView` API. However, even Chrome does not support the `DataView` API within Web Workers, which are employed in the JavaScript spectral benchmark to process the spectral analysis without blocking the user interface. Therefore, as inconvenient as it may be, the `ArrayBufferView` API was used to access and parse the digital audio samples.

The JavaScript implementation of the inner `for` loop differs considerably from the C implementation of the spectral benchmark. This part is responsible for the extraction of the audio samples according to the sample rate and for their preparation for the FFT. The restrictions of the `ArrayBufferView` API would have made it difficult, inelegant, and slow to implement the low-level C algorithm. Instead, depending on the sample size, a 16-bit or an 8-bit `ArrayBufferView` is created. In the first case, a 16-bit sample can be read from the buffer without modifications. In case of 24-bit samples, three 8-bit data elements are read, combined into a single number, and converted into the two's-complement system. To prevent unnecessary conditionals within each iteration of the `for` loop, these algorithms are implemented as functions and dynamically assigned during the execution of the JavaScript application.

Unfortunately, JavaScript does not provide an elegant means of appending a zero padding to the end of the audio samples. Depending on the size of the data window, the overlap, and the size of the audio samples, this might be necessary to avoid the overstepping past the end of the audio samples during the STFT (see Figure 6.31). Therefore, the STFT in the JavaScript implementation of the spectral benchmark omits the final audio samples, if these do not align with the data window and overlap. To ensure fairness between all benchmark implementations, this behavior was inherited by the C and NaCl implementations.

**Native Client**

Native Client, in its current state, does not provide any means of accessing files directly. It also does not support sockets, which makes it impossible to request data from a remote server within NaCl. Therefore, the NaCl implementation of the spectral benchmark was forced to rely on JavaScript in order to access the contents of the digital audio file.

The main challenge of the NaCl spectral benchmark was to determine which parts of the processing chain should be handled by NaCl. It was clear that JavaScript would be used to retrieve the audio samples from the file. Early testing revealed that it was unfeasible to transfer the data to NaCl in

---
[26]`ArrayBufferView` also supports 32-bit and 64-bit floating point numbers.

## 6.5. Spectral Benchmark

a single batch, as there was a limit on the data size that could be transferred. Therefore, the idea of processing the entire spectral analysis entirely within NaCl was discarded. On the other hand, it proved to be impractical to keep the parsing of the binary data and the nested for loops within JavaScript and to process only the FFT and the magnitude computations within NaCl. The performance impact of the marshalling[27] overhead was substantial and made it clear immediately that this approach was not worth pursuing.

In a discussion in the Native-Client-Discuss group, Michael Mortensen, a Google developer, suggested to convert the binary data into a string of numbers in order to circumvent the costly marshalling process[28]. Since strings consists of bytes (one byte per character in case of a single byte character encoding) they do not need to be marshalled like numbers. The overhead of packing the binary data into and unpacking it from the string is substantially lower than the marshalling overhead. This procedure is, without doubt, a hack that would probably not be very appealing for developers of *real* applications. Yet, for the sake of this experiment it remained the most promising approach and was implemented in the NaCl spectral benchmark.

The processing chain has been split as follows: The audio file is opened and parsed in JavaScript. Two attributes, bits per sample and block align, are required for the spectral analysis and are therefore set in NaCl as properties. The main for loop that slides the data window over the audio samples remains in JavaScript. It also packs the corresponding audio samples into the string and passes them to NaCl. The inner for loop that extracts the data according to the sample rate and converts it into the two's complement system, as well as the actual spectral analysis are performed in NaCl.

Porting a mix of the C and JavaScript implementations of the spectral benchmark to NaCl was not a difficult task. Much of the boilerplate code could be re-used from the *gears application*, although it was extended to support NaCl properties in the spectral benchmark. It should be noted that the NaCl implementation, unlike the JavaScript version, does not make use of Web Workers.

### 6.5.4. Experimental Setup

The spectral benchmark compares the performance characteristics of C, NaCl, and JavaScript during the processing of large amounts of binary data. The run time (in milliseconds) of the spectral analysis was chosen as the primary performance indicator. In addition, the CPU utilization in percent and the memory consumption in KB were measured as secondary performance indicators. The benchmarking was carried out on Ubuntu 10.10 and Mac OS 10.6.

Table 6.2.: Audio files analyzed during the spectral benchmarking process

| Audio file | Sample data in kB | Sample rate | Bits per sample |
|---|---:|---:|---:|
| LMAIntro.wav | 534,404 | 44,100 | 16 |
| Sold His Soul.wav | 8,037,228 | 44,100 | 24 |
| The Blooze.wav | 11,698,104 | 44,100 | 24 |
| LMAI.wav | 78,628,728 | 44,100 | 24 |

---

[27] Marshalling is the process of adjusting the representation of data as it is passed from one computer program or programming language to another — in this case from JavaScript to NaCl and vice versa.

[28] Discussion on the topic of *NaCl Performance Questions*, http://groups.google.com/group/native-client-discuss/browse_thread/thread/c3f193f0130b55e8, last visited on October 5, 2011.

## 6. Performance Analysis

The data base of the spectral benchmark was comprised of four RIFF/WAVE audio samples[29], differing in data size and bit rate. Their characteristics are compared in Table 6.2.

The C implementation of the spectral benchmark and its Native Client counterpart were benchmarked on Ubuntu Linux, with the Chrome browser serving as the platform for the NaCl application. The JavaScript implementation of the spectral analysis was benchmarked in the Google Chrome 9 and Mozilla Firefox 4 browsers on Ubuntu Linux and in a nightly build of the Safari browser (Webkit r83161) on Mac OS X. Unfortunately, due to its lack of support for ArrayBuffers, the Opera browser could not be included in the browser comparison.

As described in Section 6.5.3, the JavaScript implementation of the spectral benchmark makes use of Web Workers to prevent the user interface from blocking during lengthy analyses. As the experiments revealed, there are substantial differences between the web browsers in terms of their levels of Web Workers support. Google Chrome supports ArrayBuffers in Web Workers. Mozilla Firefox 4 generally supports ArrayBuffers but does not support the XMLHttpRequest API with ArrayBuffer support in Web Workers. Apple's Safari pre-release Webkit r83161 supports both, ArrayBuffers and Web Workers. NaCl generally does not yet support applications with Web Workers.

Table 6.3.: Web Workers usage in spectral benchmark implementations

| Browser | Implementation | Web Workers | No Web Workers |
|---|---|---|---|
| Chrome 9 | JavaScript | x | |
| | NaCl | | x |
| Firefox 4 | JavaScript | | x |
| Safari r83161 | JavaScript | x | |

Due to these limitations, two versions of the JavaScript spectral benchmark were developed: one with Web Workers support and one without. The web-worker-based implementation was generally favored and used where possible. Table 6.3 provides and overview of which spectral implementations were benchmarked with Web Workers.

The CPU utilization measurements were performed on Linux and Mac OS, using the `top` application. The smaps kernel interface facilitated the memory analysis on Linux, whereas the Activity Monitor provided the corresponding data on Mac OS.

### 6.5.5. Execution

The computer was rebooted before commencing the experiments and whenever switching between benchmark implementations. During the benchmarking process itself, one GNOME terminal with three tabs was executed on Linux and a single terminal window was run on Mac OS X.

The benchmarking was conducted in four rounds, one for each audio file, consisting of 12 runs of spectral analyses. After discarding the lowest and the highest aberrations, the remaining 10 valid samples were arithmetically averaged, resulting in the average duration of the spectral analysis for each audio file. The results of each run were immediately recorded in text files. For the web browser comparison, the largest audio file was omitted from the benchmarking rounds, reducing these to three.

---
[29] The audio samples were provided by the rock band *Dirty Dudes*.

## 6.5. Spectral Benchmark

A shell script was written to simplify the benchmarking process of the C spectral benchmark. Once executed with the path to the corresponding audio sample as an argument, it carried out the benchmarking and timing of the 12 runs independently. The benchmarking of NaCl and JavaScript was performed entirely by hand.

The browsers were run without arguments, except for Google Chrome, which was executed as follows:

`google-chrome --enable-nacl --enable-webgl --allow-file-access-from-files`.

The CPU utilization was measured independently from the actual benchmarking, in order to be able to focus on each process. 12 samples were recorded during the spectral analysis of the *LMAI.wav* audio file. The C implementation was an exception, since it completed the benchmark before 12 samples could be collected. Likewise, the memory analysis was conducted during the spectral analysis of the largest audio sample, *LMAI.wav*. In order to obtain a realistic representation of the memory consumption, the smaps statistics were observed until they remained fairly static and then recorded. The same applied to the memory statistics delivered by the Activity Monitor on Mac OS. During the memory analysis, the Chrome browser was run with the `--no-sandbox` flag, in order to gain access to its smaps memory statistics:

`google-chrome --enable-nacl --enable-webgl --allow-file-access-from-files --no-sandbox`.

Unlike the other implementations, the memory consumption of the NaCl spectral benchmark grew consistently with the duration of the spectral analysis. Since this is an indication for a memory leak, the issue was further examined. Repeated code reviews did not reveal a defect in the source code of the NaCl spectral benchmark implementation. In addition, the C benchmark, which shares a lot of source code with the NaCl version, did not exhibit this behavior. Further testing strengthened the implication that the memory leak was not caused by the spectral benchmark application, but somewhere else in the NaCl framework. The memory leak persisted, even with the spectral analysis code removed from the NaCl native web application. It therefore seems likely that the exorbitant memory consumption was caused during the passing and marshalling of binary data from JavaScript to NaCl. In any case, the memory analysis of the NaCl applications must be considered a snapshot at a certain time.

### 6.5.6. Results

The results of the spectral benchmark turned out to be very interesting. Again, the C implementation showed the best performance, but this time NaCl's performance dropped considerably. Figure 6.33 illustrates the results of the spectral benchmark experiments.

NaCl consistently exhibited the worst performance throughout the spectral benchmark experiments. Table 6.4 compares the running times of the spectral analysis with the data sizes of the WAVE audio files. The C implementation completed the spectral benchmark approximately three times as fast as JavaScript, which in turn was six times as fast as NaCl. The magnitude of the gap in performance between JavaScript and NaCl was immense: JavaScript processed the largest audio file, *LMAI.wav* in 89.7 seconds, while NaCl completed the analysis of *The Blooze.wav* in 81.3 seconds. It took JavaScript only 10 seconds longer to process a file that is seven times as large. Subsequently, for performance reasons, further NaCl benchmarks of the largest audio file were omitted.

The CPU utilization of the spectral benchmark implementations is compared in Figure 6.34. The

## 6. Performance Analysis

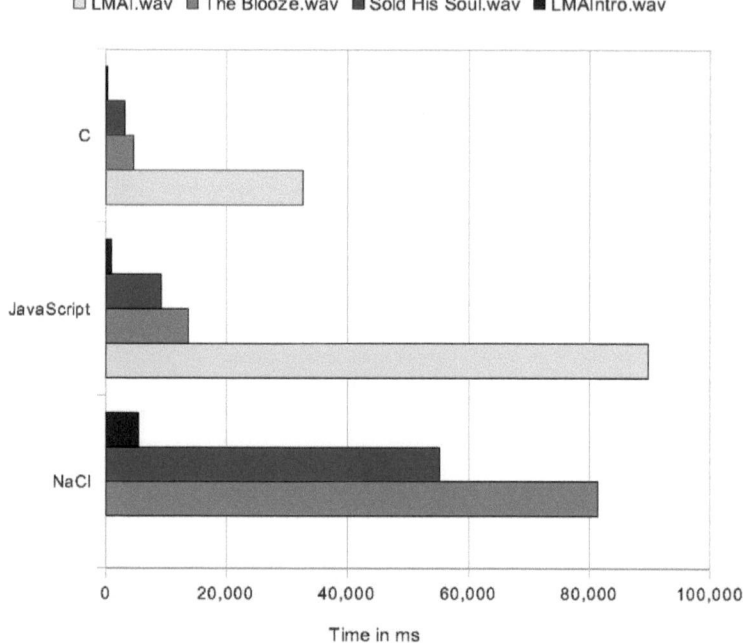

Figure 6.33.: Spectral benchmark: running times of C, NaCl, and JavaScript

Table 6.4.: Spectral benchmark: results of C, NaCl, and JavaScript

| Audio file | Data in MB | Running times in seconds | | |
|---|---|---|---|---|
| | | C | JavaScript | NaCl |
| LMAIntro.wav | 0.5 | 0.3 | 0.9 | 5.4 |
| Sold His Soul.wav | 8.0 | 3.2 | 9.3 | 55.2 |
| The Blooze.wav | 11.7 | 4.6 | 13.7 | 81.3 |
| LMAI.wav | 78.6 | 32.7 | 89.7 | - |

benchmark processes of both C and JavaScript achieved a consistently high CPU utilization of around 100%. NaCl, on the other hand, achieved lower utilizations between 87% and 94%. This is not surprising given the distribution of the workload and the repeated data transfer between the JavaScript and NaCl processes.

Figure 6.35 illustrates the memory consumption during the spectral benchmark experiments. As explained in Section 6.5.5, the memory consumption of the NaCl spectral benchmark grew linearly during the benchmarking of the *LMAI.wav* file. NaCl consumed 500 MB of private RSS memory when then memory snapshots were taken. In comparison, C consumed 76.9 MB of private RSS memory and JavaScript used 145.5 MB.

## 6.5. Spectral Benchmark

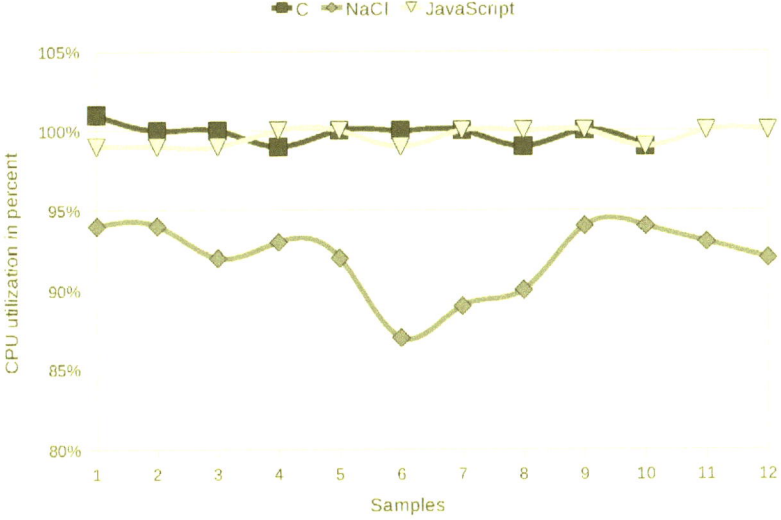

Figure 6.34.: Spectral benchmark: CPU utilization of C, NaCl, and JavaScript

In the web browser comparison, Google Chrome's JavaScript engine consistently delivered the fastest results. As shown in Figure 6.36, Chrome completed the spectral analyses roughly twice as fast as the Safari/Webkit nightly build (on Mac OS) and almost four times as fast as Mozilla Firefox 4. The results of the browser comparison are compared in Table 6.5 — the largest audio file *LMAI.wav* was omitted from the experiments.

Table 6.5.: Spectral benchmark: web browser comparison

| Audio file | Data in MB | Running times in seconds | | |
|---|---|---|---|---|
| | | Chrome | Safari | Firefox |
| LMAIntro.wav | 0.5 | 0.9 | 2.3 | 3.3 |
| Sold His Soul.wav | 8.0 | 9.3 | 22.7 | 35.7 |
| The Blooze.wav | 11.7 | 13.7 | 33 | 53.9 |

Although Firefox was by far the slowest web browser in the comparison, it still performed the spectral analyses considerably faster than NaCl.

In terms of memory consumption, Apple Safari/Webkit consumed the least private RSS memory, followed by Google Chrome and Mozilla Firefox. Figure 6.37 provides an overview of the memory consumption of the web browsers during the JavaScript spectral benchmark. During the spectral analysis of *LMAI.wav*, the largest audio file of 78.6 MB, Safari/Webkit used 107.5 MB, while Chrome consumed 145.5 MB of private RSS memory. Firefox employed 240.8 MB of private RSS memory — substantially more than Chrome and Safari/Webkit.

Figure 6.38 illustrates the CPU utilization achieved by the web browsers during the spectral bench-

## 6. Performance Analysis

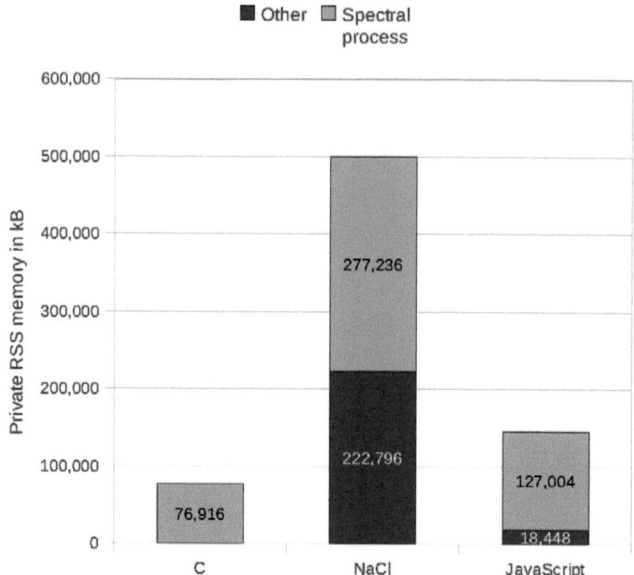

Figure 6.35.: Spectral benchmark: memory consumption of C, NaCl, and JavaScript

mark. Generally, all browsers achieved high utilizations of 98% to 100%, with the CPU utilization of the Firefox browser fluctuating more than that of the other browsers.

### 6.6. Discussion

Native Client intends to bring computational performance to web applications, specifically with a focus on simple, computationally intensive tasks. The results of the pi- and pi-MT benchmarks indicate that NaCl does indeed perform exceptionally well in number crunching tasks — it is on par with C. However, the same applies to the JavaScript engine of the Mozilla Firefox browser. According to the pi-MT benchmark, JavaScript Web Workers are able to offer a comparable level of performance to that of native application threads for simple computational tasks. On the other hand, native application threads offer much more flexibility than Web Workers, e.g. shared memory access and synchronization principles. Therefore, it must be expected that C and NaCl threads remain superior for complex parallel applications.

When it comes to high-performance 3D graphics performance, NaCl has a significant advantage over JavaScript/WebGL. NaCl's performance comes very close to that of the *glxgears* reference implementation in C. Considering that, due to the necessary port to OpenGL ES 2.0, the rendering code differs substantially between C and NaCl, the valid question remains as to whether the performance differences can (at least partially) be attributed to this fact. The JavaScript benchmark implementation uses the SetEvent() call to repeatedly call the main loop for rendering. This event-based approach obviously cannot achieve the same amount of CPU utilization as a while() loop in *glxgears* or the

## 6.6. Discussion

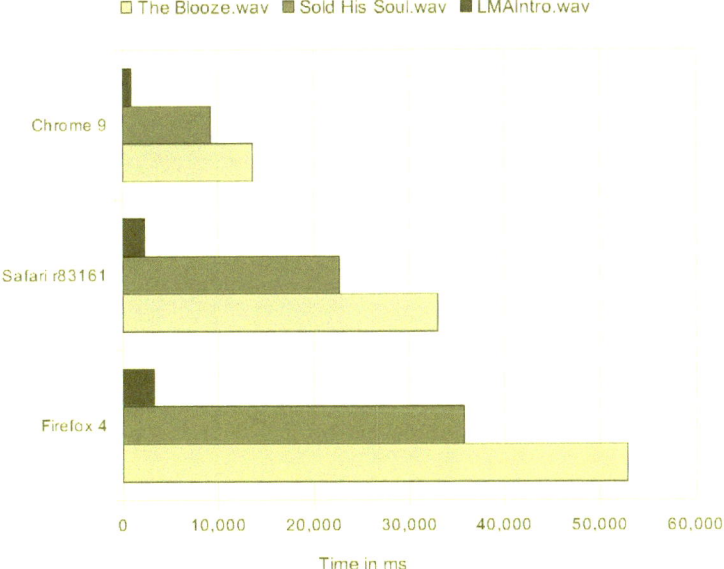

Figure 6.36.: Spectral benchmark: web browser comparison

approach employed in the NaCl gears implementation. This explains the rather consistent and limited frame rates achieved by Chrome and Firefox, despite the increases of the drawing area size. Yet, there is no doubt that the 3D graphics performance of NaCl is vastly superior to that of JavaScript/WebGL as implemented in the Chrome and Firefox browsers. However, WebGL is a very young technology that should see performance improvements as it matures.

The spectral benchmark revealed NaCl's weakness in the area of data intensive tasks. Unlike in any of the other benchmarks, NaCl was outperformed by all competitors — even by the relatively slow JavaScript engine of the Firefox web browser. These results lead to the conclusion that, in its current state, NaCl is not suitable for the processing of data intensive tasks. But why is this the case?

The Chrome browser executes core browser components, the JavaScript engine, and NaCl modules in separate OS processes, thus isolating them from each other. This concept, although robust and security effective, becomes a problem when large amounts of data are passed between the JavaScript and the NaCl layers. The two foremost reasons for NaCl's disappointing performance during spectral benchmark are:

1. The overhead of inter-process communication (IPC) is extremely costly in terms of performance.

2. There is no suitable API to pass binary data effectively.

The overhead caused by IPC when large amounts of data are transferred from one process to another is the foremost reason for NaCl's performance deficits during the spectral benchmark. Unfortunately, as NaCl does not permit file system access and does not support sockets, there is no other way of pushing data into the NaCl process, other than through the JavaScript process. Even the time required to

## 6. Performance Analysis

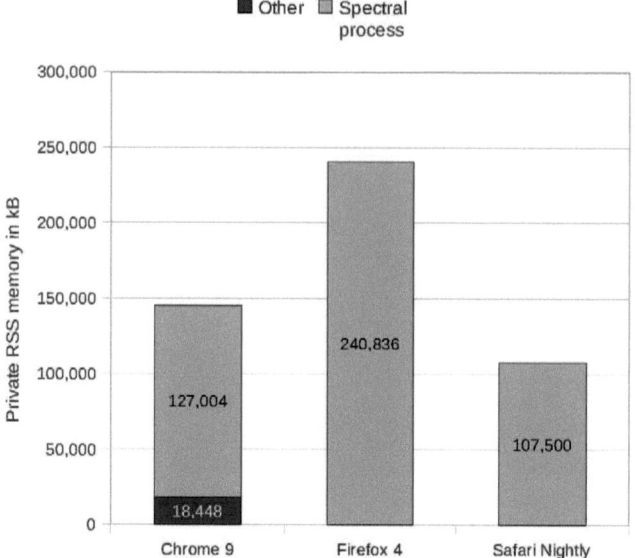

Figure 6.37.: Spectral benchmark: web browser memory consumption

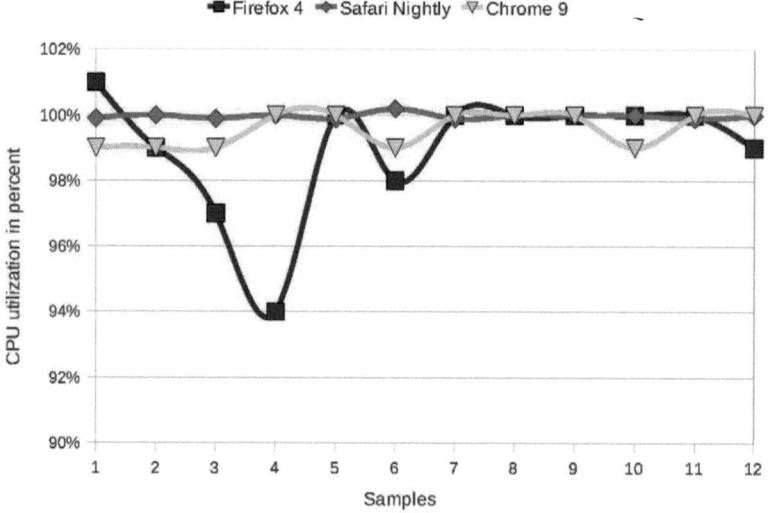

Figure 6.38.: Spectral benchmark: web browser CPU utilization

pack and unpack the binary data into a string of numbers is negligible when compared to the impact of the IPC. Anyhow, this diversion would not be necessary if NaCl provided an API that allows the passing of an `ArrayBuffer` from JavaScript to the NaCl layer. Experiments indicated that passing the audio samples[30] individually from JavaScript to NaCl resulted in a substantial marshalling overhead, as all JavaScript natural numbers are automatically converted into C/C++ integers.

With the exception of the spectral benchmark, NaCl exhibits a consistently high level of computational performance that is on par with native C applications. This cannot be said about the performance of the JavaScript engines of the Chrome and Firefox browsers. While both perform favorably and even comparably to the native applications in some benchmarks, their performance in general is rather inconsistent. More than anything, the performance of JavaScript web applications depends on the executing JavaScript engine, which could potentially fragment the user experience.

## 6.7. Further Investigations and Potential Solutions

If NaCl wants to realize its full potential as a native code extension for web applications, its shortcomings must be addressed. Data-intensive tasks are relevant for various applications that have so far not been implemented within the web browser, such as image manipulation software, or audio and video editors.

NaCl provides a very simple Remote Procedure Call (RPC) mechanism that can be used as an alternative to the NPAPI browser plugin interface for the development of NaCl services. This mechanism is called Simple Remote Procedure Call (SRPC) and it allows the implementation of NaCl modules that communicate with JavaScript through basic C/C++ data types. The SRPC mechanism does not support complex data types, such as `structs` or `unions`, and it does not require the implementation of glue code, as required by the NPAPI plugin interface. Plus, it has a distinct advantage over NPAPI: The SRPC mechanism supports shared memory in order to exchange data between JavaScript and NaCl.

The potential advantage of shared memory is that processes can share a common address space within a computer's main memory to exchange data, thus reducing the overhead of IPC. In order to evaluate whether this approach could provide superior performance over the NPAPI-based implementation, the NaCl spectral benchmark was rewritten to employ shared memory. A shared memory segment was created to exchange the audio data between JavaScript and NaCl. The basic principle was that the JavaScript process would write the audio samples into the shared memory segment, where they could be accessed by the NaCl process. Unfortunately, this approach did not provide any performance improvements over the initial implementation. Further complicating matters, it was not possible to write the contents of the JavaScript `ArrayBuffer` object into a NaCl shared memory segment. Therefore, the extra step of converting the audio samples into a string had to be inherited from the original NPAPI-based implementation of the NaCl spectral benchmark. Since the string of samples can potentially become several times larger than the binary representation within the `ArrayBuffer`, this limitation can have dramatic effects on the size and the write performance of the shared memory segment. In another attempt to remove this bottleneck, the code was modified to return a string from the `XMLHttpRequest()` call that loads the binary data into the browser. The idea was to speed up the process by writing the string directly to the shared memory segment. This was, however, not possible for unknown reasons and would result in error messages. These investigations let to the conclusion

---

[30] WAVE audio samples can be encoded in either 8-, 16-, 24-, or 32-bit sequences.

## 6. Performance Analysis

that the SRPC mechanism suffers from the same performance problems as the NPAPI interface — it was unable to provide significant advantages in practice.

As explained in Section 6.6, the reasons for NaCl's weaknesses in data processing can be attributed to the overhead of IPC and the lack of a suitable API to pass binary data efficiently. The second issue is less severe, has less impact on NaCl's data processing performance, and should be easier to solve. It can most certainly be addressed by developing a dedicated API that allows the direct passing of binary data that is stored in `ArrayBuffers` from JavaScript to NaCl. There might be technical problems to resolve, but generally there are no obvious reasons as to why a solution to this problem should not be possible, i.e. unless the data representation in JavaScript `ArrayBuffers` differs substantially from that of C binary buffers.

The first issue constitutes the core problem of data processing in NaCl. NaCl employs process isolation as a design principle for security and reliability reasons. Although work could be put into reducing the computational overhead of IPC and context switches, it remains questionable whether these alone could be sufficient to allow the transfer of large amounts of data between processes. Therefore, it seems more promising to grant NaCl applications access to sockets and/or the file system, like Microsoft Xax does. This could enable NaCl applications to acquire and process the data in the same process, thus circumventing the costly IPC. However, NaCl does not permit access to the file system or sockets for security reasons and so far there have been very good arguments for this design decision.

A possible solution to this limitation could become viable with the adoption of the *WebSocket* and *File API* HTML5 interfaces. These make it possible for JavaScript web applications to communicate with remote servers through sockets and to open, read from, and write to file resources — while retaining the security constraints otherwise applied to web applications. If this functionality becomes available to JavaScript, why should it be withheld from NaCl? NaCl already reuses several other browser mechanisms to allow the execution of compiled native modules in the web browser. Access to the File API and WebSockets would allow NaCl modules to acquire and load binary data directly into their private memory address ranges — avoiding the computational overhead of IPC altogether. This approach would make NaCl's computational advantages available for tasks like the spectral benchmark. The adoption of WebSockets and the File API remains the most promising strategy to amend NaCl's shortcomings in data processing.

# 7. Evaluation, Effects, and Opportunities

In the previous chapter, a performance analysis of native applications, JavaScript web applications, and NaCl native web applications in various areas of computing was carried out. The analysis found that native C applications offered the highest performance in number crunching, 3D graphics, and data processing. On the other hand, NaCl performed exceptionally well in number crunching and 3D graphics, but lacked severely in data processing. Finally, JavaScript was unable to achieve the performance of NaCl in 3D graphics, but matched it in number crunching and outperformed NaCl in data processing.

While the results of the performance analysis are interesting, they only focus on a single aspect of native, JavaScript, and NaCl applications: performance. In order to conduct an extensive evaluation of the advantages and disadvantages of each technology, additional factors must be taken into account. This chapter complements the performance analysis of the previous chapter by defining additional criteria for the evaluation of native applications, JavaScript web applications, and NaCl native web applications. The criteria consist of technical and non-technical items that are applied to and discussed for each technology. The key question is: Can NaCl successfully combine the strengths of native applications and JavaScript web applications, while minimizing its weaknesses?

The evaluation of native applications, JavaScript, and NaCl is followed by a discussion of the key drivers for the success of NaCl as a technology for the creation of native web applications. NaCl's adoption is not alone dependent on its computational performance. It depends on several technical, political, and strategic factors. Finally, the show-stoppers for NaCl's propagation are discussed.

## 7.1. Comparison Criteria

In order to evaluate and compare the capabilities of native applications, JavaScript web applications, and NaCl native web applications, the following ten criteria will be employed:

1. *3D graphics performance*: OpenGL performance for games and professional computer graphics applications

2. *Browser neutrality*: is the technology browser independent and supported by multiple web browsers?

3. *Computational performance*: performance during computational tasks, i.e. mathematical operations, number crunching, etc.

4. *Data processing*: performance regarding the processing large amounts of (binary) data

5. *Maturity*: is the technology considered stable and has proven itself in production use?

6. *Openness*: are decision making and development spread among several stakeholders and is the source code open source?

7. *Evaluation, Effects, and Opportunities*

7. *OS-independence*: the ability of applications to run on different operating systems, if possible without modifications
8. *Portability*: can applications be executed on different computing environments (OS and CPU architecture), if possible without modifications?
9. *Porting and code reuse*: the effort of porting an application to a new platform, while taking into account the source code that can be reused
10. *Security*: protection against malware, viruses, and other attacks

## 7.2. Evaluation

### 7.2.1. 3D Graphics Performance

3D graphics performance is important for computer games, computer aided design, and other applications that visualize three-dimensional objects. The gears benchmark (Section 6.4) revealed that native applications and NaCl native web applications have substantial advantages over JavaScript/WebGL in terms of 3D graphics performance. While NaCl was between 3% to 15% slower than the native application in the gears benchmark, it was up to 1,200% faster than JavaScript/WebGL — depending on the size of the drawing area.

While the capabilities of JavaScript/WebGL are impressive, it is unable to match the level of 3D graphics performance that NaCl can offer to web applications. However, WebGL is a novel technology that has only recently become available to web developers. It must to be expected that future revisions of WebGL in major browsers will offer improved performance and more efficient resource usage.

NaCl has another distinct advantage over JavaScript/WebGL that is related to 3D graphics performance: code reuse. A significant amount of 3D applications and libraries is written in the C/C++ programming languages. NaCl makes it possible to reuse this functionality for web application development, at a higher performance than can be achieved by porting source code to JavaScript. Higher performance and faster time to market are two very important arguments for the adoption of NaCl for applications that rely heavily on 3D graphics. It would not be surprising if NaCl could play a decisive role in bringing 3D games to the web browser.

Although it does not quite achieve the performance of native applications, NaCl offers higher 3D performance and less memory consumption than JavaScript/WebGL.

### 7.2.2. Browser Neutrality

JavaScript is omnipresent in the web browser. As outlined in Section 3.2.4, virtually all modern browsers provide support for the core JavaScript language and APIs and a runtime that allows the execution of JavaScript applications. While Adobe Flash was once the predominant web technology to construct animated web sites or to view video content in the browser, JavaScript has gained many of the capabilities required to take over these tasks natively, without the need for (proprietary) browser plugins. This is a substantial advantage — not only over Adobe Flash, Microsoft Silverlight, and JavaFX, but also over NaCl. JavaScript applications are browser neutral and will run unmodified on different web browsers. On the other hand, multi-vendor support and different implementations of JavaScript engines in the web browser have lead to a certain degree of fragmentation. This has

## 7.2. Evaluation

become obvious during the experiments in Chapter 6. Not all browsers support the same feature set of JavaScript APIs. Therefore, it can be challenging for web application developers to support all modern web browsers. Application developers must take into account the capabilities that are provided by browser vendors and, especially, by different browser versions that are being employed by consumers.

NaCl does not suffer from this fragmentation, as there currently is only a single implementation of the API and runtime. The creators of NaCl were aware that browser neutrality is important for native code extensions to web applications. They designed and implemented NaCl as a browser plugin, which, at least in theory, can allow the execution of compiled NaCl modules in other web browsers. As described in Section 5.3, current versions of NaCl require the Pepper 2 plugin interface, instead of the NPAPI interface that is supported by most major browsers and therefore is considered the de facto standard. Although from a technical standpoint it is understandable that the limitations of NPAPI mandated the development of a browser plugin interface that is better suited for NaCl's demands, the use of a custom plugin interface further raises the bar for NaCl's adoption by other browser vendors. Pepper 2 is currently only supported by the Google Chrome browser and its adoption by other leading browsers is uncertain. Mozilla[1] and Opera[2] have already declined support for NaCl, which is a major setback for the adoption of NaCl as a standard Internet technology. Apple and Microsoft have not yet publicly commented on NaCl, but it seems unlikely that they intend to embrace this technology. Unfortunately, this means that NaCl applications are currently restricted to the Google Chrome browser — with little prospect of change.

NaCl's lack of browser neutrality also affects Google's own Android platform. The web browser that ships with Android is based on the same technological foundations as the Chrome browser, but it is not identical and it does not yet support NaCl[3]. In addition, Android features its own set of APIs for the development of native applications. These facts lead to the implication that NaCl is not (yet) a top priority for the Android platform, although NaCl already supports the ARM processor architecture that is prevalent on mobile devices.

Although NaCl was designed with browser neutrality in mind, its rejection by competing browser vendors and its deep level of technical integration with the Chrome browser must lead to the conclusion that NaCl is not browser neutral. The advantage in terms of browser neutrality is clearly with JavaScript. Browser neutrality is, of course, not applicable to native applications, as these do not run inside the web browser.

### 7.2.3. Computational Performance

The performance analysis in Chapter 6 confirmed NaCl's excellent computational performance. In both the pi and pi-MT benchmarks, the performance of NaCl was comparable to that of the native C applications and roughly twice as fast as the JavaScript engine of the Chrome browser. The overhead of NaCl's security framework was barely measurable and did not have substantial impacts on application performance in practice. The Firefox browser, on the other hand, was able to provide a degree of JavaScript performance in both benchmarks that was only marginally lower than that of C and NaCl. These findings lead to the implication that JavaScript is indeed suitable for simple computational tasks — with its performance depending heavily on the web browser. This also applies to concurrent

---

[1] http://www.theregister.co.uk/2010/06/24/jay_sullivan_on_firefox/, last visited on September 9, 2011.
[2] http://www.theregister.co.uk/2010/10/01/opera_on_google_native_client/, last visited on September 9, 2011.
[3] Discussion on Android support in the Native-Client-Discuss group, https://groups.google.com/d/topic/native-client-discuss/aK6xD9Ctdj4/discussion, last visited on October 18, 2011.

## 7. Evaluation, Effects, and Opportunities

applications. Web Workers make it possible to implement efficient multithreaded applications that do not require access to shared memory.

While the results of the performance analysis imply a parity between NaCl and JavaScript in terms of computational performance, the foremost advantage of NaCl lies in the fact that it provides low-level access to the computing hardware (see Section 5.1. JavaScript is a high-level language that features automatic memory management and garbage collection, hiding many of the low-level programming details from the developer. The downside of this approach is that low-level hardware access is not available to JavaScript developers, even in cases were it would be desirable. Like native applications in C, NaCl supports features such as hand-written assembler code and instruction set extensions (e.g. SSE) — all of which JavaScript does not support. NaCl also provides capabilities for the development of multithreaded applications that are superior over those of JavaScript. Applications that make use of these features should be able to gain substantial performance advantages over JavaScript-based web applications.

In terms of computational performance, native applications clearly set the performance benchmark. However, NaCl brings a level of computational performance to web applications that is comparable to that of native applications. Although JavaScript is perfectly suitable for simple computational algorithms, which it can potentially execute as fast as native code, NaCl provides more flexibility for the development of complex, computationally intensive web applications — plus the additional benefit of being able to reuse existing legacy code.

### 7.2.4. Data Processing

Data processing is an integral field of computing, perhaps the field that motivated the widespread adoption of computers in the first place. Unfortunately, as the experimental results of the spectral benchmark in Section 6.5 proved, NaCl shows substantial performance weaknesses when processing large amounts of (binary) data. It was outperformed by both C and JavaScript in the spectral benchmark. The fastest JavaScript engine, that of the Chrome browser, completed the spectral analyses up to six times as fast as NaCl. Even the Firefox 4 browser, which featured the slowest JavaScript engine in the spectral benchmark, offered superior performance over NaCl. These results have lead to the conclusion that NaCl is currently not a suitable technology for the processing of large amounts of data in a web application.

The reasons for NaCl's poor performance in data processing were discussed in Section 6.6. The overhead of IPC between the JavaScript and NaCl processes, as well as the lack of a dedicated interface to pass binary data between both processes, had major impacts on NaCl's performance in the spectral benchmark. Section 6.7 presented further investigations and recommended the reuse of HTML5/JavaScript APIs in order to provide constrained file and socket access to NaCl applications. By accessing data sets directly, NaCl applications could ideally avoid the costly overhead of IPC altogether. It remains to be seen whether NaCl's security framework permits these modifications and whether NaCl applications can actually benefit from these improvements in practice. There is certainly potential for the enhancement of NaCl's capabilities in terms of data processing.

JavaScript showed a solid performance in the spectral benchmark and outperformed NaCl in every respect. Yet, the native C application offered three times the performance of the JavaScript web application, which is a substantial advantage, especially with large data sets. While the performance aspects of JavaScript are generally positive, the `ArrayBufferView` API leaves a lot to be desired. Although it provides a level of functionality that was until recently not available to JavaScript devel-

## 7.2. Evaluation

opers, `ArrayBufferView` is inflexible and not well suited for heterogeneous data, which is commonly found in binary files. Writing a JavaScript parser for binary data is certainly more work than accomplishing the same task in C. The `DataView` API marks an improvement over `ArrayBufferView` but it is currently not well supported by most web browsers. Overall, there is a lot of room for improvement regarding the binary data APIs available to JavaScript developers, but improvements surely will be made as JavaScript expands into the realm of binary data processing.

With NaCl's performance weaknesses and JavaScript's lack of comfortable APIs for the processing of binary data, neither technology rivals the flexibility and performance of native applications in the field of data processing. However, for the development of web application that process large amounts of binary data, JavaScript should be favored over NaCl at this point in time.

### 7.2.5. Maturity

Compared to JavaScript, which has been around since 1995, NaCl is a young technology. The project was established in the late 2000s and has not yet achieved a stable release. NaCl is still under heavy development — the technical details of its implementation and its APIs are subject to change. Until the API stabilizes, NaCl must be considered unstable, despite being very usable, and not ready for production use. Yet, NaCl is a novel approach to a long standing problem and developer interest is picking up. Several proof of concept projects have been initiated to evaluate its potential, such as Qt for NaCl[4] and NaClBox[5]. Although the NaCl project has not released a roadmap that outlines when the first stable release is expected, NaCl has recently been integrated into the beta channel of the Chrome browser. This is an indication that its APIs are stabilizing and its maturity is growing.

The JavaScript programming language, on the other hand, is a very mature technology for application development. Initially developed by Netscape in 1995, it powers the front end of numerous highly popular web applications that are being used daily by millions of users. As explained in Section 3.2.4 JavaScript has found its way into mobile phones and even server development, surpassing its initial intention as an extension for HTML pages. After years of stagnation and lack of innovation, the recent increase in competition between browser vendors has led to considerable improvements in the field of JavaScript performance. With performance having become a selling argument in advertisement, this is expected to continue — especially considering that several popular benchmarks have appeared that measure JavaScript performance.

With the HTML5 initiative, JavaScript is gaining new functionality for web application development. While JavaScript itself is a very mature technology, this is not necessarily the case for the new HTML5 APIs, which are subsequently added to modern web browsers. Like NaCl, HTML5 is very much work in progress. The final version of its specification is not expected before 2014. Security vulnerabilities such as those quoted by Microsoft Research for WebGL [MSRC Engineering 2011], or the lack of performance and memory efficiency, as discussed in Section 6.4 have to be expected. Despite these limitations, JavaScript has a clear advantage over NaCl in terms of maturity.

### 7.2.6. Openness

The overwhelming success of Apple's iOS platform has fueled discussions regarding vendor lock-in and the Open Web. The Open Web movement encourages the development and use of open and

---

[4] http://labs.qt.nokia.com/2010/06/25/qt-for-google-native-client-preview/, last visited on October 11, 2011.
[5] http://www.naclbox.com/, last visited on October 11, 2011.

## 7. Evaluation, Effects, and Opportunities

non-proprietary web technologies. The independent technological writer Tantek Çelik argues that the Open Web allows [Çelik 2010]:

1. the publishing of content and applications using open standards,
2. the implementation of web standards that empower web content and web applications,
3. the unrestricted usage of these resources.

Çelik makes the point that, in order for content and web applications to be available for everybody, open and patent-free formats should be employed when publishing them on the Web. They should further be well documented and royalty free. In addition, he concludes that cheap, unrestricted, and uncensored Internet should be available for everybody. The Open Web stands for the idea that information on the Web is accessible through open standards and not controlled by a single (commercial) entity with the ability to restrict access to this information.

NaCl is an open source project under a BSD license[6], i.e. its source code is freely available to the general public, but at foremost it is a Google project. Although external contributors are encouraged, Google is the only commercial vendor that currently funds the development of this technology. As of July 2011, virtually all contributors to NaCl are listed on the project page with either google.com or chromium.org e-mail addresses[7]. While Google deserves credit for establishing NaCl as an open source project, the company views itself as a proponent of the Open Web, a single (commercial) entity controlling an open source project is certainly not desirable and may be considered unhealthy. Successful open source projects are characterized by a strong and heterogeneous development community.

The availability of the source code does not automatically make for an open project. The decision making throughout the NaCl project is dominated by Google, which is not surprising given the company's commitment in terms of manpower and financial backing. Technical decisions are taken inside the company, primarily with the Chrome browser in mind. While this strategy allows Google's developers to act fast and to achieve results quickly, it is not a governance model that encourages participation from other companies or independent developers. The blame, however, is not entirely Google's to take. Google has made NaCl available to the general public, but not a single competing browser vendor has expressed interest — neither in the technological approach itself, nor in collaborating. Instead, Mozilla and Opera have stated that they will not support NaCl and want to push for JavaScript as the primary technology for web applications. Therefore, Google might try to take the route Netscape took with JavaScript, i.e. acting as the initial creator and establishing the technology later as a standard. This would, however, require substantial changes to the governance of the project. As it stands today, NaCl is open source and free of charge, but not a particularly open project.

HTML and JavaScript, on the other hand, are governed by organizations such as the WHATWG, W3C, and the Khronos Group. Representatives of Microsoft, Apple, Google, Mozilla, and Opera are actively involved in the drafting of new standards and features within these organizations. This does not necessarily mean that these corporations are always in agreement, for example several new JavaScript and CSS APIs were implemented in various browsers before being officially accepted into the HTML5 standard. Still, the development of HTML and JavaScript is discussed openly between the stakeholders, which is necessary as new features must be supported by all major browsers for developers to take advantage of them. The existence of these discussions puts JavaScript in a favorable position over NaCl in terms of openness.

---

[6]Berkeley Software Distribution (BSD) licenses are permissive free software licenses that declare the terms of software redistribution.
[7]http://code.google.com/p/nativeclient/people/list, last visited on October 13, 2011.

### 7.2.7. OS-Independence

"Write once, run anywhere" was a slogan conceived by Sun Microsystems to advertise the cross-platform benefits of its Java platform[8]. Whether Java ever fulfilled the promise of true OS-independence remains disputable, primarily due to incompatibilities between platforms. However, the similarities with the web browser as a platform for application development are apparent. Just like the Java virtual machine, the web browser has become the runtime for applications. JavaScript itself is OS-independent — JavaScript applications will run on any operating system that supports a capable web browser. The OS-independence of JavaScript has benefited from the simplicity of its core APIs. Unlike JavaScript, Java supports threads and other features that are closely tied to the underlying operating system. While a rich API is desirable from an application developer standpoint, the simple and compact JavaScript core APIs require less support from and less integration with the underlying operating system. Perhaps this is one of the reasons why JavaScript applications have proven to be truly OS-independent and very portable.

Like JavaScript, NaCl is OS-independent and employs the web browser as the runtime for its applications. Instead of directly accessing OS functionality, NaCl applications reuse browser functionality for the provision of application services. This makes it possible to execute compiled NaCl applications on different operating systems without requiring modifications or even recompiles of their source codes. On the other hand, NaCl provides functionality that is tied to the CPU architecture and the operating system — perhaps to a greater extent than Java. Therefore, it remains to be seen whether the NaCl runtime can be easily ported to support a greater number of operating systems and processor architectures, without suffering from the compatibility problems that Java faced. Java, JavaScript, and NaCl applications will (theoretically) run anywhere as long as their execution environment is available. For Java this is the Java virtual machine, for JavaScript web applications this is the web browser, and for NaCl this is the Chrome web browser with the NaCl plugin. As discussed in Section 3.3.1, this is one of the greatest advantages of web applications over traditional native applications, which must target one or more specific operating systems and CPU architectures directly. Between JavaScript and NaCl, neither technology has a substantial advantage over the other in terms of OS-independence — but both have considerable advantages over native applications.

### 7.2.8. Portability

A computing platform is considered OS-independent, if its applications are independent of the underlying operating system. Applications are considered portable, if they can be executed on a different computing environment, consisting of an underlying CPU architecture and an operating system, with few modifications. As presented in Section 3.3.1, traditional native applications target a specific CPU architecture. They are compiled into machine language using a compiler that is optimized for a certain processor architecture. Native applications make direct use of operating system and CPU functionality. Therefore, developing portable native applications demands a lot of work, as the differences in operating systems and compilers must be taken into account. A key element to achieve portability for native applications is the addition of an abstraction layer between the application logic and system interfaces. Ideally, this abstraction layer makes it possible to recompile the application on a different OS/CPU architecture and to execute it afterwards.

JavaScript applications are OS and processor independent and thus highly portable with minimal effort (see Section 3.2.4). They target the functionality of their runtime, i.e. the web browser or a

---
[8] http://www.java.com, last visited on October 11, 2011.

## 7. Evaluation, Effects, and Opportunities

stand alone JavaScript engine, instead of the system interfaces. The browser runtime is responsible for the execution of the JavaScript applications. The details of the CPU architecture are handled by the runtime and opaque to the web application. Therefore, JavaScript applications can run unmodified on computers, phones, and other mobile devices — as long as a suitable web browser or another JavaScript runtime are available. This is an enormous advantage over native applications, as the worldwide use of mobile computing increases and as computing devices become increasingly heterogeneous (compare with Section 4.1). Due its nature of a dynamic language, JavaScript applications are not statically compiled before deployment, but dynamically compiled before execution. This overhead causes a performance penalty compared to native applications. However, as the experiments in Chapter 6 have shown, this penalty is not necessarily substantial.

In terms to OS-independence and portability, NaCl exhibits some the advantages of JavaScript and some of the disadvantages of native applications (see Section 5.3). NaCl applications can run unmodified on any operating that supports the Chrome web browser. In this respect they are highly portable. However, since NaCl applications are compiled into machine language for dedicated CPU architectures, like traditional native applications, precompiled binaries for every supported CPU architecture must be deployed. As described in Section 5.3.4, the web browser automatically determines the CPU architecture, downloads the correct application binary, and inserts it into the NaCl runtime for execution. In addition, NaCl applications must be recompiled in order to support new processor architectures or instruction set extensions. If NaCl should eventually support more CPU architectures, the amount of binaries that must be deployed will increase — this could cause additional work during testing and deployment. While NaCl applications are highly portable, they are currently restricted to three CPU architectures: Intel x86 32-bit, x86 64-bit, and ARM. In order to extend this support to additional processor architectures, not only the web browser must be ported (as would be sufficient in the case of JavaScript), but the development tools as well. This is the downside of native code execution, which NaCl shares with traditional native applications.

Overall, the support for compiled native code execution in the web browser comes at an expense that was previously unknown from JavaScript. NaCl applications provide a high level of portability by supporting the major consumer CPU architectures, but they require more maintenance during deployment. It is also unclear how long compiled NaCl modules will be supported. Whether these restrictions remain theoretical, or perhaps turn into practical problems, will be determined in the future. The PNaCl project that facilitates the creation of processor independent application binaries could elevate the portability of NaCl applications to the level JavaScript applications. Today, JavaScript is at slight advantage over NaCl — both technologies offer a degree of portability that is far superior over that of native applications.

### 7.2.9. Porting and Code Reuse

If an application was not designed with portability in mind but should be made available to a new computing environment, it must be ported. The effort of porting an application to a new platform depends on several factors. First of all, the porting effort can be greatly reduced, if the application was well designed and structured. If the original programming language can be retained, e.g. when porting a C application from the Microsoft Windows platform to the Apple Mac OS platform, this greatly reduces the porting effort. The same applies to the compiler suite and build tools. Perhaps the most difficult task of porting an application to a new platform is when neither the original development tools, nor the programming language are available. This is the case when porting native applications to JavaScript web applications.

JavaScript shares a lot of syntax similarities with C/C++. This fact can make it easier for C/C++ developer to get started with JavaScript. Yet, when porting a C application to JavaScript, the application logic must be translated into the JavaScript syntax — this is even more the case with other programming languages that differ significantly in syntax, for example Python. In addition, JavaScript features a very reduced and simplified core API with little functionality. Therefore, the supporting libraries commonly associated with a native application must either be replaced by JavaScript alternatives outside the core API, or reimplemented altogether. JavaScript does not permit the reuse of existing application code (written in another programming language). As a result, porting the C implementation of the gears benchmark (Section 6.4) to JavaScript was found to be fairly straightforward, but a lot of work. The resulting web application differs substantially from its native application counterpart.

Porting/code reuse is one of the most prominent advantages of NaCl over JavaScript — at least in respect to C/C++ applications. The experiments in Chapter 6 confirmed that porting native applications from C to NaCl is generally straightforward. The majority of the original C source code could be reused without modifications. Many C/C++ libraries have already been ported to NaCl and a lot of the functionality that developers have become accustomed to is already available. In addition to saving time, code reuse also reduces the amount of programming bugs[9] that are introduced as new code is written. NaCl embraces the GNU compiler collection and many common C/C++ development tools that are especially popular on the Apple Mac OS and Linux platforms. This keeps the learning barrier low and makes it very easy for many C/C++ developers to get started with NaCl application development. NaCl is not necessarily limited to the C and C++ programming languages. Its architecture allows the addition of other programming languages that can be compiled to native code. These advantages make NaCl attractive to developers of native applications that want to leverage existing functionality and code for new web applications. Popular applications such as Adobe Photoshop and Apple Logic could, theoretically, be able to take advantage of these capabilities. If this advantage is paired with NaCl's outstanding OpenGL performance, NaCl could become a very appealing platform for computer aided design and game development. The complex and performance critical components of modern games are commonly written in C/C++. In theory, these could be easily ported to NaCl. Second, game development has been one of the areas that has suffered from JavaScript's performance problems and the lack of hardware accelerated 3D support. Both of these areas have seen improvements but, as the results of the gears benchmark indicate, WebGL still lacks the performance capabilities of NaCl. Whether developers can and will take advantage of NaCl's possibilities in terms of code reuse and portability will be seen. However, there is no doubt that the advantages NaCl provides in terms of code reuse and portability are compelling.

### 7.2.10. Security

Security is an important and omnipresent subject in modern computing. This has not always been the case. Before computing devices were interconnected through the Internet, security considerations were often treated secondary to features. When computers and mobile devices went online and became generally accessible, malware and viruses became a serious problem. Microsoft, the market leader in operating systems and web browsers, repeatedly made the headlines due to exploits and hacks affecting its products. The company has since successfully put a lot of effort into security. Although every computer program is subject to programming errors and security flaws, web browsers and web applications are under a particular security focus — perhaps due to their history of exploits and

---

[9]In software development, the term bug is commonly used to describe a programming error.

## 7. Evaluation, Effects, and Opportunities

attacks. The perception of security in information technology varies. Some consider JavaScript itself a security nightmare and recommend disabling it altogether. Others praise security improvements of modern web browsers, such as process isolation and sandboxing, which were outlined in Section 4.3.1.

The *Web Application Security Trends Report Q3-Q4 2010* of Cenzic Inc., a company that specializes in security solutions, comes to the conclusion that, in the year 2010, browser companies have fixed most reported security vulnerabilities in a timely manner — often proactively by offering bounties [Khera et al. 2011]. It seems the lessons of the past were well learned by the browser vendors. The report further states that web application development flaws were the root cause for most reported attacks. Web application vulnerabilities were found to account for 57% of the total vulnerabilities and those related to web technologies. Clearly, security is an issue in the growing field of web applications. The most common flaws were caused by "critical application-layer injection flaws, such as Cross Site Scripting (XSS), and SQL Injection" [Khera et al. 2011]. These flaws are classical programming errors that are well known in the realm of native application development.

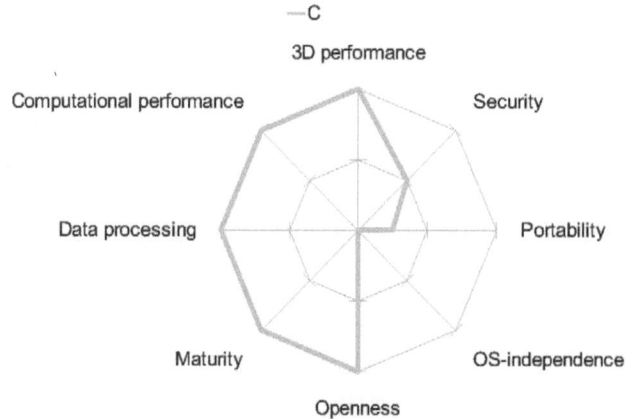

Figure 7.1.: The spider web of native application pros and cons

NaCl was designed from the ground up with a strong focus on security. It employs two sandboxing layers to isolate untrusted native application code from the NaCl runtime and the underlying operating system (see Section 5.3.1). Software fault isolation and segmented memory are employed to restrict data and instruction memory references. Untrusted application code is disassembled and statically analyzed prior to execution — a validator ensures that only legal machine instructions are issued. Overall, the security framework that was conceptualized and implemented for NaCl is impressive. If Google discovers and fixes NaCl vulnerabilities at the same rate as for the Chrome browser, there is no substantial reason to believe that NaCl is inherently less secure than JavaScript in this browser. On the contrary, neither modern JavaScript engines, which are sandboxed to prevent unwanted side effects, nor native applications offer security mechanisms that involve static analysis and reliable disassembly of arbitrary application binaries.

Table 7.1.: Evaluation of C, JavaScript, and NaCl

|  | C | JavaScript | Native Client |
|---|---|---|---|
| 3D performance | ++ | o | ++ |
| Browser neutrality | N/A | ++ | -- |
| Computational performance | ++ | + | ++ |
| Data processing | ++ | + | -- |
| Maturity | ++ | + | o |
| Openness | ++ | ++ | o |
| OS-independence | -- | ++ | ++ |
| Portability | - | ++ | + |
| Porting and code reuse | N/A | o | ++ |
| Security | o | o | + |

| | |
|---|---|
| ++ | Very good |
| ++ | Good |
| o | Average |
| - | Poor |
| -- | Insufficient |

### 7.2.11. Conclusion

Table 7.1 compares the results of the evaluation for native C applications, JavaScript web applications, and NaCl native web applications. Native applications written in the C programming language generally have their strong points in performance, i.e. 3D performance, computational performance, and data processing. They also portray a great level of openness and maturity: C is standardized and several independent implementations exist. On the other hand, due to their tight integration with operating systems and CPU architectures, native applications exhibit deficits in OS-independence and portability. The development of portable native applications demands that the details of OS mechanisms and CPU architectures are abstracted away, which is time-consuming and difficult. However, even portable native applications must be recompiled to run on a different operating system. Like all other computer programs, native applications are subject to programming errors that can result in security vulnerabilities. Native applications do not provide their own security mechanisms, but rely on the underlying OS to prevent unwanted side effects. Therefore, it is debatable whether they have actual technical advantages over web applications in terms of security. Figure 7.1 illustrates the strengths and weakness of native applications. It omits browser neutrality and code reuse, which are not applicable to native applications.

The strengths and weaknesses of JavaScript web applications are well balanced. They are illustrated in Figure 7.2. JavaScript excels in browser and OS-independence, as well in portability and openness. Although it lacks serious shortcomings, its 3D performance, porting/code reuse, and security capabilities are merely average. The fact that JavaScript targets the web browser as the runtime for its applications allows these to be used with virtually every Internet-enabled computing device — this alone is perhaps JavaScript's greatest advantage. The development of JavaScript is open and

## 7. Evaluation, Effects, and Opportunities

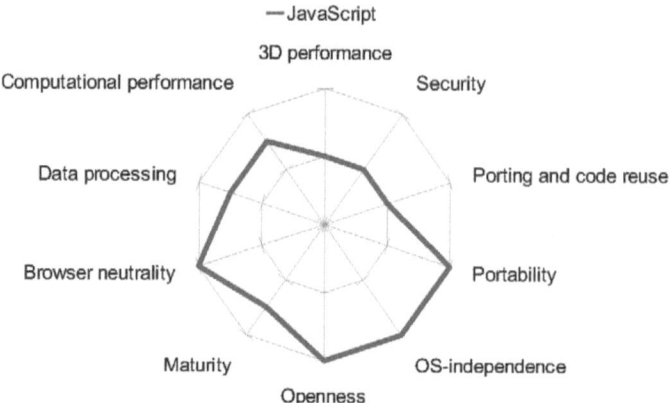

Figure 7.2.: The spider web of JavaScript strengths and weaknesses

not controlled by a single (commercial) entity. In addition, it is well supported by various modern browsers. In spite of claims that attribute JavaScript a lack of computational performance and general slowness, the performance analysis in Chapter 6 indicates the opposite. Although JavaScript was unable to match the performance of C and NaCl, especially in terms of 3D graphics performance, it showed a solid level of computational and data processing performance. However, the results varied considerably between web browsers.

The strong points of NaCl native web applications are computational performance, 3D graphics performance, OS-independence, and the ability to reuse existing C/C++ source code. NaCl offers a level of computational performance that is superior over that of JavaScript and comparable with native applications. The same applies to 3D graphics performance, where the performance gap between NaCl and JavaScript is substantial. NaCl excels in OS-independence and makes it possible to execute native web applications on Linux, MacOS, and Windows operating systems, without modifications. This level of OS-independence is unprecedented by native applications. The ability to reuse legacy code for the development of native web applications is one of NaCl's foremost advantages.

NaCl's most substantial shortcomings are in browser neutrality and data processing — although this might be addressed with architectural changes and improvements in future revisions. The lack of support through other browser vendors is a serious setback for NaCl's chances of adoption as a defining Internet technology. It will remain to be seen whether Google alone can generate enough developer and user interest to entrench NaCl in the market. Yet, the fact that NaCl is dependent on the Chrome browser is a practical limitation. The strengths and weaknesses of NaCl are illustrated in Figure 7.3.

While the source code of NaCl was released under an open source license, the lack of open project governance and third-party engagement is a disadvantage. The same applies to NaCl's lack of maturity. NaCl is currently available in the beta channel of the Chrome browser — a stable release is still pending. NaCl performs exceptionally well when compared to their native application counterparts in terms of portability, but still falls short in comparison with JavaScript. NaCl's security framework, on the other hand, is remarkable. It provides more security measures that native applications and modern JavaScript engines. The future will provide insight into its practical capabilities.

## 7.3. Drivers for NaCl's Adoption

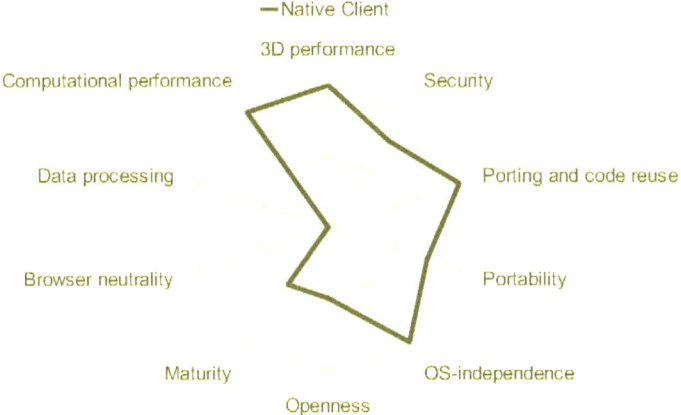

Figure 7.3.: The spider web of NaCl strengths and weaknesses

As graphically displayed by the spider web Figures, NaCl is not quite able to combine the strengths of native and JavaScript web applications. It fails to merge the advantages of JavaScript in browser neutrality with the excellent data processing performance of native applications. In addition, NaCl is less open than the C and JavaScript programming frameworks.

## 7.3. Drivers for NaCl's Adoption

Unlike Xax, which is a research project, NaCl will soon become available to web developers around the world. It has officially been included and enabled in the beta channel of Chrome 14, which means that the first stable release of NaCl will happen shortly. NaCl's foremost advantages are the provision of computational performance to web applications, the ability to employ legacy code for web application development, and the reuse of browser components to achieve OS-independence. Its major challenge, however, will be to reach critical mass: a wide level of adoption among users and developers. This section discusses the technical, political, and strategical drivers that can help NaCl achieve the goal of becoming the defining technology framework for the development of native web applications.

### 7.3.1. Technical Drivers

Several technical drivers for NaCl's adoption can directly be extracted from the shortcomings that were revealed during the evaluation in Section 7.2. In order to fully utilize its potential, NaCl's weaknesses in data processing must be addressed. A technical solution must be devised and implemented that reduces or avoids the computational overhead of IPC when processing large amounts of (binary) data. As stated in Section 6.7, the provision of the HTML5/JavaScript File API and WebSocket interfaces to NaCl applications remains the most promising approach. The solution to the problem of data processing is one of the foremost technical drivers for the improvement of NaCl.

Another technical driver related to the aforementioned problem is maturity. NaCl's feature set is

## 7. Evaluation, Effects, and Opportunities

not yet complete, e.g. hardware accelerated 3D graphics are currently unavailable — they have been disabled with the move to the Pepper 2 plugin interface. NaCl also does not yet support HTML5 Web Workers and does not provide access to camera devices or microphones[10]. Due to the reuse of browser functionality for the provision of services to native modules, the evolution of NaCl will depend largely on the evolution of HTML5/JavaScript APIs in the web browser. The first stable release of NaCl is a major step towards maturity, especially since it guarantees a stable ABI for future versions, but a clear roadmap would further benefit NaCl's adoption and its maturity.

In order to drive the adoption of NaCl by developers, the technical documentation and development tools should be improved. Although the NaCl SDK includes source code examples, and additional information can be found on the NaCl project website, the overall documentation is rather scarce. In addition to describing the APIs and toolchain, the documentation should also include best-practices that inform developers how to approach certain tasks and how to work around NaCl's limitations or performance bottlenecks, e.g. in the area of data processing. The NaCl SDK does not yet support debugging or profiling. Although it is possible to compile and execute a NaCl application as a standalone native application, which allows the use of debuggers and profilers, this limitation should be addressed. Developers of native applications have become used to powerful development tools and will continue to expect these from NaCl. Both documentation and development tools are important technical drivers for NaCl's adoption by software engineers.

The completion of the PNaCl project could be a major technical driver for NaCl. As described in Section 5.3.3, PNaCl allows the creation of CPU-independent application binaries. Instead of compiling native modules for three different CPU architectures, PNaCl targets the LLVM intermediate bytecode format. The separation of the bytecode format from the underlying CPU architecture not only allows the support of additional CPU architectures, it also reduces the amount of application binaries that must be distributed to exactly one: the LLVM version. In the long run, PNaCl may also be able to provide backward compatibility for older application binaries that target CPU architectures that have gone out of fashion. With the help of PNaCl, NaCl could ultimately gain a level of portability that is equivalent to that of JavaScript.

Although HTML5 adds several much needed features to the Web as a platform, the completion of the specification is years away — the final version of HTML5 is not expected before 2014 (see Section 3.3.2). NaCl promises to bring a much quicker technological boost to web application development. It could serve as a bridge technology until the shortcomings of JavaScript have been amended, or until it is replaced with a more powerful successor. Perhaps the most crucial limitation of current web applications is their lack of offline support, i.e. the ability to function without an active Internet connection. Offline support is a substantial opportunity for NaCl, especially since NaCl requires the downloading of native modules prior to execution. Wireless connectivity is not yet ubiquitous everywhere in the world, therefore offline support can become a major driver for NaCl.

### 7.3.2. Political Drivers

In order to drive the adoption of NaCl on a political level, Google, the creator of NaCl, has two major options:

1. force NaCl into the market as is, by using Google's reach and market strength,
2. standardize NaCl, establish open governance, and take the diplomatic approach.

---

[10]http://code.google.com/intl/de/chrome/nativeclient/faq.html, last visited on October 12, 2011.

## 7.3. Drivers for NaCl's Adoption

In the first scenario, Google would remain fully in control of NaCl's governance and technological direction. Instead of depending on the support of other browser vendors to establish NaCl as a technology for web application development, the strategy would be to encourage the adoption of NaCl by providing a compelling platform for the development, deployment, and monetization of NaCl applications. Chrome OS, Google's new web-application-only operating system, is a logical vehicle for this approach: an independent platform with a web application store that allows the monetization of NaCl applications. Chrome OS would gain additional value through NaCl. NaCl, in turn, would gain exposure through the Chrome OS platform, which would raise its attractiveness for developers. Although Google might succeed in driving NaCl into the market by itself, it remains questionable whether this will suffice in order to establish NaCl as a base technology for the extension of common web applications with native code.

In the second scenario, Google could attempt to standardize NaCl, much like Netscape did with JavaScript, in order to drive its adoption by other browser vendors. A single-vendor controlled technology that aims to become a standard on the Web is problematic and not likely to be adopted by third parties. Therefore, in this approach, openness would become a key political driver for NaCl's adoption by other browser vendors, in turn leading to greater propagation. By opening up the development and governance of NaCl, and not just the source code, Google could make its technology much more appealing to third parties — maybe eventually turning it into a web standard.

Since NaCl is implemented as a browser plugin that targets the Pepper 2 plugin API, Google should at least attempt to advertise and standardize this new plugin API as a successor to the aging NPAPI. So far, only the the Chrome browser supports Pepper 2, but NaCl could become available to other browsers, should these adopt Pepper 2. The implementation of Pepper 2 could be a resource problem, especially for Mozilla and Opera that are focused on the implementation of HTML5 APIs and tablet versions of their browsers. Google could go as far as providing patches to the Firefox browser, which is open source, to add support for Pepper 2. This approach, although politically difficult, could double the potential user base of the NaCl platform.

It is out of the question that the second route, attempting to standardize NaCl and placing it under open government, is most certainly the more tedious and time consuming approach. In addition, it could potentially slow down technological innovation, with more time being spent on diplomatic matters. However, in order to achieve the highest possible adoption of NaCl as a technology for native web applications, the diplomatic approach remains compelling.

### 7.3.3. Strategical Drivers

The creation of a strong platform with a large user base and the ability to monetize applications is one of the key strategical drivers for NaCl. For Google, this platform is the Chrome browser, including the Chrome OS web-application-only operating system. According to the browser statistics illustrated in Figure 6.1, Chrome already owns 16% of the global desktop web browser market share. In May 2011, Chrome has passed the staggering number of 160 million active users[11]. In addition, the Chrome platform features the Web Store, which allows the discovery and monetization of web applications. The Web Store is a perfect distribution channel for NaCl web applications, which are currently restricted to the Chrome browser. The market would surely adopt a new technology that allows richer web applications, enables the reuse of legacy code, and possibly opens new markets, such

---

[11] http://googleblog.blogspot.com/2011/05/new-kind-of-computer-chromebook.html, last visited on October 13, 2011.

## 7. Evaluation, Effects, and Opportunities

as 3D games in the web browser — but its success among developers and corporations will depend on the ability to monetize.

Another key strategical driver for the success of NaCl are partnerships with operators of application platforms. For example, in order encourage the adoption of NaCl for creators of computer games, Google could attempt to bring the Unity 3D engine[12] and the Steam[13] platform to NaCl. Complex 3D games have not yet become available as web applications, due to the computational shortcomings of JavaScript. NaCl provides the technological capabilities of bringing complex 3D games to the web browser and, at the same time, allows cost-savings due to the reuse of legacy code. The ability to share code between desktop, mobile, and web applications is a compelling advantage for game developers. There is an opportunity for NaCl in the area of computer games that is far greater than a niche.

Despite these partnerships, Google should advertise its NaCl technology by creating exiting new applications that show off NaCl's capabilities. "Firstly, users care about availability of popular content (see Angry Birds, Skype and Facebook) most of which are not available as web apps often due to HTML technology limitations" [Vision Mobile 2011]. Some of these limitations can be circumvented with NaCl. By creating full-featured NaCl applications such as Skype or Google Earth in the web browser, Google could generate a hype around NaCl as a technology. The creation of innovative NaCl native web applications to generate interest among users and developers is a strategical driver for the adoption of NaCl.

Web-only operating systems, such as Google Chrome OS or Mozilla's Boot to Gecko (B2G)[14] projects may be ahead of their time in the consumer space, but could become compelling offerings for enterprises. By dismissing the execution of native applications and allowing only web applications, these projects provide benefits such as: simplicity, automatic updates, and enhanced security. Since user profiles and data are stored in the cloud, computers may be shared between employees or replaced without requiring a tedious and time consuming setup process. These advantages may well translate into a substantially reduced total cost of ownership (TCO) per computer. Missing native applications could be made possible through NaCl, with NaCl's security framework providing several advantages over conventional native application platforms and operating systems. By prohibiting the installation of arbitrary native applications and allowing only dual-sandboxed NaCl native web applications, corporations can lock down the machines used by their employees — thus reducing problems caused by viruses and other malware, without sacrificing functionality. Success in the enterprise sector is a major strategical driver for NaCl as part of the Chrome OS platform.

### 7.3.4. Show-Stoppers

There are many drivers for NaCl's success, but the technology faces two show-stoppers:

1. Market penetration
2. Limitations in data processing

If NaCl does not achieve a critical level of market penetration and adoption by developers, it could remain a niche technology for very specific applications — restricted to the Chrome web browser. In

---

[12] The Unity 3D engine provides the technological foundations for the creation of 3D games; http://unity3d.com, last visited on October 13, 2011.

[13] Steam is an online gaming platform that allows the sale and distribution of computer games; http://store.steampowered.com, last visited on October 13, 2011.

[14] Boot to Gecko is an attempt to create an open source OS for HTML5 web applications only; https://wiki.mozilla.org/B2G, last visited on October 19, 2011.

this case, it is unlikely that Google would continue to support NaCl in the long term, making the lack of market penetration the most relevant show-stopper for native web applications.

Perhaps less severe, but also a show-stopper in respect to realizing its full potential, are NaCl's technical limitations in the area of data processing. NaCl is not yet a general purpose technology for the development of native web applications, but could become one if these limitations are overcome.

# 8. Conclusion and Outlook

The World Wide Web has become a significant platform for the development of web applications. However, JavaScript, the leading web programming language, is not expected to be able to provide a comparable level of computational performance to that of compiled native code. This shortcoming has prevented the creation of browser-based applications demanding high performance and low-level access to hardware, e.g. scientific simulations, 3D computer games, and high-resolution scene rendering. The Native Client project (NaCl) attempts to bring computational performance to the Web, by facilitating native web applications: web applications that are extended with compiled native code. The primary goals of native web applications are computational performance, security, OS-independence, and code reuse — they aim to combine the strengths of native applications and web applications.

This doctoral thesis has discussed the effects and opportunities of compiled native code, as an extension for computationally demanding web applications. A performance analysis of native C applications, JavaScript web applications, and NaCl native web applications was carried out in order to answer the following questions:

1. How does JavaScript performance compare to that of traditional native applications and native web applications?

2. Is JavaScript fast enough to enable web applications of the future or is an alternative needed?

3. What are the benefits and drawbacks of extending JavaScript web applications with compiled native code?

Four application benchmarks measuring different performance aspects were introduced. The *pi benchmark* evaluated number crunching performance during the evaluation of simple mathematical terms. The *pi-MT benchmark* was an evolution of the pi benchmark. It employed parallel programming to distribute the computation of $\pi$ among several processing cores. The *gears benchmark* evaluated 3D computer graphics performance and rendered a simple scene with three animated mechanical gears. Finally, the *spectral benchmark* focused on the processing of large amounts of binary data. It performed a spectral analysis of digital audio samples.

As expected, the native C applications consistently delivered the highest performance throughout the benchmarking process. NaCl offered a comparable level of performance in the computational and 3D performance benchmarks, but exhibited significant shortcomings in data processing. JavaScript performance varied considerably between web browsers. The fastest JavaScript engines completed the pi and pi-MT benchmarks only marginally slower than NaCl and outperformed NaCl in the spectral benchmark. However, JavaScript generally lacked in 3D graphics performance.

NaCl's limitations in data processing were attributed to the computational overhead of inter-process communication (IPC). NaCl applications consist of a JavaScript and a NaCl module — both modules run in separate processes in order to increase robustness through isolation. Since NaCl modules do not have direct access to the local file system or the network, data must first be acquired using JavaScript and then transferred to NaCl for processing. This step incurs a substantial overhead in IPC that was responsible for the inadequate performance of NaCl in the spectral benchmark. This doctoral thesis

## 8. Conclusion and Outlook

discussed several possible solutions to this problem. The reuse of the HTML5/JavaScript File API and WebSocket interfaces was recommended in order to permit file and socket access to NaCl applications. Meanwhile, the initial stable release of NaCl has implemented one of these recommendations, underlining its feasibility: Using File API, NaCl applications can now directly access the file system and should be able to avoid the performance-critical IPC altogether[1].

To evaluate the strengths and weaknesses of native and web technologies, a set of technical and non-technical evaluation criteria were defined: 3D performance, browser neutrality, computational performance, data processing, maturity, openness, OS neutrality, portability, porting/code reuse, and security. A comparison of C, JavaScript, and NaCl was undertaken in order to complement the results of the performance analysis. NaCl excelled in 3D graphics and computational performance, OS neutrality, and code reuse. Its weaknesses were ascertained in the areas of data processing and browser neutrality — NaCl is only supported by a single web browser. The pros and cons of JavaScript were more evenly balanced. It showed a decent level of performance in number crunching and data processing, with its strong points in browser neutrality, OS-independence, maturity, and openness.

Following the evaluation, the technical, political, and strategical drivers for NaCl's adoption were discussed. In order to reach critical market penetration and general acceptance, NaCl must overcome its technical limitations, gain widespread support among developers, multi-browser support, and additional corporate backing. While the technical issues can be resolved, the fact that NaCl is a single-vendor controlled technology is problematic and may hinder its adoption as a universal Internet technology. Google, NaCl's creator, has the options of using its market strength to establish NaCl or to pursue the route of open governance for the NaCl project. While Apple and Microsoft have yet to comment, the other major browser vendors, Mozilla and Opera, have already declined support for NaCl. They intend to focus on the further development of JavaScript instead. This is a serious setback for NaCl's propagation in the browser space. As a result, two show-stoppers for the success of NaCl were identified: lack of market penetration and its limitations in data processing.

The findings of this doctoral thesis leave several opportunities for future work. The benchmark applications, for example, could be expanded to incorporate additional performance aspects not considered in this document. The performance analysis could be repeated on other computing platforms, e.g. Chrome OS, in order to determine whether native code execution can provide additional advantages on less powerful machines. The Dart programming language[2], introduced by Google in October 2011 as a possible successor to JavaScript, could be evaluated in terms of computational performance. Dart addresses some of the architectural shortcomings of JavaScript and aims to improve web application performance. Once a Dart runtime is implemented in the Chrome browser, it would be interesting to determine whether Dart can rival the speed of compiled native code. The technical feasibility and complexity of adding support for the Pepper 2 plugin interface, and thus NaCl, to the Firefox web browser could be researched. Although this is a challenging subject, the fact that both the Chrome and Firefox browsers are open source projects facilitates this investigation. Likewise, the opportunities of porting additional programming languages or application frameworks to NaCl could be investigated. For example, the The Mono project has recently added support for NaCl, allowing the execution of its virtual machine, garbage collector, and just-in-time compiler inside a NaCl module[3]. This makes it possible to execute programs written in .NET programming languages, e.g. C#

---

[1] http://chrome.blogspot.com/2011/09/new-stable-release-of-chrome-expanding.html, last visited on October 13, 2011.

[2] http://www.dartlang.org/, last visited on October 25, 2011.

[3] Mono is an open source implementation of ECMA standardized components of the Microsoft .NET platform; http://www.mono-project.com/Release_Notes_Mono_2.10#Google_Native_Client_Support, last visited on October 25, 2011.

and Visual Basic, on top of inside the web browser — in a constrained execution environment. The addition of programming languages and application frameworks to NaCl has the potential of enabling new applications and attracting additional developers. These effects could be investigated. Finally, the state of the HTML5/JavaScript application framework and its progress compared to native and mobile application frameworks could provide an interesting research topic. In addition to comparing the levels of functionality, the rate of innovation and standardization of HTML5/JavaScript could be critically examined. Ideally, approaches could be developed that promote innovation and faster time to market.

The research carried out in this doctoral thesis leads to the conclusion that JavaScript is a mature web technology, able to provide a decent level of computational performance for general purpose web applications. However, as revealed during the performance analysis, JavaScript's capabilities are fragmented and depend heavily on the web browser and its underlying JavaScript engine. For example, the Firefox browser was able to match the performance of compiled native code in the pi and pi-MT benchmarks, but its performance dropped behind that of other browsers in the gears and spectral benchmarks. 3D graphics performance was found to be a weak spot of JavaScript, although this might change as the WebGL technology matures. The Web as a platform certainly needs more innovation. HTML5 is a step in the right direction, but its final version is not expected before 2014. Native and mobile platforms still have advantages over the Web in terms of functionality and this will remain the case, despite HTML5. The Web as a platform lacks focus and a unified future vision, which is not surprising as different stakeholders have different priorities. It is questionable whether the standardization bodies that govern HTML and JavaScript have the potential to innovate at a pace that rivals that of competing platforms.

Native Client is an innovative web technology that achieves most of the goals of native web applications. It implements a sophisticated security framework and provides a level of OS-independence that was previously unknown from compiled native code. NaCl's computational and 3D graphics performance is excellent and comparable to that of native applications. Due to its support for multithreading and code reuse, NaCl is equipped with compelling advantages over JavaScript — especially for complex parallel applications. NaCl's primary technical weakness was found to be in the processing of large amounts of binary data. The rectification of this shortcoming can turn NaCl into a general purpose technology for the development of computationally demanding browser-based applications.

The question remains whether the Web as a platform *needs* native code extensions. A comparison with the mobile space could make for an interesting argument. When presented to the World in 2007, the original iPhone was restricted to web applications. The ongoing demand of developers to program the device to its full potential caused Apple to rethink its strategy. Subsequently, Apple released an SDK and provided public access to the iPhone's low-level native APIs. Today, every current mobile OS, including iOS, Android, and WebOS, provides low-level native APIs for the development of applications in the need of more computational performance — most notably games. If compiled native code has allowed the creation of computationally demanding and feature-rich mobile applications, why should this option not be explored for web applications?

NaCl's most significant challenge is to achieve widespread adoption. If it proves unable to reach this goal, NaCl will remain a niche technology, restricted to the Chrome platform, for special tasks that cannot be accomplished with JavaScript. Nevertheless, Native Client has the potential to empower a new generation of web applications — turning the Web into the primary platform for application development.

# Appendix A. Benchmarking Data

## A.1. Pi Benchmark

Pi benchmark: Running measurements for $10^7$ to $10^8$ iterations in milliseconds

| | 10,000,000 | 20,000,000 | 30,000,000 | 40,000,000 | 50,000,000 | 60,000,000 | 70,000,000 | 80,000,000 | 90,000,000 | 100,000,000 |
|---|---|---|---|---|---|---|---|---|---|---|
| C | 99 | 198 | 297 | 397 | 494 | 594 | 690 | 789 | 888 | 984 |
| NaCl | 108 | 205 | 301 | 399 | 497 | 594 | 692 | 790 | 888 | 985 |
| JavaScript | 199 | 388 | 572 | 759 | 948 | 1133 | 1319 | 1507 | 1695 | 1886 |
| Firefox 4 | 110 | 211 | 308 | 409 | 507 | 606 | 704 | 804 | 910 | 1025 |
| Opera 11 | 111 | 227 | 333 | 440 | 552 | 656 | 763 | 873 | 978 | 1112 |
| Chrome 9 | 199 | 388 | 572 | 759 | 948 | 1133 | 1319 | 1507 | 1695 | 1886 |
| Safari 5 | 165 | 327 | 488 | 650 | 811 | 973 | 1134 | 1296 | 1458 | 1618 |

Pi benchmark: CPU utilization data of 12 samples in percent

| | | | | | | | | | | |
|---|---|---|---|---|---|---|---|---|---|---|
| C | 99% | 100% | 100% | 100% | 100% | 100% | 100% | 100% | 100% | 100% |
| NaCl | 100% | 100% | 100% | 100% | 100% | 100% | 100% | 100% | 100% | 100% |
| JavaScript | 99% | 100% | 100% | 100% | 100% | 100% | 100% | 100% | 100% | 100% |
| Firefox 4 | 101% | 100% | 100% | 100% | 100% | 100% | 100% | 100% | 100% | 100% |
| Opera 11 | 99% | 100% | 100% | 100% | 100% | 100% | 100% | 100% | 100% | 100% |
| Safari 5 | 100% | 100% | 100% | 100% | 100% | 100% | 100% | 100% | 99% | 100% |
| Chrome 9 | 99% | 100% | 100% | 100% | 100% | 100% | 100% | 100% | 100% | 100% |

Pi benchmark: memory footprint in KB during 1.000.000.000 iterations

| | C | NaCl | JavaScript | Chrome 9 | Firefox 4 | Opera 11 | Safari 5 |
|---|---|---|---|---|---|---|---|
| Other processes | | 11,108 | 12,108 | 12,108 | | | |
| | | 952 | 964 | 964 | | | |
| | | 376 | 592 | 592 | | | |
| | | 7,208 | 5,240 | 5,240 | | | |
| Sum other | | 19,644 | 18,904 | 18,904 | | | |
| Pi process | 88 | 2,412 | 4,876 | 4,876 | 46,600 | 37,956 | 16,500 |
| Total | 88 | 22,056 | 23,780 | 23,780 | 46,600 | 37,956 | 16,500 |

*Appendix A. Benchmarking Data*

## A.2. Pi-MT Benchmark

| Pi-MT benchmark: running time measurements for $10^7$ to $10^8$ iterations in milliseconds | | | | | | | | | | |
|---|---|---|---|---|---|---|---|---|---|---|
| | 10,000,000 | 20,000,000 | 30,000,000 | 40,000,000 | 50,000,000 | 60,000,000 | 70,000,000 | 80,000,000 | 90,000,000 | 100,000,000 |
| C | 56 | 113 | 159 | 218 | 256 | 303 | 353 | 407 | 450 | 493 |
| NaCl | 59 | 108 | 160 | 208 | 262 | 308 | 359 | 415 | 457 | 509 |
| JavaScript | 109 | 203 | 299 | 395 | 496 | 584 | 683 | 781 | 877 | 973 |
| Firefox 4 | 66 | 116 | 169 | 216 | 264 | 315 | 365 | 416 | 465 | 516 |
| Opera 11 | 118 | 225 | 333 | 440 | 549 | 655 | 762 | 869 | 977 | 1080 |
| Chrome 9 | 109 | 203 | 299 | 395 | 496 | 584 | 683 | 781 | 877 | 973 |
| Safari 5 | 91 | 176 | 262 | 348 | 433 | 520 | 604 | 690 | 775 | 866 |

| Pi-MT benchmark: CPU utilization data of 12 samples on 2 CPUs in percent | | | | | | | | | | |
|---|---|---|---|---|---|---|---|---|---|---|
| C | 194% | 195% | 196% | 196% | 196% | 195% | 192% | 196% | 195% | 195% |
| NaCl | 194% | 195% | 196% | 196% | 198% | 196% | 199% | 199% | 197% | 199% |
| JavaScript | 198% | 194% | 197% | 197% | 198% | 198% | 198% | 198% | 198% | 197% |
| Firefox 4 | 199% | 196% | 199% | 199% | 199% | 199% | 199% | 199% | 199% | 199% |
| Opera 11 | 100% | 99% | 100% | 100% | 100% | 100% | 100% | 100% | 100% | 100% |
| Chrome 9 | 198% | 194% | 198% | 197% | 198% | 198% | 198% | 198% | 198% | 197% |
| Safari 5 | 194% | 196% | 195% | 198% | 194% | 196% | 195% | 196% | 194% | 197% |

| Pi-MT benchmark: memory footprint in KB during 1,000,000,000 iterations | | | | | | | |
|---|---|---|---|---|---|---|---|
| | C | NaCl | JavaScript | Chrome 9 | Firefox 4 | Opera 11 | Safari 5 |
| Other processes | | 11,264 | 12,068 | 12,068 | | | |
| | | 944 | 972 | 972 | | | |
| | | 580 | 572 | 572 | | | |
| | | 5284 | 5316 | 5316 | | | |
| Sum other | | 18,072 | 18,928 | 18,928 | | | |
| Pi processes | | 4,880 | 4,852 | 4,852 | | | |
| | | 4,880 | 4,848 | 4,848 | | | |
| Sum pi processes | 132 | 9,760 | 9,700 | 9,700 | 56,912 | 38,660 | 18,000 |
| Total | 132 | 27,832 | 28,628 | 28,628 | 56,912 | 38,660 | 18,000 |

136

## A.3. Gears Benchmark

Gears benchmark: frames per second according to drawing area size in pixels

|            | 300x300 | 400x400 | 500x500 | 600x600 | 700x700 |
|------------|---------|---------|---------|---------|---------|
| C          | 3195    | 2063    | 1413    | 983     | 731     |
| NaCl       | 2736    | 1878    | 1309    | 921     | 711     |
| JavaScript | 208     | 196     | 192     | 159     | 132     |
| Firefox 4  | 99      | 99      | 98      | 99      | 96      |
| Firefox 4 Mesa | 80  | 50      | 36      | 29      | 22      |
| Chrome 9   | 208     | 196     | 192     | 159     | 132     |
| Safari Nightly | 118 | 60      | 59      | 60      | 60      |

Gears benchmark: Average CPU utilization in percent

|            | 300x300 | 400x400 | 500x500 | 600x600 | 700x700 |
|------------|---------|---------|---------|---------|---------|
| C          | 99.90%  | 100.00% | 99.90%  | 99.60%  | 99.90%  |
| NaCl       | 40.20%  | 47.80%  | 62.90%  | 69.40%  | 76.60%  |
| JavaScript | 34.90%  | 49.10%  | 53.00%  | 85.90%  | 88.40%  |
| Firefox 4  | 57.10%  | 65.40%  | 70.50%  | 65.40%  | 77.90%  |
| Firefox 4 Mesa | 92.70% | 81.60% | 82.90% | 91.90%  | 81.20%  |
| Chrome 9   | 34.90%  | 49.10%  | 53.00%  | 85.90%  | 88.40%  |
| Safari Nightly | 23.36% | 14.69% | 15.29% | 15.78%  | 18.69%  |

Gears benchmark: memory footprint in KB at 500x500 pixels

|                 | C     | NaCl   | JavaScript | Chrome 9 | Firefox 4 | Firefox 4 Mesa | Safari Nightly |
|-----------------|-------|--------|------------|----------|-----------|----------------|----------------|
| Other processes |       | 11,456 | 12,740     | 12,740   |           |                |                |
|                 |       | 952    | 988        | 988      |           |                |                |
|                 |       | 380    | 956        | 956      |           |                |                |
|                 |       | 13,768 | 44,216     | 44,216   |           |                |                |
|                 |       | 2,672  |            |          |           |                |                |
| Sum other       |       | 29,228 | 58,900     | 58,900   |           |                |                |
| OpenGL process  | 9,740 | 19,460 | 35,668     | 35,668   | 103,860   | 103,696        | 27,800         |
| Total           | 9,740 | 48,688 | 94,568     | 94,568   | 103,860   | 103,696        | 27,800         |

Appendix A. Benchmarking Data

## A.4. Spectral Benchmark

Spectral benchmark: running times of spectral analyses in milliseconds per audio file

| | LMAIntro.wav 0.5 MB | Sold His Soul.wav 8 MB | The Blooze.wav 11.7 MB | LMAI.wav 78.6 MB |
|---|---|---|---|---|
| Chrome 9 | 921 | 9,313 | 13,687 | 89,706 |
| Safari r83161 | 2,281 | 22,676 | 32,986 | |
| Firefox 4 | 3,315 | 35,746 | 52,929 | |
| NaCl | 5,440 | 55,217 | 81,330 | |
| JavaScript | 921 | 9,313 | 13,687 | 89,706 |
| C | 327 | 3,262 | 4,619 | 32,724 |

Spectral benchmark: CPU utilization of 12 samples during the analysis of LMAI.wav

| | | | | | | | | |
|---|---|---|---|---|---|---|---|---|
| C | 101,0% | 100,0% | 99,0% | 100,0% | 100,0% | 99,0% | 100,0% | 99,0% |
| NaCl | 94,0% | 92,0% | 93,0% | 92,0% | 87,0% | 89,0% | 94,0% | 94,0% | 93,0% |
| JavaScript | 99,0% | 99,0% | 100,0% | 100,0% | 99,0% | 100,0% | 100,0% | 100,0% | 100,0% | 92,0% |
| Firefox 4 | 101,0% | 97,0% | 94,0% | 100,0% | 98,0% | 100,0% | 100,0% | 100,0% | 100,0% | 100,0% |
| Safari Nightly | 99,9% | 99,9% | 100,0% | 99,9% | 100,2% | 99,9% | 100,0% | 99,9% | 99,0% |
| Chrome 9 | 99,0% | 99,0% | 100,0% | 100,0% | 99,0% | 100,0% | 100,0% | 100,0% | 100,0% |

Spectral benchmark: memory footprint in KB during the analysis of LMAI.wav

| | C | NaCl | JavaScript | Chrome 9 | Firefox 4 | Safari Nightly |
|---|---|---|---|---|---|---|
| Other processes | | 14,508 | 11,596 | 11,596 | | |
| | | 1,016 | 944 | 944 | | |
| | | 388 | 624 | 624 | | |
| | | 206,884 | 5,284 | 5,284 | | |
| Sum other | | 222,796 | 18,448 | 18,448 | | |
| Spectral process | 76,916 | 277,236 | 127,004 | 127,004 | 240,836 | 107,500 |
| Total | 76,916 | 500,032 | 145,452 | 145,452 | 240,836 | 107,500 |

# Bibliography

Jont B. Allen and Lawrence R. Rabiner. A unified approach to short-time fourier analysis and synthesis. *Proceedings of the IEEE*, 65, No. 11, November 1977.

Marc Andreessen. The three kinds of platforms you meet on the internet. *blog.pmarca.com*, October 2009. URL http://pmarca-archive.posterous.com/the-three-kinds-of-platforms-you-meet-on-the-0, last visited on October 26, 2011.

AppData. Top developers leaderboard, 2010. URL http://www.appdata.com/leaderboard/developers?metric_select=mau, last visited on October 26, 2011.

Michael Armbrust, Armando Fox, Rean Griffith, Anthony D. Joseph, Randy H. Katz, Andrew Konwinski, Gunho Lee, David A. Patterson, Ariel Rabkin, Ion Stoica, and Matei Zaharia. Above the clouds: A berkeley view of cloud computing. Technical Report UCB/EECS-2009-28, EECS Department, University of California, Berkeley, Feb 2009. URL http://www.eecs.berkeley.edu/Pubs/TechRpts/2009/EECS-2009-28.html.

Michael Armbrust, Armando Fox, Rean Griffith, Anthony D. Joseph, Randy Katz, Andy Konwinski, Gunho Lee, David Patterson, Ariel Rabkin, Ion Stoica, and Matei Zaharia. A view of cloud computing. *Commun. ACM*, 53:50 58, April 2010. ISSN 0001-0782. URL http://doi.acm.org/10.1145/1721654.1721672.

David H. Bailey, Jonathan M. Borwein, Peter B. Borwein, and Simon Plouffe. The quest for pi. *Mathematical Intelligencer*, 19:19 1, 1997.

Adam Barth, Collin Jackson, and Charles Reis. The security architecture of the Chromium browser. *Proceedings of WWW 2009*, 2008.

Adam Barth, Adrienne Porter Felt, Prateek Saxena, and Aaron Boodman. Protecting browsers from extension vulnerabilities. Technical Report UCB/EECS-2009-185, EECS Department, University of California, Berkeley, Dec 2009. URL http://www.eecs.berkeley.edu/Pubs/TechRpts/2009/EECS-2009-185.html.

Tim Berners-Lee. Worldwideweb: Summary, 1991. URL http://groups.google.com/group/alt.hypertext/msg/395f282a67a1916c, last visited on October 26, 2011.

Tim Berners-Lee. Long live the web: A call for continued open standards and neutrality. *Scientific American Magazine*, November 2010. URL http://www.scientificamerican.com/article.cfm?id=long-live-the-web, last visited on October 26, 2011.

Jon Brodkin. 10,000-core linux supercomputer built in amazon cloud. *Network World*, April 2011. URL http://www.networkworld.com/news/2011/040611-linux-supercomputer.html, last visited on September 29, 2011.

Nicholas Carr. *The Big Switch: Rewiring the World, from Edison to Google*. W. W. Norton & Company, January 2008. ISBN 978-0-393-06228-1.

*Bibliography*

Josh Catone. Platforms on the web are platforms on a platform. *ReadWriteWeb*, September 2007. URL http://www.readwriteweb.com/archives/platforms_on_the_web_are_platforms_on_a_platform.php, last visited on October 26, 2011.

Tantek Çelik. What is the open web?, 2010. URL http://tantek.com/2010/281/b1/what-is-the-open-web, last visited on October 26, 2011.

Michael Cerna and Audrey F. Harvey. The fundamentals of fft-based signal analysis and measurement. Technical report, National Instruments, 2009. URL http://zone.ni.com/devzone/cda/tut/p/id/4278, last visited on September 26, 2011.

Mason Chang, Edwin Smith, Rick Reitmaier, Michael Bebenita, Andreas Gal, Christian Wimmer, Brendan Eich, and Michael Franz. Tracing for web 3.0: trace compilation for the next generation web applications. In *Proceedings of the 2009 ACM SIGPLAN/SIGOPS international conference on Virtual execution environments*, VEE '09, pages 71–80, New York, NY, USA, 2009. ACM. ISBN 978-1-60558-375-4. URL http://doi.acm.org/10.1145/1508293.1508304.

Thomas Claburn. Google's 'gov cloud' wins $7.2 million los angeles contract. *Informationweek.com*, October 2009. URL http://www.informationweek.com/news/services/saas/221100129, last visited on October 26, 2011.

Sharon Cohen and Rob Franco. Activex security: Improvements and best practices, 2006. URL http://msdn.microsoft.com/en-us/library/bb250471(v=vs.85).aspx, last visited on October 26, 2011.

James Cooley and John Tukey. An algorithm for the machine calculation of complex fourier series. *Mathematics of Computation*, 19(90):297–301, 1965.

Richard S. Cox, Steven D. Gribble, Henry M. Levy, and Jacob Gorm Hansen. A safety-oriented platform for web applications. In *Proceedings of the 2006 IEEE Symposium on Security and Privacy*, pages 350–364, Washington, DC, USA, 2006. IEEE Computer Society. ISBN 0-7695-2574-1. URL http://dx.doi.org/10.1109/SP.2006.4.

Douglas Crockford. The application/json media type for javascript object notation (json), 2006. URL https://tools.ietf.org/html/rfc4627, last visited on October 26, 2011.

Alexis Deveria. Compatibility tables for support of html5, css3, svg and more in desktop and mobile browsers, 2011. URL http://caniuse.com/, last visited on October 26, 2011.

M. D. Dikaiakos, D. Katsaros, P. Mehra, G. Pallis, and A. Vakali. Cloud Computing: Distributed Internet Computing for IT and Scientific Research. *Internet Computing, IEEE*, 13(5):10–13, September 2009. URL http://dx.doi.org/10.1109/MIC.2009.103.

Alan Donovan, Robert Muth, Brad Chen, and David Sehr. PNaCl: Portable native client executables. Technical report, Google Inc., 2010.

John R. Douceur, Jeremy Elson, Jon Howell, and Jacob R. Lorch. Leveraging legacy code to deploy desktop applications on the web. In *Proceedings of the 8th USENIX conference on Operating systems design and implementation*, OSDI'08, pages 339–354, Berkeley, CA, USA, 2008. USENIX Association. URL http://portal.acm.org/citation.cfm?id=1855741.1855765.

EU. European Union protection of personal data website, 2010. URL http://europa.eu/legislation_summaries/information_society/l14012_en.htm, last visited on October 26, 2011.

# Bibliography

Philip J. Fleming and John J. Wallace. How not to lie with statistics: the correct way to summarize benchmark results. *Commun. ACM*, 29:218–221, March 1986. ISSN 0001-0782. URL http://doi.acm.org/10.1145/5666.5673.

Bryan Ford and Russ Cox. Vx32: Lightweight userlevel sandboxing on the x86. In *In Proceedings of the USENIX Annual Technical Conference*, 2008.

Forrester Consulting. Strategies to improve it efficiency in 2010. Technical report, Forrester Research Inc., 2010. URL http://teamquest.com/pdfs/whitepaper/forrester-it-efficiency-2010.pdf, last visited on October 26, 2011.

Chris Grier, Shuo Tang, and Samuel T. King. Secure web browsing with the op web browser. In *Proceedings of the 2008 IEEE Symposium on Security and Privacy*, pages 402–416, Washington, DC, USA, 2008. IEEE Computer Society. ISBN 978-0-7695-3168-7. URL http://dx.doi.org/10.1109/SP.2008.19.

Chris Grier, Samuel T. King, and Dan S. Wallach. How i learned to stop worrying and love plugins. In *In Web 2.0 Security and Privacy*, 2009.

Brian Hayes. Cloud computing. *Commun. ACM*, 51:9–11, July 2008. ISSN 0001-0782. URL http://doi.acm.org/10.1145/1364782.1364786.

Miguel Helft. Will zynga become the google of games? *The New York Times*, July 2010. URL http://www.nytimes.com/2010/07/25/business/25zynga.html?pagewanted=1&_r=1&dbk, last visited on October 26, 2011.

Ian Hickson. Html5 (including next generation additions stillin development). Technical report, WHATWG, 2010. URL http://www.whatwg.org/specs/web-apps/current-work/multipage/, last visited on October 26, 2011.

David Hopwood. A comparison between java and activex security. *Network Security*, 1997(12):15–20, 1997. ISSN 1353-4858. URL http://dx.doi.org/10.1016/S1353-4858(97)88552-2.

IBM Corporation. Dispelling the vapor around cloud computing. Technical Report CIW03062-USEN-01, IBM Corporation, January 2010.

Bruce Jacob and Trevor Mudge. Notes on calculating computer performance. Technical report, University of Michigan, 1995.

Peter Kabal. Wave file specifications, 2011. URL http://www-mmsp.ece.mcgill.ca/Documents/AudioFormats/WAVE/WAVE.html, last visited on October 26, 2011.

Kevin Kelly. We are the web. *Wired*, 13(8), August 2005. URL http://www.wired.com/wired/archive/13.08/tech.html, last visited on September 26, 2011.

Mandeep Khera, Sameer Dixit, Kulesa Faul, Erin Swanson, and Strategic Data Command. Web application security trends report q3-q4 2010. Technical report, Cenzic Inc., 2011.

Khronos Group. OpenGL - the industry standard for high performance graphics, 2011a. URL http://www.opengl.org/, last visited on October 26, 2011.

Khronos Group. WebGL - OpenGL ES 2.0 for the web, 2011b. URL http://www.khronos.org/webgl/, last visited on October 26, 2011.

*Bibliography*

Nathan Kirsch. Benchmarking javascript performance on 15 internet browsers. *legitreviews.com*, June 2010. URL http://legitreviews.com/article/1347/1/, last visited on October 26, 2011.

Kirk L. Kroeker. Toward native web execution. *Commun. ACM*, 52(7):16–17, 2009. ISSN 0001-0782. URL http://doi.acm.org/10.1145/1538788.1538795.

Scott Laningham. Developerworks interviews: Tim berners-lee. *IBM DeveloperWorks*, August 2006. URL http://www.ibm.com/developerworks/podcast/dwi/cm-int082206txt.html, last visited on October 26, 2011.

Chris Lattner and Vikram Adve. Llvm: A compilation framework for lifelong program analysis & transformation. In *Proceedings of the international symposium on Code generation and optimization: feedback-directed and runtime optimization*, CGO '04, pages 75–, Washington, DC, USA, 2004. IEEE Computer Society. ISBN 0-7695-2102-9. URL http://dx.doi.org/10.1109/CGO.2004.1281665.

LleteratePrograms. Cooley-Tukey FFT algorithm (c) - literateprograms, 2008. URL http://en.literateprograms.org/Cooley-Tukey_FFT_algorithm_(C), last visited on October 26, 2011.

Richard G. Lyons. *Understanding Digital Signal Processing (2nd Edition)*. Prentice Hall PTR, Upper Saddle River, NJ, USA, 2004. ISBN 978-0-13-108989-1.

Paul McFedries. The cloud is the computer. *IEEE Spectrum Online*, August 2008. URL http://spectrum.ieee.org/computing/hardware/the-cloud-is-the-computer, last visited on September 27, 2011.

Peter Mell and Tim Grance. Nist definition of cloud computing. Technical report, National Institute of Standards and Technology, 2011. URL http://csrc.nist.gov/publications/PubsSPs.html, last visited on October 28, 2011.

Tommi Mikkonen and Antero Taivalsaari. Using javascript as a real programming language. Technical Report SMLI TR-2007-168, Sun Microsystems, Inc., Mountain View, CA, USA, 2007.

Mozilla Developer Center. Arraybuffer - mdc doc center, 2011a. URL https://developer.mozilla.org/en/JavaScript_typed_arrays/ArrayBuffer, last visited on October 26, 2011.

Mozilla Developer Center. Dataview - mdc doc center, 2011b. URL https://developer.mozilla.org/en/JavaScript_typed_arrays/DataView, last visited on October 26, 2011.

Mozilla Developer Center. Using web workers - mdc doc center, 2011c. URL https://developer.mozilla.org/En/Using_web_workers, last visited on October 26, 2011.

Mozilla Developer Network. Plugins - MDN docs, 2011. URL https://developer.mozilla.org/En/Plugins, last visited on October 26, 2011.

Mozilla Foundation. Mozilla foundation announces more open, scriptable plugins, 2004. URL http://www-archive.mozilla.org/press/mozilla-2004-06-30.html, last visited on October 26, 2011.

Mozilla Foundation. B2G - MozillaWiki, 2011. URL https://wiki.mozilla.org/B2G, last visited on September 26, 2011.

MSRC Engineering. WebGL considered harmful, 2011. http://blogs.technet.com/b/srd/archive/2011/06/16/webgl-considered-harmful.aspx, last visited on October 26, 2011.

# Bibliography

Aaftab Munshi, Dan Ginsburg, and Dave Shreiner. *OpenGL(R) ES 2.0 Programming Guide*. Addison-Wesley Professional, 1 edition, 2008. ISBN 978-0-32150279-7.

Net Applications. Market share for browsers, operating systems and search engines, 2011. URL http://marketshare.hitslink.com, last visited on October 10, 2011.

Tim O'Reilly. What is web 2.0. *O'Reilly Media, Inc.*, September 2005. URL http://oreilly.com/web2/archive/what-is-web-20.html, last visited on October 26, 2011.

Tim O'Reilly. Web 2.0 compact definition: Trying again. *O'Reilly Radar*, October 2006. URL http://radar.oreilly.com/archives/2006/12/web-20-compact.html, last visited on October 26, 2011.

Tim O'Reilly. Google bets big on html 5: News from google i/o. *O'Reilly Radar*, May 2009. URL http://radar.oreilly.com/2009/05/google-bets-big-on-html-5.html, last visited on October 26, 2011.

Ryan Paul. Chrome web store: a solution in search of a problem? *Ars-Technica*, December 2010. URL http://arstechnica.com/web/news/2010/12/thoughts-on-the-chrome-store-does-the-web-need-an-app-delivery-channel.ars, last visited on October 26, 2011.

Linda Dailey Paulson. Building rich web applications with ajax. *Computer*, 38:14–17, October 2005. ISSN 0018-9162. URL http://portal.acm.org/citation.cfm?id=1092230.1092278.

William H. Press, Saul A. Teukolsky, William T. Vetterling, and Brian P. Flannery. *Numerical Recipes 3rd Edition: The Art of Scientific Computing*, chapter 13 Fourier and Spectral Applications. Cambridge University Press, New York, NY, USA, 3 edition, 2007. ISBN 978-0-521-88068-8.

Niels Provos. Improving host security with system call policies. In *Proceedings of the 12th conference on USENIX Security Symposium - Volume 12*, pages 18–18, Berkeley, CA, USA, 2003. USENIX Association. URL http://portal.acm.org/citation.cfm?id=1251353.1251371.

Q-Success. W3techs - world wide web technology surveys, 2011. URL http://w3techs.com, last visited on October 26, 2011.

Paruj Ratanaworabhan, Benjamin Livshits, and Benjamin G. Zorn. Jsmeter: comparing the behavior of javascript benchmarks with real web applications. In *Proceedings of the 2010 USENIX conference on Web application development*, WebApps'10, pages 3–3, Berkeley, CA, USA, 2010. USENIX Association. URL http://portal.acm.org/citation.cfm?id=1863166.1863169.

Charles Reis and Steven D. Gribble. Isolating web programs in modern browser architectures. In *Proceedings of the 4th ACM European conference on Computer systems*, EuroSys '09, pages 219–232, New York, NY, USA, 2009. ACM. ISBN 978-1-60558-482-9. URL http://doi.acm.org/10.1145/1519065.1519090.

Charles Reis, Adam Barth, and Carlos Pizano. Browser security: lessons from google chrome. *Commun. ACM*, 52:45–49, August 2009. ISSN 0001-0782. URL http://doi.acm.org/10.1145/1536616.1536634.

Gregor Richards, Sylvain Lebresne, Brian Burg, and Jan Vitek. An analysis of the dynamic behavior of javascript programs. In *Proceedings of the 2010 ACM SIGPLAN conference on Programming language design and implementation*, PLDI '10, pages 1–12, New York, NY, USA, 2010. ACM. ISBN 978-1-4503-0019-3. URL http://doi.acm.org/10.1145/1806596.1806598.

*Bibliography*

Rightscale. Amazon usage estimates, 2009. URL http://blog.rightscale.com/2009/10/05/amazon-usage-estimates/, last visited on October 26, 2011.

Gary Rivlin. A retail revolution turns 10. *New York Times*, July 2005. URL http://www.nytimes.com/2005/07/10/business/yourmoney/10amazon.html, last visited on October 26, 2011.

Aviel D. Rubin and Daniel E. Geer. Mobile code security. *IEEE Internet Computing*, 2, 1998.

Salesforce.com. The force.com multitenant architecture. Technical Report WP_Force-MT_101508, Salesforce.com, 2008. URL http://www.apexdevnet.com/media/ForcedotcomBookLibrary/Force.com_Multitenancy_WP_101508.pdf, last visited on October 26, 2011.

Craig Stuart Sapp. Microsoft wave soundfile format, 2003. URL https://ccrma.stanford.edu/courses/422/projects/WaveFormat/, last visited on October 26, 2011.

Justin Schuh and Carlos Pizano. Rolling out a sandbox for adobe flash player, 2010. URL http://blog.chromium.org/2010/12/rolling-out-sandbox-for-adobe-flash.html, last visited on October 26, 2011.

David Sehr, Robert Muth, Cliff Biffle, Victor Khimenko, Egor Pasko, Karl Schimpf, Bennet Yee, and Brad Chen. Adapting software fault isolation to contemporary cpu architectures. In *Proceedings of the 19th USENIX conference on Security*, USENIX Security'10, pages 1–1, Berkeley, CA, USA, 2010. USENIX Association. ISBN 888-7-6666-5555-4. URL http://portal.acm.org/citation.cfm?id=1929820.1929822.

J. E. Smith. Characterizing computer performance with a single number. *Commun. ACM*, 31:1202–1206, October 1988. ISSN 0001-0782. URL http://doi.acm.org/10.1145/63039.63043.

Steve Souders. High-performance web sites. *Commun. ACM*, 51:36–41, December 2008. ISSN 0001-0782. URL http://doi.acm.org/10.1145/1409360.1409374.

StatOwl. Statowl.com - statistical analysis and market research of internet usage trends, 2011. URL http://www.statowl.com, last visited on October 26, 2011.

Nicolas Sylvain. A new approach to browser security: the Google Chrome sandbox, 2008. URL http://blog.chromium.org/2008/10/new-approach-to-browser-security-google.html, last visited on October 26, 2011.

Colleen Taylor. The HTML5 boom is coming. fast., 2011. URL http://gigaom.com/2011/07/22/the-html5-boom-is-coming-fast/, last visited on October 26, 2011.

Anne van Kesteren. HTML5 differences from HTML4. Technical report, W3C, 2011. URL http://www.w3.org/TR/html5-diff/, last visited on October 26, 2011.

Vision Mobile. HTML5 and what it means for the mobile industry, 2011. URL http://www.visionmobile.com/blog/2011/06/html5-and-what-it-means-for-the-mobile-industry/, last visited on October 26, 2011.

Helen J. Wang, Chris Grier, Alexander Moshchuk, Samuel T. King, Piali Choudhury, and Herman Venter. The multi-principal os construction of the gazelle web browser. In *Proceedings of the 18th conference on USENIX security symposium*, SSYM'09, pages 417–432, Berkeley, CA, USA, 2009. USENIX Association. URL http://portal.acm.org/citation.cfm?id=1855768.1855794.

# Bibliography

Fred Wilson. Andreessen on platforms. *AVC Musings of a VC on NYC Blog*, September 2007. URL http://avc.blogs.com/a_vc/2007/09/andreessen-on-p.html, last visited on October 26, 2011.

Andy Wingo. Reducing the footprint of python applications, 2007. URL http://wingolog.org/archives/2007/11/27/reducing-the-footprint-of-python-applications, last visited on October 26, 2011.

Bennet Yee, David Sehr, Gregory Dardyk, J. Bradley Chen, Robert Muth, Tavis Orm, Shiki Okasaka, Neha Narula, Nicholas Fullagar, and Google Inc. Native client: A sandbox for portable, untrusted x86 native code. In *In Proceedings of the 2009 IEEE Symposium on Security and Privacy*, 2009.

YouTube. Youtube - broadcast yourself, 2011. URL http://www.youtube.com/t/press_statistics, last visited on October 26, 2011.

Mark Zuckerberg. 500 million stories. *The Facebook Blog*, July 2010. URL http://blog.facebook.com/blog.php?post=409753352130, last visited on October 26, 2011.

# i want morebooks!

Buy your books fast and straightforward online - at one of world's fastest growing online book stores! Environmentally sound due to Print-on-Demand technologies.

## Buy your books online at
## www.get-morebooks.com

Kaufen Sie Ihre Bücher schnell und unkompliziert online – auf einer der am schnellsten wachsenden Buchhandelsplattformen weltweit! Dank Print-On-Demand umwelt- und ressourcenschonend produziert.

## Bücher schneller online kaufen
## www.morebooks.de

VDM Verlagsservicegesellschaft mbH
Heinrich-Böcking-Str. 6-8    Telefon: +49 681 3720 174    info@vdm-vsg.de
D - 66121 Saarbrücken         Telefax: +49 681 3720 1749   www.vdm-vsg.de

Printed by Books on Demand GmbH, Norderstedt / Germany